Road Atlas

UNITED STATES • CANADA • MEXICO

REISEPLANER

INHALT

National Parks Photography:
pp. E–H:
Acadia, Great Smoky Mountains, Shenandoah, and Rocky Mountain / National Park Service ; Everglades, Glacier, and Yellowstone NPs, and Sasquatch sign / U.S. Landmarks and Travel/Getty Images ; Grand Teton, Grand Canyon, Olympic, Yosemite, and Zion / U.S. Landmarks and Travel 2/Getty Images ; Soaring eagle / Nature, Wildlife and the Environment/Getty Images ; Black bear, Mountain lion / Lions, Tigers and Bears/Getty Images ; Howling wolf / Getty Images

A Gebrauchsanweisung für diesen Atlas

Nationalparks

S. C–L

Die wichtigsten Nationalparks werden detailliert beschrieben. Vergrößerte Kartenausschnitte zeigen die Hauptwanderwege, Berge und Sehenswürdigkeiten in geschummerten Reliefkarten. Es gibt Kurzinfos über Besucherzentren, Öffnungszeiten, Eintrittspreise, Telefonnummern u.a. Braune Suchmarken verweisen auf die entsprechenden Karten im Atlas.

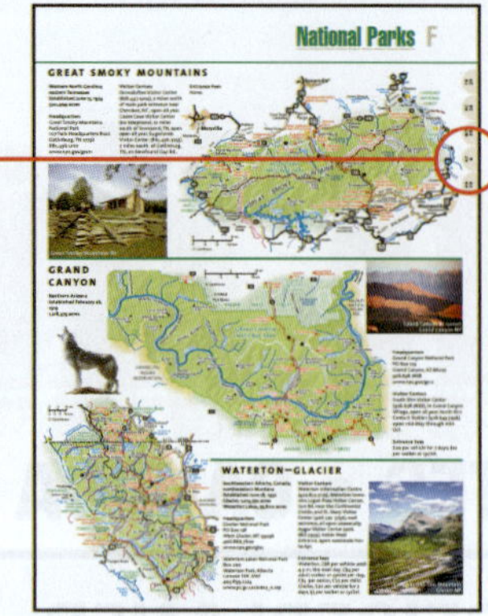

Straßenkarten S. 4–68

Straßenkarten für alle 50 Bundesstaaten, die kanadischen Provinzen und Mexiko in alphabetischer Reihenfolge

Rote Rahmenkästen

Rote umrandete Kästchen bei Großstädten verweisen auf die Seiten, auf denen die entsprechenden Stadtpläne zu finden sind.

Registerverweise

Auf jeder Staatenkarte verweisen blaue Suchmarken am Rand auf die Seitenzahl des entsprechenden Ortsverzeichnisses.

Stadtpläne S.69–85

Die vergrößerten Maßstäbe der Stadtpläne ermöglichen die Navigation in den Metropolen und erleichtern die Suche nach dem gewünschten Ziel.

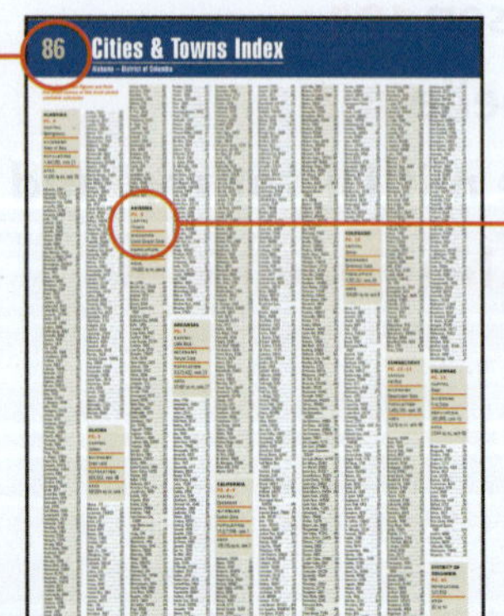

Index S. 86–93

Einfache Suche nach bestimmten Orten. Die rote Zahl verweist auf die Seite der entsprechenden Karte, die Zahlen hinter den Ortsnamen auf die Einwohnerzahl. Die Koordinaten erleichtern die Suche nach Orten und Straßen auf der Karte.

Legende zum Straßenatlas

VERKEHR

AUTOBAHNEN

- Gebührenfreier Highway
- Tollway (mautpflichtig)
- Im Bau
- Kreuzungen und Ausfahrtnummern

ANDERE STRASSEN

- Highway erster Ordnung
- Highway zweiter Ordnung
- Geteilter Highway
- Andere asphaltierte Straße
- Nicht asphaltierte Straße

STRASSENSIGNATUREN

- Interstate Autobahn
- U.S. Highway (Bundesstraße)
- Staats- bzw. Provinzstraße
- Regionale Staats- bzw. Bezirksstraße
- Trans-Canada Highway (Autobahn)
- Kanadische Provinzstraße
- Mexikanischer Highway

ANDERE SYMBOLE

- Entf. zw. Orten und Hwy.-Kreuzungen
  Meilen in USA, Kilometer in Kanada und Mexiko
- Tunnel, Pass
- Autofähre; Personenfähre

ERHOLUNG

- Nationalpark
- Staatliches Wald- und Weideland
- Andere Parks oder Erholungsgebiete
- Andere Staatsparks mit oder ohne Campingplatz
- Militärisches Sperrgebiet
- Indianerreservat
- Wanderweg, Bergpfad
- Skigebiet
- Sehenswürdigkeit

STÄDTE

- Bundeshauptstadt
- Staats- (USA) oder Prov.-Hauptstadt (Kan.
- Städte und Siedlungsgebiete
  Schriftgröße verweist auf relative Größe
- Städtische Siedlungsräume
- Großstädte

SONSTIGE KARTENMERKMALE

- Grenze der Zeitzonen
- Berggipfel; Höhenangabe in Fuß (Mt. Olympus 7,965)
- Fluss (permanent, periodisch)

Kartenverzeichnis B

US-STAATEN

KANADISCHE PROVINZEN

US-STÄDTE

KANADISCHE STÄDTE

MEXIKANISCHE STÄDTE

NATIONALPARKS

C

Nationalparks

Das Nationalparksystem schützt natürliche und historisch bedeutende Gebiete in den USA – von landschaftlich schönen Flüssen bis zu historischen Schlachtfeldern. Über die 54 Nationalparks hinaus verwaltet das Parksystem noch so diverse Schauplätze wie eine Viehranch in Montana und das Unabhängigkeitsgebäude in Philadelphia.

Abkürzungen

IHS	International Historic Site
NB	National Battlefield
NBP	National Battlefield Park
NBS	National Battlefield Site
NHA	National Historic Area
NHP	National Historical Park
NHP & PRES	National Historical Park & Preserve
NH RES	National Historical Reserve
NHS	National Historic Site
NL	National Lakeshore
NM	National Monument
NM & PRES	National Monument & Preserve

Nationalparks D

NMP	National Military Park	**N RES**	National Reserve
N MEM	National Memorial	**NS**	National Seashore
NP	National Park	**NST**	National Scenic Trail
NP & PRES	National Park & Preserve	**PKWY**	Parkway
N PRES	National Preserve		
NR	National River		
NRA	National Recreation Area		
NRRA	National River & Recreation Area		

Boston Area
Adams NHS
Boston African American NHS
Boston Harbor Islands NRA
Boston NHP
Frederick Law Olmstead NHS
John F. Kennedy NHS
Longfellow NHS
Lowell NHP
Minute Man NHP
Salem Maritime NHS
Saugus Iron Works NHS

New York City Area
African Burial Ground NM
Castle Clinton NM
Edison NHS
Federal Hall N MEM
General Grant N MEM
Hamilton Grange N MEM
Sagamore Hill NHS
Saint Paul's Church NHS
Statue of Liberty NM
Theodore Roosevelt Birthplace NHS

Philadelphia Area
Edgar Allan Poe NHS
Independence NHP
Thaddeus Kosciuszko N MEM

Baltimore Area
Ft. McHenry NM and Historic Shrine
Hampton NHS

District of Columbia
Anacostia Park
Carter G. Woodson Home NHS
Constitution Gardens
Ford's Theatre NHS
Franklin Delano Roosevelt Memorial
Frederick Douglass NHS
George Mason Memorial
Korean War Veterans Memorial
Lincoln Memorial
Mary McLeod Bethune Council House NHS
National Mall
National World War II Memorial
Pennsylvania Avenue NHS
Rock Creek Park
Sewall-Belmont House NHS
Thomas Jefferson Memorial
Vietnam Veterans Memorial
Washington Monument
White House

Maryland
Chesapeake and Ohio Canal NHP
Clara Barton NHS
Fort Washington Park
Greenbelt Park
Monocacy NB
Piscataway Park

Virginia
Arlington House
George Washington Memorial PKWY
Wolf Trap NP for the Performing Arts

Der Nationalpark des amerikanischen Samoa und der Geschichtspark des Krieges im Pazifik werden ebenfalls vom Nationalparksystem verwaltet, erscheinen aber nicht auf der nebenstehenden Karte.

E Nationalparks

WY 55
ME 24
FL 14

ACADIA

Zentralküste von Maine
Gegründet am 26. Februar, 1919, 141 km²

Hauptverwaltung
Acadia National Park
PO Box 177
Eagle Lake Rd.
Bar Harbor, ME 04609
✆ (207) 288-3338
www.nps.gov/acad

Besucherzentren
Hulls Cove Visitor Center, ✆ (207) 288-3338, Rte. 3, kurz vor der Einfahrt zur Park Loop Rd., Mai–Okt. geöffnet. Mount Desert Information Center, Rte. 3, kurz vor der Auffahrt zu Mt. Desert Island, während der Saison geöffnet.

Eintrittspreise
$ 20 pro Auto für 7 Tage; $ 5 für Fußgänger oder Radfahrer, Nov.–April kostenlos.

Seaside cliffs in winter
Acadia NP

GRAND TETON

Nordwest-Wyoming
Gegründet am 26. Februar 1929, 1 253 km²

Hauptverwaltung
Grand Teton National Park
PO Drawer 170
Moose, WY 83012
✆ (307) 739-3300
www.nps.gov/grte

Besucherzentren
Moose Visitor Center, ✆ (307) 739-3594, 12 Meilen nördlich von Jackson via Rte. 89/191/287, tägl. außer Weihnachten geöffnet. Colter Bay Visitor Center, ✆ (307) 739-3594, am Jackson Lake, von Mitte Mai bis Ende Sept. geöffnet. Jenny Lake Visitor Center, ✆ (307) 739-3343, 8 Meilen nördlich vom Moose Visitor Center, von Juni bis Sept. geöffnet. Flagg Ranch Informationsbüro, 16 Meilen nördlich der Colter-Bay-Kreuzung, auf Rte. 89/191/287, Juni–Sept. geöffnet.

Eintrittspreise
$ 20 pro Auto für 7 Tage (gilt auch für Yellowstone).

Snake River and Grand Tetons
Grand Teton NP

EVERGLADES

Süd-Florida
Gegründet am 6. Dezember 1947
6 107 km²

Hauptverwaltung
Everglades National Park
40001 State Road 9336
Homestead, FL 33034
✆ (305) 242-7700
www.nps.gov/ever

Besucherzentren
Ernest F. Coe Visitor Center, ✆ (305) 242-7700, 12 Meilen westlich von Florida City. Royal Palm Visitor Center, ✆ (305) 242-7700, 4 Meilen hinter dem Coe Visitor Center. Flamingo Visitor Center, ✆ (239) 695-2945, 38 Meilen hinter dem Coe Visitor Center. Shark Valley Visitor Center, ✆ (305) 221-8776, 30 Meilen westlich vom Florida Turnpike an US 41. Gulf Coast Visitor Center, ✆ (239) 695-3311, 3 Meilen südlich der US 51 am Hwy. 29. Alle tägl. geöffnet (Nov.–April) außer Flamingo.

Eintrittspreise
$ 10 pro Auto für 7 Tage und $ 5 für Fußgänger oder Radfahrer am Haupteingang. $ 10 pro Auto für 7 Tage und $ 5 für Fußgänger und Radfahrer am Shark Valley Eingang.

Tidelands
Everglades NP

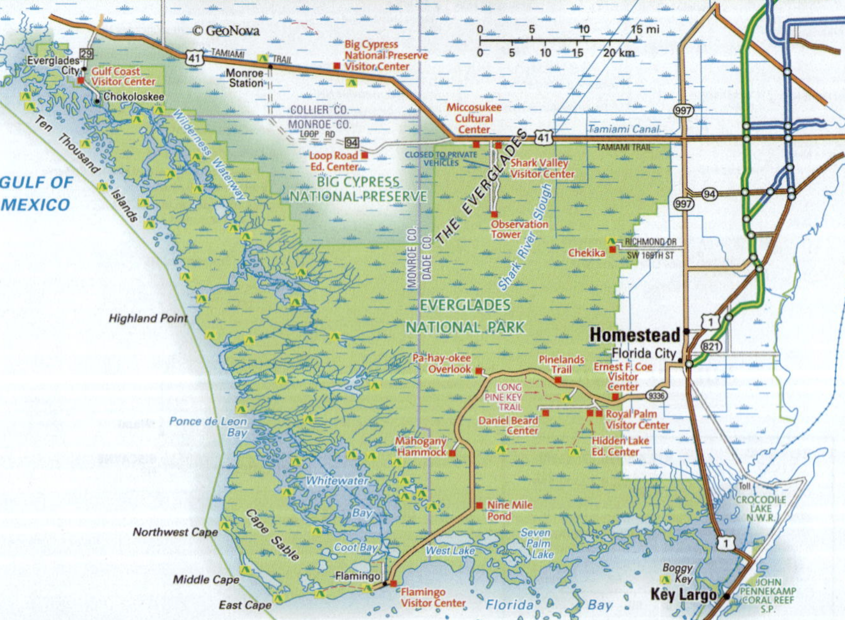

TN 20
NC 38
MT 30
AZ 6
AB 59

GREAT SMOKY MOUNTAINS

West-North-Carolina; Ost-Tennessee
Gegründet am 15. Juni 1934
2 106 km²

Hauptverwaltung
Great Smoky Mountains National Park
107 Park Headquarters Road
Gatlinburg, TN 37738
✆ (865) 436-1200
www.nps.gov/grsm

Besucherzentren
Oconaluftee Visitor Center, ✆ (828) 497-1904, 2 Meilen nördlich des Haupteingangs in der Nähe von Cherokee, NC, ganzjährig geöffnet. Cades Cove Visitor Center, kein Telefon, 12 Meilen südlich von Townsend, TN, ganzjährig geöffnet. Sugarlands Visitor Center, ✆ (865) 436-3255, 2 Meilen nördlich von Gatlinburg, TN, an der Newfound Gap Rd., ganzjährig geöffnet.

Eintrittspreise keine

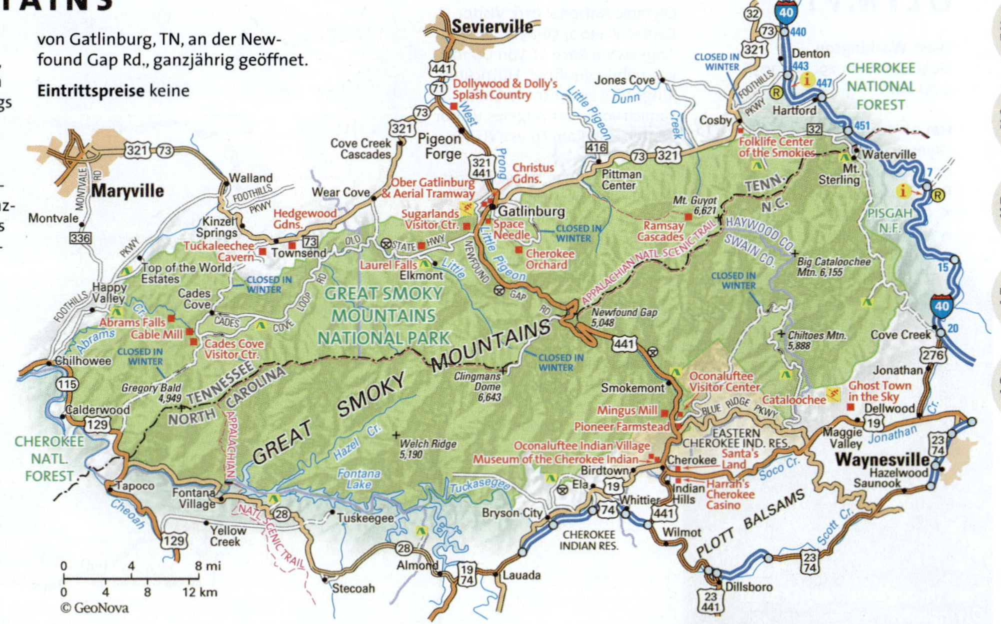

Great Smoky Mountains NP

GRAND CANYON

Nord-Arizona
Gegründet am 26. Februar 1919
4 931 km²

Grand Canyon at sunset
Grand Canyon NP

Hauptverwaltung
Grand Canyon National Park
PO Box 129
Grand Canyon, AZ 86023
✆ (928) 638-7888
www.nps.gov/grca

Besucherzentren
South Rim Visitor Center, ✆ (928) 638-7888, im Grand Canyon Village, ganzjährig geöffnet. North Rim Contact Station, ✆ (928) 638-7298, Mitte Mai–Mitte Okt. geöffnet.

Eintrittspreise
$ 20 pro Auto für 7 Tage, $ 10 für Fußgänger oder Radfahrer.

WATERTON–GLACIER

Südwest-Alberta, Kanada; Nordwest-Montana
Gegründet am 18. Juni 1932
Glacier: 4 102 km²
Waterton Lakes: 299 km²

Hauptverwaltung
Glacier National Park
PO Box 128
West Glacier, MT 59936
✆ (406) 888-7800
www.nps.gov/glac

Waterton Lakes National Park
Waterton Park, Alberta
Canada T0K 2M0
✆ (403) 859-2224
www.pc.gc.ca/index_e.asp

Besucherzentren
Waterton Information Centre, ✆ (403) 859-5133) im Ort Waterton. Logan Pass Visitor Center, Sun Rd., Nähe der kontinentalen Wasserscheide. St. Mary Visitor Center, ✆ (406) 732-7750, Osteingang. Alle haben während der Saison geöffnet. Apgar Visitor Center ✆ (406) 888-7939, Westeingang, geöffnet an den Wochenenden Nov.–April.

Eintrittspreise
Waterton: C$ 8 pro Auto bis 16 Uhr des nächsten Tages, C$ 4 für erwachsene Fußgänger oder Radfahrer pro Tag, C$ 3 für Senioren, C$ 2 für Kinder. Glacier: $ 20 pro Auto für 7 Tage, $ 5 für Fußgänger oder Radfahrer.

Going-to-the-Sun Mountain
Glacier NP

G Nationalparks

WA 51

VA 52

CO 10

OLYMPIC

West-Washington
Gegründet am 29. Juni 1938
3 731 km²

Hauptverwaltung
Olympic National Park
600 East Park Avenue
Port Angeles, WA 98362
✆ (360) 565-3132
www.nps.gov/olym

Trail through Hoh Rain Forest
Olympic NP

Besucherzentren
Olympic National Park Visitor Center, ✆ (360) 565-3132, in Port Angeles via Race St. von US 101, ganzjährig geöffnet. Hurricane Ridge Visitor Center, 17 Meilen südlich vom Port Angeles Visitor Center. Hoh Rain Forest Visitor Center,
✆ (360) 374-6925, 19 Meilen östlich der US 101 auf der Westseite des Parks, ganzjährig geöffnet (von Wetter und Straßenzustand abhängig). Zwischen Herbst und Frühjahr ggf. Selbstbedienung, da unbesetzt.

Eintrittspreise
$ 10 pro Auto, 7 Tage gültig; $ 5 für Radfahrer, Fußgänger oder Busreisende.

SASQUATCH XING

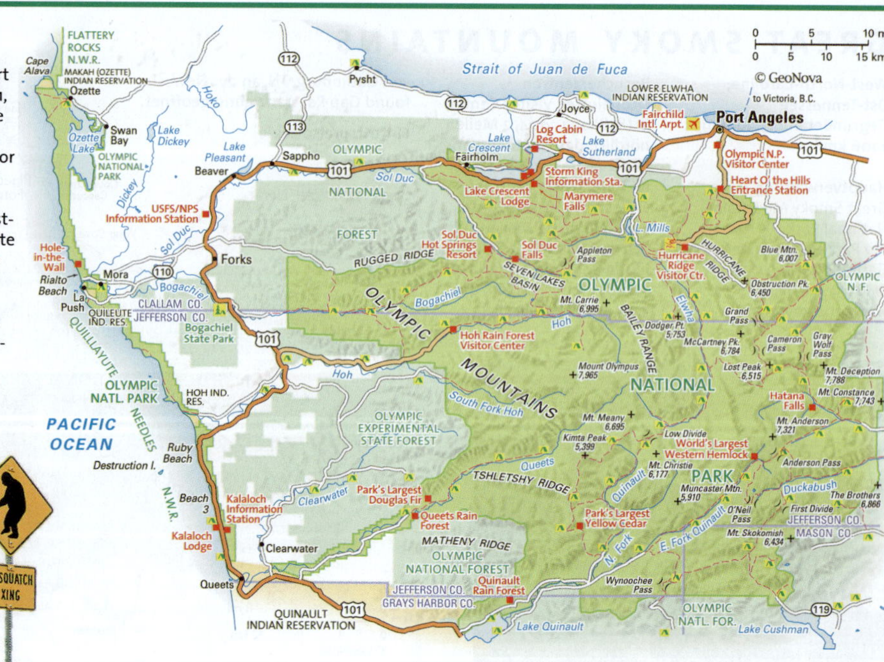

SHENANDOAH

Nord-Virginia
Gegründet am 26. Dezember 1935, 793 km²

Hauptverwaltung
Shenandoah National Park
3655 U. S. Highway 211E
Luray, VA 22835
✆ (540) 999-3500
www.nps.gov/shen

Besucherzentren
Dickey Ridge Visitor Center, ✆ (540) 635-3566, bei Meile 4.6. Harry F. Byrd, Sr. Visitor Center, ✆ (540) 999-3283, bei Meile 51, von Frühjahr bis Spätherbst geöffnet.
Die Meilensteine auf dem Skyline Drive, die von Nord nach Süd nummeriert sind, helfen dem Besucher, die Einrichtungen und Sehenswürdigkeiten des Parks zu finden.

Eintrittspreise
$ 10 pro Auto für 7 Tage; $ 5 für Fußgänger oder Radfahrer.

Shenandoah NP

Rocky Mountain NP

ROCKY MOUNTAIN

Nord-Colorado
Gegründet am 26. Januar 1915
1 075 km²

Hauptverwaltung
Rocky Mountain National Park
1000 Highway 36
Estes Park, CO 80517
✆ (970) 586-1206
www.nps.gov/romo

Besucherzentren
Headquarters Visitor Center, ✆ (970) 586-1206, US 36 am Osteingang, und Kawuneeche Visitor Center, ✆ (970) 586-1513, US 34 nördlich von Grand Lake, ganzjährig geöffnet. Alpine Visitor Center, US 34, und Moraine Park Museum und Visitor Center, ✆ (970) 586-1206, Bear Lake Rd., südlich des Beaver-Meadows-Eingangs, Mitte Mai–Mitte Okt. geöffnet.

Eintrittspreise
$ 15 pro Auto; $ 5 für Fußgänger oder Radfahrer.

YELLOWSTONE

Nordwest-Wyoming, zum Teil übergreifend in den Südwesten von Montana und ins östliche Idaho
Gegründet am 1. März 1872
8 991 km²

Lower Falls of the Yellowstone River
Yellowstone NP

Hauptverwaltung
Yellowstone National Park
PO Box 168
Yellowstone National Park, WY 82190
✆ (307) 344-7381
www.nps.gov/yell

Besucherzentren
Albright Visitor Center, ✆ (307) 344-2263, in Mammoth Hot Springs, ganzjährig geöffnet. Old Faithful Visitor Center, ✆ (307) 545-2750, Mitte April–Ende Okt. und Mitte Dez.–Mitte März geöffnet. Canyon Visitor Center, ✆ (307) 242-2550, Fishing Bridge Visitor Center, ✆ (307) 242-2450 und Grant Village Visitor Center, ✆ (307) 242-2650 alle von Mitte Mai–Sept. geöffnet. West Thumb Information Station, Anfang Juni–Sept. geöffnet.

Eintrittspreise
$ 20 pro Auto für 7 Tage (gilt auch für Grand Teton); $ 15 pro Snowmobil oder Motorrad; $ 10 für Fußgänger, Radfahrer oder Skiläufer.

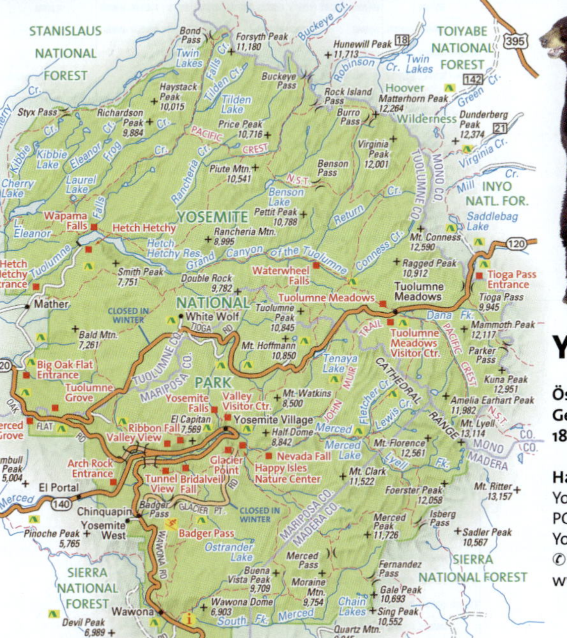

YOSEMITE

Östliches Zentralkalifornien
Gegründet am 1. Oktober 1890, 3 027 km²

Hauptverwaltung
Yosemite National Park
PO Box 577
Yosemite, CA 95389
✆ (209).372-0200
www.nps.gov/yose

Besucherzentren
Yosemite Valley Visitor Center und Yosemite Valley sind ganzjährig geöffnet. Wawona Information Station, ✆ (209) 375-9531, Mai–Sept. geöffnet. Big Oak Flat Information Station, ✆ (209) 379-1899, in der Nähe des Parkeingangs am Hwy. 120, Juni–Aug. geöffnet. Tuolumne Meadows Visitor Center, ✆ (209) 372-0263, an der Tioga Rd., öffnet wie der Tioga-Pass im Sommer.

Eintrittspreise
$ 20 pro Auto für 7 Tage; $ 10 für Fußgänger, Radfahrer oder Busreisende.

El Capitan and Merced River
Yosemite NP

The peaceful Virgin River
Zion NP

ZION

Südwest-Utah
Gegründet am 19. November 1919, 593 km²

Hauptverwaltung
Zion National Park
State Route 9
Springdale Park, UT 84767
✆ (435).772-3256
www.nps.gov/zion

Besucherzentren
Zion Canyon Visitor Center, ✆ (435) 772-3256, in der Nähe des Südeingangs an Utah Rte. 9 und Kolob Canyons Visitor Center, ✆ (435) 586-9548, in der Nordwestecke des Parks via Exit 40 von der I-15, ganzjährig geöffnet außer an Hauptfeiertagen. Visitor Center am Watchman Campground, ✆ 1-800-365-CAMP, April–Okt. geöffnet.

Eintrittspreise
$ 20 pro Auto für 7 Tage; $ 10 für Fußgänger oder Radfahrer.

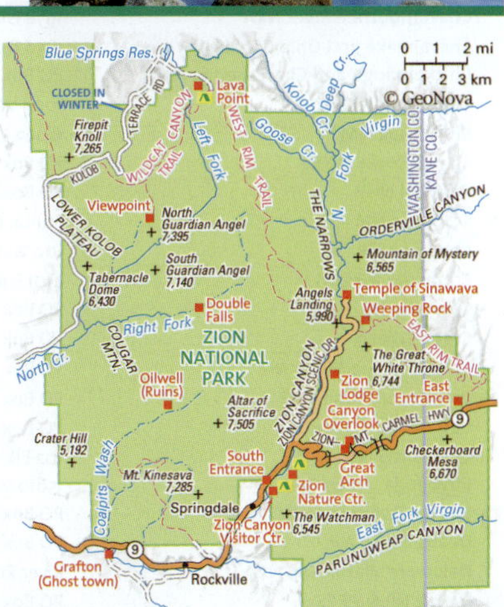

Nationalparks

ABKÜRZUNGEN

NB	National Battlefield	NMP	National Military Park	NS	National Seashore
NBP	National Battlefield Park	NP	National Park	NSR	National Scenic River/ Riverway
NHP	National Historical Park	N PRES	National Preserve	PKWY	Parkway
NHS	National Historic Site	NRA	National Recreation Area	WSR	Wild and Scenic River
NL	National Lakeshore	NRRA	National River and Recreation Area		
N MEM	National Memorial	N RES	National Reserve		
NM	National Monument				

	Park	Address	Fees	(Disabled Access) Visitor Center	Programs and Tours	Picnic area	(Disabled Access) Campground	Hiking	Horse Trail	Swimming	Boating	Fishing	Hunting	Bicycle Trail	Cabin Rental	Hotel, Motel, Lodge	Restaurant, Snacks
A	Abraham Lincoln Birthplace NHS	2995 Lincoln Farm Road, Hodgenville, KY 42748 270-358-3137		x (DA)		x		x									
	Acadia NP	PO Box 177, Eagle Lake Rd, Bar Harbor, ME 04609 207-288-3338	x	x (DA)	x	x	x (DA)	x	x	x	x	x		x			x
	Adams NHP	135 Adams St, Quincy, MA 02169 617-770-1175	x	x (DA)	x												
	Agate Fossil Beds NM	301 River Road, Harrison, NE 69346 308-668-2211	x	x (DA)	x	x		x				x					
	Allegheny Portage Railroad NHS	110 Federal Park, Gallitzin, PA 16641 814-886-6150	x	x (DA)	x	x		x									
	Amistad NRA	4121 Hwy 90 West, Del Rio, TX 78840 830-775-7491	x		x	x	x (DA)	x		x	x	x	x				
	Andersonville NHS	496 Cemetery Road, Andersonville, GA 31711 229-924-0343		x (DA)	x	x											
	Andrew Johnson NHS	121 Monument Avenue, Greeneville, TN 37743 423-638-3551	x	x (DA)	x												
	Antietam NB	PO Box 158, Sharpsburg, MD 21782 301-432-5124	x	x (DA)	x			x				x					
	Apostle Islands NL	415 Washington Ave, Bayfield, WI 54814 715-779-3397	x	x (DA)	x	x	x	x		x	x	x	x				
	Appomattox Court House NHP	PO Box 218 Route 24, Appomattox, VA 24522 434-352-8987, ext 26	x	x (DA)		x		x									
	Arches NP	PO Box 907, Moab, UT 84532 435-719-2299	x	x (DA)	x	x	x (DA)	x									
	Arkansas Post N MEM	1741 Old Post Road, Gillett, AR 72055 870-548-2207		x (DA)	x	x		x				x					
	Assateague Island NS	7206 National Seashore Lane, Berlin, MD 21811 410-641-1441	x	x (DA)	x	x	x (DA)	x		x	x	x	x	x			
	Aztec Ruins NM	84 County Road, Aztec, NM 87410 505-334-6174, ext 30	x	x (DA)		x											
B	Badlands NP	PO Box 6, Interior, SD 57750 605-433-5361	x	x (DA)	x	x	x (DA)	x							x	x	x
	Bandelier NM	15 Entrance Rd, Los Alamos, NM 87544 505-672-0343	x	x (DA)	x	x	x (DA)	x									x
	Bent's Old Fort NHS	35110 Hwy 194 East, La Junta, CO 81050 719-383-5010	x		x	x											
	Big Bend NP	PO Box 129, Big Bend National Park, TX 79834 432-477-2251	x	x (DA)	x	x	x	x	x		x	x				x	x
	Big Cypress N PRES	33100 Tamiami Trail, Ochopee, FL 34141 239-695-1201	x	x (DA)	x	x	x	x	x		x	x	x	x			
	Big Hole NB	PO Box 237, Wisdom, MT 59761 406-689-3155	x	x (DA)	x	x						x					
	Big South Fork NRRA	4564 Leatherwood Road, Oneida, TN 37841 423-286-7275		x (DA)		x	x (DA)	x	x	x	x	x	x	x		x	
	Big Thicket N PRES	6044 FM420, Kountze, TX 77625 409-951-6725		x (DA)	x	x		x	x		x	x	x	x			
	Biscayne NP	9709 SW 328 Street, Homestead, FL 33033 305-230-7275	x	x (DA)	x	x	x				x	x					
	Black Canyon of the Gunnison NP	102 Elk Creek, Gunnison, CO 81230 970-641-2337 ext 205	x	x (DA)	x	x	x (DA)	x				x				x	x
	Blue Ridge PKWY	199 Hemphill Knob Road, Asheville, NC 28803 828-298-0398		x (DA)	x	x	x (DA)	x	x		x	x		x	x	x	x
	Bluestone NSR	PO Box 246, Glen Jean, WV 25846 304-465-0508			x			x			x	x	x				
	Booker T. Washington NM	12130 Booker T. Washington Hwy, Hardy, VA 24101 540-721-2094		x (DA)	x	x		x									
	Boston African American NHS	14 Beacon Street, Suite 503, Boston, MA 02108 617-742-5415			x												
	Boston NHP	Charlestown Navy Yard, Boston, MA 02129 617-242-5601	x	x (DA)	x	x											x
	Bryce Canyon NP	PO Box 640201, Bryce Canyon, UT 84764 435-834-5322	x	x (DA)	x	x	x (DA)	x	x						x	x	x
	Buffalo NR	402 N. Walnut, Suite 136, Harrison, AR 72601 870-741-5443	x	x (DA)	x	x	x (DA)	x	x	x	x	x	x		x		x
C	Cabrillo NM	1800 Cabrillo Memorial Drive, San Diego, CA 92106 619-557-5450	x	x (DA)	x	x		x				x					
	Canaveral NS	308 Julia Street, Titusville, FL 32796 321-267-1110	x	x (DA)	x	x		x	x	x	x	x	x				
	Canyon de Chelly NM	PO Box 588, Chinle, AZ 86503 928-674-5500		x (DA)	x	x	x (DA)	x	x							x	x
	Canyonlands NP	2282 S West Resource Blvd, Moab, UT 84532 435-719-2313	x	x (DA)	x	x	x	x			x						
	Cape Cod NS	99 Marconi Site Road, Wellfleet, MA 02667 508-255-3421	x	x (DA)	x	x		x		x	x	x	x	x		x	x
	Cape Hatteras NS	1401 National Park Drive, Manteo, NC 27954 252-995-4474	x	x (DA)	x	x	x (DA)	x	x	x	x	x	x		x	x	x
	Cape Lookout NS	131 Charles Street, Harkers Island, NC 28531 252-728-2250		x (DA)		x		x			x	x	x		x		
	Capitol Reef NP	HC 70 Box 15, Torrey, UT 84775 435-425-3791	x	x (DA)	x	x	x (DA)	x	x								
	Capulin Volcano NM	PO Box 40, Capulin, NM 88414 505-278-2201	x	x (DA)	x	x		x									
	Carl Sandburg Home NHS	81 Carl Sandburg Lane, Flat Rock, NC 28731 828-693-4178	x	x (DA)	x	x		x									
	Carlsbad Caverns NP	3225 National Parks Hwy, Carlsbad, NM 88220 505-785-2232	x	x (DA)	x	x		x									x
	Casa Grande Ruins NM	1100 Ruins Drive, Coolidge, AZ 85228 520-723-3172	x	x (DA)	x	x											
	Castillo de San Marcos NM	1 South Castillo Drive, St. Augustine, FL 32084 904-829-6506	x		x												
	Castle Clinton NM	1 Bowling Green, New York, NY 10005 212-344-7220		x (DA)	x												
	Cedar Breaks NM	2390 W Hwy 56, Suite 11, Cedar City, UT 84720 435-586-9451	x	x (DA)	x	x	x (DA)	x									
	Chaco Culture NHP	PO Box 220, Nageezi, NM 87037 505-786-7014	x	x	x	x	x (DA)	x						x			
	Chamizal N MEM	800 S San Marcial Street, El Paso, TX 79905 915-532-7273		x (DA)	x	x											
	Channel Islands NP	1901 Spinnaker Drive, Ventura, CA 93001 805-658-5700		x (DA)	x	x	x	x		x	x	x					
	Charles Pinckney NHS	1214 Middle Street, Sullivans Island, SC 29482 843-881-5516		x (DA)	x												
	Chattahoochee River NRA	1978 Island Ford Pkwy, Atlanta, GA 30350 678-538-1200	x		x	x		x	x		x	x		x			x
	Chesapeake and Ohio Canal NHP	1850 Dual Hwy, Suite 100, Hagerstown, MD 21740 301-739-4200	x	x (DA)	x	x	x (DA)	x	x		x	x		x			x
	Chickamauga and Chattanooga NMP	PO Box 2128, Fort Oglethorpe, GA 30742 706-866-9241	x	x (DA)	x	x		x	x								
	Chickasaw NRA	1008 W Second Street, Sulphur, OK 73086 580-622-3165		x (DA)	x	x	x (DA)	x		x	x	x	x				
	Chiricahua NM	13063 E Bonita Canyon Road, Willcox, AZ 85643 520-824-3560	x	x (DA)	x	x	x (DA)	x	x								
	City of Rocks N RES	PO Box 169, Almo, ID 83312 208-824-5519	x	x (DA)	x	x	x (DA)	x	x				x	x			
	Colonial NHP	PO Box 210, Yorktown, VA 23690 757-898-2410	x	x (DA)	x	x		x				x		x			
	Colorado NM	Fruita, CO 81521 970-858-3617	x	x (DA)	x	x	x (DA)	x	x								
	Congaree NP	100 National Park Road, Hopkins, SC 29061 803-776-4396		x (DA)	x	x		x			x	x					
	Coronado N MEM	4101 E Montezuma Canyon Road, Hereford, AZ 85615 520-366-5515		x (DA)		x		x									
	Cowpens NB	PO Box 308, Chesnee, SC 29323 864-461-2828		x (DA)		x											
	Crater Lake NP	PO Box 7, Crater Lake, OR 97604 541-594-3100	x	x (DA)	x	x	x (DA)	x	x			x				x	x
	Craters of the Moon NM	PO Box 29, Arco, ID 83213 208-527-3257	x	x (DA)	x	x	x	x									
	Cumberland Gap NHP	PO Box 1848, Middlesboro, KY 40965 606-248-2817	x	x (DA)	x	x	x (DA)	x	x		x			x			
	Cumberland Island NS	PO Box 806, St. Marys, GA 31558 888-817-3421	x	x (DA)	x	x	x (DA)	x		x		x	x				
	Curecanti NRA	102 Elk Creek, Gunnison, CO 81230 970-641-2337, ext 205	x	x (DA)	x	x	x (DA)	x	x	x	x	x	x				x
	Cuyahoga Valley NP	15610 Vaughn Road, Brecksville, OH 44141 216-524-1497		x (DA)	x	x		x	x	x		x		x		x	x
D	Dayton Aviation Heritage NHP	PO Box 9280, Wright Brothers Station, Dayton, OH 45409 937-225-7705	x		x									x			
	Death Valley NP	PO Box 579, Death Valley, CA 92328 760-786-3200	x	x (DA)	x	x	x (DA)	x	x	x				x	x	x	x
	Delaware Water Gap NRA	River Rd, Bushkill, PA 18324 570-588-2451	x	x (DA)	x	x	x	x	x	x	x	x	x	x			
	Denali NP & PRES	PO Box 9, Denali Park, AK 99755 907-683-2294	x	x (DA)	x	x	x (DA)	x				x	x			x	x

ABKÜRZUNGEN

NB	National Battlefield	NMP	National Military Park	NS	National Seashore
NBP	National Battlefield Park	NP	National Park	NSR	National Scenic River/ Riverway
NHP	National Historical Park	N PRES	National Preserve	PKWY	Parkway
NHS	National Historic Site	NRA	National Recreation Area	WSR	Wild and Scenic River
NL	National Lakeshore	NRRA	National River and Recreation Area		
N MEM	National Memorial	N RES	National Reserve		
NM	National Monument				

(● = available; ● DA = with disabled access)

			Fees	(Disabled Access) Visitor Center	Programs and Tours	Picnic area	(Disabled Access) Campground	Hiking	Horse Trail	Swimming	Boating	Fishing	Hunting	Bicycle Trail	Cabin Rental	Hotel, Motel, Lodge	Restaurant, Snacks
	De Soto N MEM	PO Box 15390, Bradenton, FL 34280 941-792-0458		● DA	●							●					
	Devils Postpile NM	PO Box 3999, Mammoth Lakes, CA 93546 760-934-2289	●	● DA	●	●	●	●	●			●					
	Devils Tower NM	PO Box 10, Devils Tower, WY 82714 307-467-5283	●	● DA	●	●	● DA	●				●					
	Dinosaur NM	4545 E Hwy 40, Dinosaur, CO 81610 970-374-3000	●	● DA	●	●	● DA	●			●	●					
	Dry Tortugas NP	P.O. Box 6208, Key West, FL 33031 305-242-7700	●	● DA	●	●	●			●	●	●					
E	Edison NHS	Main Street and Lakeside Avenue, West Orange, NJ 07052 973-736-0551	●	● DA	●												
	Effigy Mounds NM	151 Hwy 76, Harpers Ferry, IA 52146 563-873-3491	●	● DA	●			●				●					
	Eisenhower NHS	97 Taneytown Road, Gettysburg, PA 17325 717-338-9114	●	● DA	●												
	Eleanor Roosevelt NHS	4097 Albany Post Road, Hyde Park, NY 12538 845-229-9115	●		●	●		●									
	Everglades NP	40001 State Road 9336, Homestead, FL 33034 305-242-7700	●	● DA	●	●	● DA	●	●		●	●		●	●	●	●
F	Federal Hall N MEM	26 Wall Street, New York, NY 10005 212-825-6888		● DA	●												
	Fire Island NS	120 Laurel Street, Patchogue, NY 11772 631-289-4810	●	● DA	●	●	● DA	●		●	●	●	●				●
	Florissant Fossil Beds NM	PO Box 185, Florissant, CO 80816 719-748-3253	●	● DA	●	●		●									
	Ford's Theatre NHS	900 Ohio Drive SW, Washington, DC 20024 202-426-6924		●	●												
	Fort Caroline N MEM	12713 Fort Caroline Road, Jacksonville, FL 32225 904-641-7155		● DA	●	●		●									
	Fort Davis NHS	PO Box 1379, Fort Davis, TX 79734 432-426-3224	●	● DA													
	Fort Donelson NB	PO Box 434, Dover, TN 37058 931-232-5706		● DA		●		●									
	Fort Frederica NM	6515 Frederica Road, St. Simons Island, GA 31522 912-638-3639	●	● DA	●			●				●					
	Fort Laramie NHS	965 Gray Rocks Road, Fort Laramie, WY 82212 307-837-2221	●	● DA	●	●						●					
	Fort Larned NHS	RR 3 Box 69, Larned, KS 67550 620-285-6911	●	● DA	●	●											
	Fort Matanzas NM	8635 A1A South, St. Augustine, FL 32080 904-471-0116		● DA	●					●	●	●					
	Fort McHenry NM and Historic Shrine	2400 East Fort Avenue, Baltimore, MD 21230 410-962-4290	●	● DA	●	●											
	Fort Necessity NB	1 Washington Pkwy, Farmington, PA 15437 724-329-5512	●	● DA	●	●		●									
	Fort Point NHS	Long Ave & Marine Dr, Presidio of San Francisco, CA 94129 415-556-1693		● DA	●							●		●			
	Fort Pulaski NM	PO Box 30757,Hwy 80 East, Savannah, GA 31410 912-786-5787	●	● DA	●	●		●			●	●		●			
	Fort Raleigh NHS	1401 National Park Drive, Manteo, NC 27954 252-473-5772		● DA	●	●		●								●	●
	Fort Scott NHS	PO Box 918, Fort Scott, KS 66701 620-223-0310	●	● DA	●	●											
	Fort Smith NHS	301 Parker Avenue, Fort Smith, AR 72901 479-783-3961	●	● DA	●												
	Fort Stanwix NM	112 E Park Street, Rome, NY 13440 315-336-2090	●	● DA	●												
	Fort Sumter NM	1214 Middle Street, Sullivans Island, SC 29482 843-883-3123	●	● DA	●	●						●					
	Fort Union NM	PO Box 127, Watrous, NM 87753 505-425-8025	●	● DA	●	●											
	Fort Union Trading Post NHS	15550 Hwy 1804, Williston, ND 58801 701-572-9083		● DA	●	●						●					
	Fort Vancouver NHS	612 E Reserve Street, Vancouver, WA 98661 360-816-6230	●	● DA	●	●											
	Fossil Butte NM	PO Box 592, Kemmerer, WY 83101 307-877-4455		● DA	●	●		●									
	Franklin Delano Roosevelt Memorial	NCP Central, 900 Ohio Drive SW, Washington, DC 20024 202-426-6841			●												
	Frederick Douglass NHS	1411 W St SE, Washington, DC 20020 202-426-5961	●	● DA	●												
	Fredericksburg and Spotsylvania NMP	120 Chatham Lane, Fredericksburg, VA 22405 540-371-6122	●	● DA	●	●		●									
	Friendship Hill NHS	1 Washington Pkwy, Farmington, PA 15437 724-725-9190		● DA	●	●		●				●					
G	Gates of the Arctic NP & PRES	PO Box 26030, Bettles Field, AK 99726 907-692-5494		●	●			●			●	●	●				
	Gateway NRA	210 New York Avenue, Staten Island, NY 10305 718-354-4500		● DA	●	●	●	●	●	●	●	●		●			●
	Gauley River NRA	PO Box 246, Glen Jean, WV 25846 304-465-0508					●	●			●	●	●				
	General Grant N MEM	122nd Street and Riverside Drive, New York, NY 10027 212-666-1640		●	●												
	George Rogers Clark NHP	401 S 2nd Street, Vincennes, IN 47591 812-882-1776, ext 110	●	● DA	●	●											
	George Washington Birthplace NM	1732 Popes Creek Road, Colonial Beach, VA 22443 804-224-1732	●	● DA	●	●		●				●					
	George Washington Carver NM	5646 Carver Road, Diamond, MO 64840 417-325-4151	●	● DA	●	●											
	George Washington MEM PKWY	Turkey Run Park, McLean, VA 22101 703-289-2500	●	●	●	●		●	●		●	●		●			●
	Gettysburg NMP	97 Taneytown Road, Gettysburg, PA 17325 717-334-1124		● DA	●	●		●									
	Gila Cliff Dwellings NM	HC 68 Box 100, Silver City, NM 88061 505-536-9461		● DA	●	●	● DA	●	●			●					
	Glacier Bay NP & PRES	PO Box 140, Gustavus, AK 99826 907-697-2230		● DA	●		●	●			●	●	●			●	●
	Glacier NP	PO Box 128, West Glacier, MT 59936 406-888-7800	●	● DA	●	●	● DA	●	●	●	●	●		●	●	●	●
	Glen Canyon NRA	PO Box 1507, Page, AZ 86040 928-608-6404	●	● DA	●	●	●	●	●	●	●	●	●	●		●	●
	Golden Gate NRA	Fort Mason, Building 201, San Francisco, CA 94123 415-561-4700	●	● DA	●	●	●	●	●	●	●	●		●		●	●
	Golden Spike NHS	PO Box 897, Brigham City, UT 84302 435-471-2209, ext 29	●	● DA	●	●		●						●			
	Grand Canyon NP	PO Box 129, Grand Canyon, AZ 86023 928-638-7888	●	● DA	●	●	● DA	●	●			●			●	●	●
	Grand Portage NM	PO Box 668, Grand Marais, MN 55604 218-387-2788	●		●	●		●				●					
	Grand Teton NP	PO Drawer 170, Moose, WY 83012 307-739-3300	●	● DA	●	●	● DA	●	●	●	●	●			●	●	●
	Grant-Kohrs Ranch NHS	266 Warren Lane, Deer Lodge, MT 59722 406-846-2070	●	● DA	●												
	Great Basin NP	100 Great Basin National Park, Baker, NV 89311 775-234-7331	●	● DA	●	●	● DA	●	●			●					●
	Great Sand Dunes NP & N PRES	11500 Hwy 150, Mosca, CO 81146 719-378-6399	●	● DA	●	●	● DA	●									●
	Great Smoky Mountains NP	107 Park Headquarters Road, Gatlinburg, TN 37738 865-436-1200	●	● DA	●	●	● DA	●	●			●		●		●	
	Guadalupe Mountains NP	HC 60 Box 400, Salt Flat, TX 79847 915-828-3251		● DA	●	●	● DA	●	●								
	Guilford Courthouse NMP	2332 New Garden Road, Greensboro, NC 27410 336-288-1776		● DA	●			●						●			
	Gulf Islands NS (Florida District)	1801 Gulf Breeze PKWY, Gulf Breeze, FL 32563 850-934-2600	●	● DA	●	●	● DA	●		●	●	●	●	●			●
	Gulf Islands NS (Mississippi District)	3500 Park Road, Ocean Springs, MS 39564 228-875-9057		● DA	●	●	● DA	●		●	●	●		●			●
H	Haleakala NP	PO Box 369, Makawao, HI 96768 808-572-4400	●	● DA	●	●	● DA	●	●	●					●		
	Hampton NHS	535 Hampton Lane, Towson, MD 21286 410-823-1309	●	●	●												●
	Harpers Ferry NHP	PO Box 65, Harpers Ferry, WV 25425 304-535-6029	●	● DA	●	●		●				●					
	Harry S Truman NHS	223 N Main Street, Independence, MO 64050 816-254-9929	●	● DA	●												
	Hawaii Volcanoes NP	PO Box 52, Hawaii National Park, HI 96718 808-985-6000	●	● DA	●	●	● DA	●	●					●	●	●	●
	Herbert Hoover NHS	PO Box 607, West Branch, IA 52358 319-643-2541	●	● DA	●	●		●									
	Home of Franklin D. Roosevelt NHS	4097 Albany Post Road, Hyde Park, NY 12538 845-229-9115	●	● DA		●		●									
	Homestead NM of America	8523 W State Hwy 4, Beatrice, NE 68310 402-223-3514		● DA	●	●											

K Nationalparks

ABKÜRZUNGEN

NB	National Battlefield	NMP	National Military Park	NS	National Seashore
NBP	National Battlefield Park	NP	National Park	NSR	National Scenic River/ Riverway
NHP	National Historical Park	N PRES	National Preserve		
NHS	National Historic Site	NRA	National Recreation Area	PKWY	Parkway
NL	National Lakeshore	NRRA	National River and Recreation Area	WSR	Wild and Scenic River
N MEM	National Memorial				
NM	National Monument	N RES	National Reserve		

Fees · (Disabled Access) Visitor Center · Programs and Tours · Picnic area · (Disabled Access) Campground · Hiking · Horse Trail · Swimming · Boating · Fishing · Hunting · Bicycle Trail · Cabin Rental · Hotel, Motel, Lodge · Restaurant, Snacks

H	Hopewell Culture NHP	16062 State Route 104, Chillicothe, OH 45601	740-774-1125
	Hopewell Furnace NHS	2 Mark Bird Lane, Elverson, PA 19520	610-582-8773
	Horseshoe Bend NMP	11288 Horseshoe Bend Road, Daviston, AL 36256	265-234-7111
	Hot Springs NP	101 Reserve Street, Hot Springs, AR 71902	501-624-2701
	Hovenweep NM	McElmo Route, Cortez, CO 81321	970-562-4282
	Hubbell Trading Post NHS	PO Box 150, Ganado, AZ 86505	928-755-3475
I	Independence NHP	143 South Third Street, Philadelphia, PA 19106	215-965-2305
	Indiana Dunes NL	1100 N Mineral Springs Road, Porter, IN 46304	219-926-7561, ext 225
	Isle Royale NP	800 E Lakeshore Drive, Houghton, MI 49931	906-482-0984
J	Jean Lafitte NHP & PRES	419 Decatur Street, New Orleans, LA 70130	504-589-3882
	Jefferson National Expansion Memorial	11 N 4th Street, St. Louis, MO 63102	314-655-1700
	Jewel Cave NM	11149 Bldg B12, US Hwy 16, Custer, SD 57730	605-673-2288
	Jimmy Carter NHS	300 N Bond Street, Plains, GA 31780	229-824-4104
	John Day Fossil Beds NM	32651 Highway 19, Kimberly, OR 97848	541-987-2333
	John Muir NHS	4202 Alhambra Avenue, Martinez, CA 94553	925-228-8860
	Johnstown Flood N MEM	733 Lake Road, South Fork, PA 15956	814-495-4643
	Joshua Tree NP	74485 National Park Drive, Twentynine Palms, CA 92277	760-367-5500
K	Kalaupapa NHP	PO Box 2222, Kalaupapa, HI 96742	808-567-6802
	Kaloko-Honokohau NHP	73-4786 Kanalani, Street #14, Kailua-Kona, HI 96740	808-329-6881
	Katmai NP & PRES	PO Box 7, King Salmon, AK 99613	907-246-3305
	Kenai Fjords NP	PO Box 1727, Seward, AK 99664	907-224-7500
	Kennesaw Mountain NBP	900 Kennesaw Mountain Drive, Kennesaw, GA 30152	770-427-4686
	Kings Canyon NP	47050 Generals Hwy, Three Rivers, CA 93271	559-565-3341
	Kings Mountain NMP	2625 Park Road, Blacksburg, SC 29702	864-936-7921
	Klondike Gold Rush NHP-Alaska	PO Box 517, Skagway, AK 99840	907-983-2921
	Klondike Gold Rush NHP-Seattle	319 Second Avenue, Seattle, WA 98104	206-220-4240
	Knife River Indian Villages NHS	PO Box 9, Stanton, ND 58571	701-745-3300
	Kobuk Valley NP	PO Box 1029, Kotzebue, AK 99752	907-442-3890
	Korean War Veterans Memorial	NCP Central, 900 Ohio Drive SW, Washington, DC 20024	202-426-6841
L	Lake Chelan NRA	810 State Route 20, Sedro-Woolley, WA 98284	360-856-5700
	Lake Clark NP & PRES	4230 University Drive, Suite 311, Anchorage, AK 99508	907-781-2218
	Lake Mead NRA	601 Nevada Hwy, Boulder City, NV 89005	702-293-8990
	Lake Meredith NRA	PO Box 1460, Fritch, TX 79036	806-857-3151
	Lake Roosevelt NRA	1008 Crest Drive, Coulee Dam, WA 99116	509-633-9441
	Lassen Volcanic NP	PO Box 100, Mineral, CA 96063	530-595-4444
	Lava Beds NM	1 Indian Well Headquarters, Tulelake, CA 96134	530-667-8100
	Lewis & Clark NHP	92343 Fort Clatsop Road, Astoria, OR 97103	503-861-2471
	Lincoln Boyhood N MEM	PO Box 1816, Lincoln City, IN 47552	812-937-4541
	Lincoln Home NHS	413 S 8th Street, Springfield, IL 62701	217-492-4241, ext 221
	Lincoln Memorial	900 Ohio Drive SW, Washington, DC 20024	202-426-6841
	Little Bighorn Battlefield NM	PO Box 39, Crow Agency, MT 59022	406-638-3204
	Lowell NHP	67 Kirk Street, Lowell, MA 01852	978-970-5000
	Lyndon B. Johnson NHP	PO Box 329, Johnson City, TX 78636	830-868-7128, ext 244
M	Mammoth Cave NP	PO Box 7, Mammoth Cave, KY 42259	270-758-2180
	Manassas NBP	12521 Lee Highway, Manassas, VA 20109	703-361-1339
	Martin Luther King, Jr., NHS	450 Auburn Avenue NE, Atlanta, GA 30312	404-331-5190
	Martin Van Buren NHS	1013 Old Post Road, Kinderhook, NY 12106	518-758-9689
	Mesa Verde NP	PO Box 8, Mesa Verde, CO 81330	970-529-4465
	Minute Man NHP	174 Liberty Street, Concord, MA 01742	978-369-6993
	Mojave N PRES	2701 Barstow Road, Barstow, CA 92311	760-252-6100
	Montezuma Castle NM	PO Box 219, Camp Verde, AZ 86322	928-567-3322
	Moores Creek NB	40 Patriots Hall Drive, Currie, NC 28435	910-283-5591
	Morristown NHP	30 Washington Place, Morristown, NJ 07960	908-766-8215
	Mount Rainier NP	Tahoma Woods, Star Route, Ashford, WA 98304	360-569-2211
	Mount Rushmore N MEM	13000 Highway 244, Building 31, Suite 1, Keystone, SD 57751	605-574-2523
	Muir Woods NM	Mill Valley, CA 94941	415-388-2596
N	Natchez NHP	640 S Canal Street, Box E, Natchez, MS 39120	601-442-7047
	Natchez Trace PKWY	2680 Natchez Trace Pkwy, Tupelo, MS 38804	800-305-7417
	Natural Bridges NM	HC 60, Box 1, Lake Powell, UT 84533	435-692-1234
	Navajo NM	HC 71, Box 3, Tonalea, AZ 86044	928-672-2700
	New River Gorge NR	PO Box 246, Glen Jean, WV 25846	304-465-0508
	Nez Perce NHP	39063 US Hwy, Spalding, ID 83540	208-843-7001
	Ninety Six NHS	PO Box 496, Ninety Six, SC 29666	864-543-4068
	North Cascades NP	810 State Route 20, Sedro-Woolley, WA 98284	360-856-5700
O	Obed WSR	PO Box 429, Wartburg, TN 37887	423-346-6294
	Ocmulgee NM	1207 Emery Hwy, Macon, GA 31217	478-752-8257
	Olympic NP	600 E Park Avenue, Port Angeles, WA 98362	360-565-3130
	Oregon Caves NM	19000 Caves Hwy, Cave Junction, OR 97523	541-592-2100
	Organ Pipe Cactus NM	10 Organ Pipe Drive, Ajo, AZ 85321	520-387-6849
	Ozark NSR	PO Box 490, Van Buren, MO 63965	573-323-4236
P	Padre Island NS	PO Box 181300, Corpus Christi, TX 78480	361-949-8068
	Pea Ridge NMP	15930 Highway 62, Pea Ridge, AR 72751	479-451-8122

Nationalparks

ABKÜRZUNGEN

NB	National Battlefield	NMP	National Military Park	NS	National Seashore
NBP	National Battlefield Park	NP	National Park	NSR	National Scenic River/ Riverway
NHP	National Historical Park	N PRES	National Preserve	PKWY	Parkway
NHS	National Historic Site	NRA	National Recreation Area	WSR	Wild and Scenic River
NL	National Lakeshore	NRRA	National River and Recreation Area		
N MEM	National Memorial	N RES	National Reserve		
NM	National Monument				

			Fees	(Disabled Access) Visitor Center	Programs and Tours	Picnic area	(Disabled Access) Campground	Hiking	Horse Trail	Swimming	Boating	Fishing	Hunting	Bicycle Trail	Cabin Rental	Hotel, Motel, Lodge	Restaurant, Snacks
	Pecos NHP	PO Box 418, Pecos, NM 87552 505-757-6414, ext 1	x	DA	x	x											
	Perry's Victory & International Peace Memorial	PO Box 549, Put-in-Bay, OH 43456 419-285-2184	x	DA	x							x					
	Petersburg NB	1539 Hickory Hill Road, Petersburg, VA 23803 804-732-3531	x	DA	x	x		x	x			x		x			
	Petrified Forest NP	PO Box 2217, Petrified Forest, AZ 86028 928-524-6228	x	DA	x	x		x									x
	Petroglyph NM	6001 Unser Blvd NW, Albuquerque, NM 87120 505-899-0205	x	DA	x	x		x	x								
	Pictured Rocks NL	PO Box 40, Munising, MI 49862 906-387-3700	x	DA		x	DA	x		x	x	x	x				
	Pinnacles NM	5000 Hwy 146, Paicines, CA 95043 831-389-4485	x	DA	x	x	DA	x									
	Pipe Spring NM	HC 65 Box 5, Fredonia, AZ 86022 928-643-7105	x	DA	x			x									x
	Pipestone NM	36 Reservation Avenue, Pipestone, MN 56164 507-825-5464	x	DA		x		x									
	Point Reyes NS	1 Bear Valley Rd, Point Reyes Station, CA 94956 415-464-5100	x	DA	x	x	x	x	x	x		x		x			x
	Pu'uhonua o Honaunau NHP	PO Box 129, Honaunau, HI 96726 808-328-2288	x	DA	x	x		x		x		x					
	Puukohola Heiau NHS	62-3601 Kawaihae Road, Kawaihae, HI 96743 808-882-7218		DA	x												
R	Rainbow Bridge NM	PO Box 1507, Page, AZ 86040 928-608-6404			x						x						
	Redwood NP	1111 2nd Street, Crescent City, CA 95531 707-464-6101		DA	x	x	DA	x	x	x	x	x		x			
	Richmond NBP	3215 E Broad Street, Richmond, VA 23223 804-226-1981		DA	x	x											
	Rocky Mountain NP	1000 Highway 36, Estes Park, CO 80517 970-586-1206	x	DA	x	x	DA	x	x			x					x
	Roger Williams N MEM	282 N Main Street, Providence, RI 02903 401-521-7266		DA		x											
	Ross Lake NRA	810 State Route 20, Sedro-Woolley, WA 98284 360-856-5700	x	DA	x	x	DA	x	x		x	x	x		x		
	Russell Cave NM	3729 County Road 98, Bridgeport, AL 35740 256-495-2672		DA	x	x		x									
S	Sagamore Hill NHS	20 Sagamore Hill Road, Oyster Bay, NY 11771 516-922-4788	x	DA	x	x											
	Saguaro NP	3693 S Old Spanish Trail, Tucson, AZ 85730 520-733-5153	x	DA	x	x		x	x					x			
	Saint Croix NSR	PO Box 708, St. Croix Falls, WI 54024 715-483-3284		DA	x	x	DA	x			x	x	x				
	Saint-Gaudens NHS	139 Saint Gaudens Road, Cornish, NH 03745 603-675-2175	x		x	x		x									
	Salem Maritime NHS	174 Derby Street, Salem, MA 01970 978-740-1650	x	DA	x	x											
	Salinas Pueblo Missions NM	PO Box 517, Mountainair, NM 87036 505-847-2585, ext 20		DA	x	x											
	San Antonio Missions NHP	2202 Roosevelt Avenue, San Antonio, TX 78210 210-932-1001		DA	x	x		x						x			
	San Francisco Maritime NHP	Building E, Fort Mason Center, San Francisco, CA 94123 415-447-5000	x		x	x				x				x			
	San Juan Island NHP	PO Box 429, Friday Harbor, WA 98250-0429 360-378-2240		DA	x	x		x									
	San Juan NHS	501 Norzagaray Street, San Juan, PR 00901 787-729-6777	x	DA	x												
	Santa Monica Mountains NRA	401 W Hillcrest Drive, Thousand Oaks, CA 91360 805-370-2301		DA	x	x	DA	x	x	x				x		x	x
	Saratoga NHP	648 Route 32, Stillwater, NY 12170 518-664-9821, ext 224	x	DA		x		x	x								
	Scotts Bluff NM	PO Box 27, 190276 Hwy 92, Gering, NE 69341 308-436-4340	x	DA	x	x		x						x			
	Sequoia NP	47050 Generals Hwy, Three Rivers, CA 93271 559-565-3341	x	DA	x	x	DA	x	x			x			x	x	x
	Shenandoah NP	3655 US Hwy 211 E, Luray, VA 22835 540-999-3500	x	DA	x	x	DA	x	x			x			x	x	x
	Shiloh NMP	1055 Pittsburg Landing Road, Shiloh, TN 38376 731-689-5696	x	DA		x		x									
	Sitka NHP	103 Monastery Street, Sitka, AK 99835 907-747-0110	x	DA	x	x		x				x					
	Sleeping Bear Dunes NL	9922 Front Street, Empire, MI 49630 231-326-5134	x	DA	x	x	DA	x	x	x	x	x	x				
	Statue of Liberty NM and Ellis Island	Liberty Island, New York, NY 10004 212-363-3200		DA	x	x											x
	Steamtown NHS	150 S Washington Avenue, Scranton, PA 18503 888-693-9391	x	DA	x	x											
	Sunset Crater Volcano NM	6400 N. Highway 89, Flagstaff, AZ 86004 928-526-0502	x	x	x	x	DA	x									
T	Theodore Roosevelt Birthplace NHS	28 E 20th Street, New York, NY 10003 212-260-1616	x	x	x												
	Theodore Roosevelt Island	G.W. Mem Pkwy, Turkey Run Park, McLean, VA 22101 703-289-2500			x			x				x					
	Theodore Roosevelt NP	PO Box 7, Medora, ND 58645 701-623-4466	x	DA	x	x	DA	x	x		x	x					
	Thomas Jefferson Memorial	900 Ohio Drive SW, Washington, DC 20024 202-426-6841			x	x						x					x
	Timpanogos Cave NM	RR 3 Box 200, American Fork, UT 84003 801-756-5238	x	DA	x	x		x				x					x
	Tonto NM	HC 02 Box 4602, Roosevelt, AZ 85545 928-467-2241	x	DA	x	x											
	Tumacacori NHP	PO Box 67, Tumacacori, AZ 85640 520-398-2341	x	DA	x	x		x									
	Tuskegee Institute NHS	1212 West Montgomery Rd, Tuskegee Institute, Tuskegee, AL 36088 334-727-3200		DA	x											x	x
	Tuzigoot NM	PO Box 219, Camp Verde, AZ 86322 928-634-5564	x	DA													
U	USS Arizona Memorial	1 Arizona Memorial Place, Honolulu, HI 96818 808-422-0561		DA	x												
V	Valley Forge NHP	1400 North Outerline Dr, King of Prussia, PA 19406 610-783-1000	x	DA		x		x	x		x	x		x			x
	Vanderbilt Mansion NHS	4097 Albany Post Road, Hyde Park, NY 12538 845-229-9115	x	DA		x		x									
	Vicksburg NMP	3201 Clay Street, Vicksburg, MS 39183 601-636-0583	x	DA		x		x									
	Vietnam Veterans Memorial	900 Ohio Drive SW, Washington, DC 20024 202-426-6841			x												x
	Virgin Islands NP	1300 Cruz Bay Creek, St. John, VI 00830 340-776-6201		DA	x	x	DA	x		x	x	x				x	x
	Voyageurs NP	3131 Hwy 53, South International Falls, MN 56649 218-283-9821		DA	x	x	DA	x		x	x	x			x	x	x
W	Walnut Canyon NM	6400 N. Hwy 89, Flagstaff, AZ 86004 928-526-3367	x	x	x	x											
	Washington Monument	900 Ohio Drive SW, Washington, DC 20024 202-426-6841			x												x
	Whiskeytown-Shasta-Trinity NRA	PO Box 188, Whiskeytown, CA 96095 530-242-3400	x	DA	x	x	DA	x	x	x	x	x	x	x			
	White House	1450 Pennsylvania Avenue NW, Room 1894, Washington, DC 20230 202-208-1631		DA	x												x
	White Sands NM	PO Box 1086, Holloman AFB, NM 88330 505-479-6124	x	DA	x	x		x	x								x
	Whitman Mission NHS	328 Whitman Mission Road, Walla Walla, WA 99362 509-529-6357	x	DA	x	x											
	Wilson's Creek NB	6424 W Farm Road 182, Republic, MO 65738 417-732-2662	x	DA		x		x	x								
	Wind Cave NP	RR 1 Box 190, Hot Springs, SD 57747 605-745-4600	x	DA	x	x	DA	x	x								
	Wolf Trap NP for the Performing Arts	1551 Trap Road, Vienna, VA 22182 703-255-1800			x	x											x
	Women's Rights NHP	136 Fall Street, Seneca Falls, NY 13148 315-568-2991	x	DA	x												
	Wrangell-St. Elias NP & PRES	PO Box 439, Copper Center, AK 99573 907-822-5234		DA		x		x	x		x	x	x	x	x	x	x
	Wright Brothers N MEM	1401 National Park Drive, Manteo, NC 27954 252-441-7430	x	DA	x											x	x
	Wupatki NM	6400 N Hwy 89, Flagstaff, AZ 86004 928-679-2365	x	DA	x	x		x									
Y	Yellowstone NP	PO Box 168, Yellowstone National Park, WY 82190 307-344-7381	x	DA	x	x	DA	x	x	x	x	x		x	x	x	x
	Yosemite NP	PO Box 577, Yosemite National Park, CA 95389 209-372-0200	x	DA	x	x	DA	x	x	x	x	x		x	x	x	x
Z	Zion NP	SR 9, Springdale, UT 84767 435-772-3256	x	x	x	x	DA	x	x					x	x	x	x

M Events

JANUARY

CALIFORNIA
Tournament of Roses Parade, Pasadena.
It's ten times more fun in person than watching it on TV. Most folks come the night before and camp on the sidewalk, waiting for the passing parade of the best floats in the world.
626.449.4100

COLORADO
National Western Stock Show and Rodeo, Denver.
What do ranchers do in the middle of winter? They go to Denver to exhibit–and buy–horses and cattle. Sheep, hogs, llamas, and a vast array of farm machinery are also on display. This is the largest livestock show in the world.
800.336.6977

FLORIDA
Annual Florida Citrus Festival and Polk County Fair, Winter Haven.
An 11-day celebration of the citrus industry is set in a country-fair atmosphere, with livestock exhibits, quilt shows, and entertainment.
863.292.9810

MINNESOTA
St. Paul Winter Carnival, St. Paul.
In North America's oldest and largest winter carnival, the frigid depths of a Twin Cities winter come to life for a week with antique sleigh and cutter parades, fireworks, car races on ice, and ice-carving and snow-sculpting competitions.
651.223.4700, 800.488.4023

NEVADA
National Cowboy Poetry Gathering, Elko.
An institution in its own right, the "granddaddy of all poetry gatherings" is a weeklong celebration of the Old West, complete with dances, workshops on rawhide braiding and the like, guitar-and-fiddle jams into the small hours, and, of course, poetry readings.
775.738.7508

PENNSYLVANIA
Mummers Parade, Philadelphia.
The world-famous New Year's Day parade features 30,000 spectacularly costumed mummers, including string bands and comics.
215.336.3050

UTAH
Sundance Film Festival, Park City.
Hollywood pulls on its snow pants to find the next big thing at Robert Redford's annual showcase of independent film.
801.328.3456

FEBRUARY

CALIFORNIA
Chinese New Year Festival, San Francisco.
Dancing dragons, fireworks, and great food in celebration of the lunar New Year, and the best time to visit San Francisco's famed Chinatown.
415.982.3071

COLORADO
Steamboat Springs Winter Carnival, Steamboat Springs.
Almost like a rodeo on ice, with strange events like snow-shovel racing, broomball, and a parade on skis.
970.879.0880

FLORIDA
Speed Weeks, Daytona.
The world's best road racers and stock-car drivers converge on the Daytona International Speedway for some of motor sport's biggest events from the Rolex 24 through the Daytona 500.
386.254.2700

LOUISIANA
Mardi Gras, New Orleans.
Rollicking, raucous, and ritualistic, Mardi Gras is New Orleans's legendary carnival, featuring freewheeling street celebrations, formal masquerade balls, and the famous parade in which the "Krewes" try to outdo each other's floats and costumes.
504.566.5003, 877.791.8272

MANITOBA
Le Festival du Voyageur, Winnipeg.
Manitoba commemorates its French-Canadian heritage, when fur traders were king, with this ten-day winter carnival that includes period costumes, arts and crafts, and a downtown street party.
204.237.7692

QUÉBEC
Winter Carnival of Québec City.
A citywide celebration of winter for the whole family, with art exhibits, sporting events such as the famed canoe race across the ice-choked St. Lawrence, ice sculptures (and an ice palace), and general bonhomie.
418.626.3716

TEXAS
Charro Days Fiesta, Brownsville.
Starting with the traditional *grito* yell and a blast of mariachi music, this southernmost Texas city celebrates the *charro*–skilled horseman, hero of neighboring Mexico's folklore–with parades, street dances, and carnivals . . . not to mention great food. Begins last Thursday of the month.
956.542.4245

MARCH

ALASKA
Iditarod Trail Sled Dog Race, Anchorage to Nome.
The world's longest dogsled race heads through the streets of Anchorage, mushes through mountains and ice-locked seas, and ends 9 to 13 days later in Nome.
907.376.5155

ARIZONA
Scottsdale Arts Festival, Scottsdale.
Arts and crafts from across the nation abound at this annual event in an upscale Phoenix suburb that has become a major center for Western, Native American, and contemporary art.
480.994.2787

MAINE
Maine Maple Sunday
The Governor kicks off this statewide event with a proclamation, and several dozen maple-sugar producers open their doors for tours and sampling. Savor the traditional snack of sugar on snow" (that's syrup poured on shaved ice, for out-of-towners) with plain doughnuts.
207.287.3491

NEBRASKA
Sandhill Crane Spring Migration, Platte.
One of the most magnificent sights anywhere in the Great Plains is watching half a million sandhill cranes swoop over the Platte River as they return to the adjoining wetlands in spring. Special sunrise and sunset crane tours are organized by a volunteer group, Wings Over the Platte.
800.658.3178

NEW YORK
St. Patrick's Day, New York City.
New Yorkers have their own unique ways of celebrating St. Patrick's Day. More than 150,000 marchers, representing the various Irish societies of the city, participate in the parade up 5th Avenue from 44th to 86th Streets.

SOUTH CAROLINA
Festival of Houses and Gardens, Charleston.
The historic neighborhoods and private gardens of one of America's most beautiful cities reveal themselves to visitors during this monthlong event.
843.722.3405

APRIL

DISTRICT OF COLUMBIA
National Cherry Blossom Festival, Washington, D.C.
Washingtonians celebrate the blossoming of more than 6,000 Japanese cherry trees with festivities that include the crowning of the Cherry Blossom Festival Queen and a parade.
202.547.1500

HAWAII
Merrie Monarch Festival, Hilo, Big Island
The premier hula competition and event of the year, this festival draws a multitude of hula *halau* (schools) to Hilo, where performers dance ancient and modern hula, perform traditional chanting, and play ancient Hawaiian instruments.
808.935.9168

KENTUCKY
American Quilter's Society National Show and Contest, Paducah.
Quilters from around the country gather for one of the nation's largest shows of its kind.
502.898.7903

MASSACHUSETTS
Boston Marathon, Boston.
The Patriot's Day 26.2-mile course starts in Hopkinton, winds through eight cities and towns, and finishes near Copley Square.
617.236.1652

ONTARIO
The Shaw Festival, Niagara-on-the-Lake.
From April through October the works of George Bernard Shaw and his contemporaries come alive on three stages in the heart of Ontario's wine country.
800.511.7429

TEXAS
Fiesta San Antonio, San Antonio.
The city's Hispanic roots come out in full force during this boisterous, exuberant, city-wide party that includes parades, costume balls with revelers in historical outfits, and great Tex-Mex food.
210.227.5191

WASHINGTON
Washington State Apple Blossom Festival, Wenatchee.
Here in the fruit basket of the Northwest, a vast array of produce thrives–but the apple is still king. Wenatchee becomes a wonderland of blossoms in late April and early May, and dozens of events celebrate the flowering of commercial orchards.
509.662.3616

MAY

DELAWARE
Winterthur Point-to-Point Races, Winterthur.
Exciting amateur competitions include steeplechase and flat races. The day includes a parade of antique horse-drawn carriages, canine demonstrations, and pony races, as well as a tailgate-picnic competition.
800.448.3883

KENTUCKY
Kentucky Derby and Derby Festival, Louisville.
Festivities leading up to the legendary horse race, which is held each year on the first Saturday in May, begin two weeks before the event.
800.928.3378

INDIANA
500 Festival, Indianapolis.
Before the racers start their engines and embark on 3 plus hours of counter-clockwise spectacle, visitors can drive their own cars on the fabled oval and glimpse drivers and celebrities in the Festival Parade.
800.638.4296

NORTH CAROLINA
Ole Time Fiddler's & Bluegrass Festival, Union Grove.
The oldest festival of its kind in North America, this down-home, family-oriented get-together highlights traditional American music through fiddle contests, informal jam sessions, and workshops.
828.478.3735

SOUTH CAROLINA
Spoleto Festival U.S.A., Charleston.
Originally founded by composer Gian Carlo Menotti, this 17-day festival fills Charleston's historic churches and theaters with more than 120 performances of opera, dance, theater, jazz and classical music.
843.722.2764

TENNESSEE
Beale Street Music Festival. Memphis
American blues, as irresistible as the neighboring Mississippi River, and blues-inspired music streams from the celebrated Beale Street clubs and temporary stages, performed by "legends" and newcomers.
901.525.4611

WASHINGTON
Northwest Folklife Festival, Seattle.
Billed as the largest festival of its kind in the U. S., Folklife is an ethnic extravaganza celebrating traditional arts, with participatory dancing (square, swing), jam sessions, craft demonstrations, and music workshops.
206.684.7300

JUNE

ALASKA
Midnight Sun Festival, Fairbanks.
What do you do on the summer solstice with more than 22 hours of direct sunlight? Celebrate with sporting events, a parade, lots of street activities, and baseball played under the midnight sun.
907.452.8671

MASSACHUSETTS
Jacob's Pillow, Becket.
From late June through early August, the United States' oldest dance festival attracts dancers and troupes from around the world.
413.243.0745

Scooper Bowl, Boston.
The nation's largest all-you-can eat ice cream festival unofficially kicks off summer in Boston to help the Jimmy Fund's fight against cancer.
617.632.4215

MICHIGAN
The Frankenmuth Bavarian Festival, Frankenmuth.
Michigan's "Little Bavaria" rolls out the *willkommen* mat for its annual multiday heritage celebration, hosting some of the nation's best polka bands and serving up locally brewed ale, homemade bratwurst, and pretzels.
800.386.3378

OKLAHOMA
Red Earth Festival, Oklahoma City.
Representatives from a hundred tribes in Oklahoma and throughout the U. S. and Canada gather for competitions, displays of traditional crafts and fine arts, and dancing contests.
405.427.5228

OREGON
Portland Rose Festival, Portland.
The Grand Floral Parade is the second largest in the country. Eighty events in 25 days, including parties, music, and celebration, with a special welcome mat laid out for the Navy crews docked downtown.
503.227.2681

Oregon Shakespeare Festival, Ashland.
It's definitely worth the trip to this eclectic town of Victorian homes and galleries to catch its Tony Award-winning festival of the Bard's best. Productions run February through October, but the Elizabethan outdoor stage opens in June.
541.482.4331

JULY

ALBERTA
Calgary Exhibition and Stampede, Calgary.
This wild celebration of the West has been held since 1912. Highlights include the chuck-wagon race at Stampede Park and one of the biggest rodeos in Canada.
800.661.1260

CALIFORNIA
Gilroy Garlic Festival, Gilroy.
Garlic ice cream, garlic cheesecake, even chocolate-covered garlic. This harvest festival celebrates 101 uses for the pungent herb.
408.842.1625

DISTRICT OF COLUMBIA
Independence Day Celebration, Washington, D.C.
Activities include colonial military maneuvers, a parade down Constitution Avenue, free entertainment, and a concert by the National Symphony Orchestra followed by fireworks over the Washington Monument.
202.619.7222

MICHIGAN
National Cherry Festival, Traverse City.
In the Grand Traverse region, known for the world's greatest concentration of tart cherries, this summer resort town hosts a multiday celebration that includes parades, fireworks, big-name entertainers, and tasty cherry pies.
231.947.4230, 800.968.3380

MISSOURI
Tom Sawyer Days, Hannibal.
The childhood home of Mark Twain – known then as Samuel Clemens – celebrates with a mighty frog-jumping contest and a just-for-fun fence-painting championship. Take a look at the author's boyhood home while you're there.
866.263.4825

WISCONSIN
EAA AirVenture, Oshkosh.
Annual gathering of some 12,000 homebuilt, antique and aerobatic planes, as well as military and general aviation aircraft.
800.564.6322
800.843.3612

WYOMING
Cheyenne Frontier Days, Cheyenne.
A hefty prize purse – the largest for any outdoor rodeo in the world – draws the best to this celebration, which also includes country-western entertainment and parades.
800.227.6336

AUGUST

BRITISH COLUMBIA
Peach Festival, Penticton.
The Okanagan Valley celebrates its biggest agriculture crop with a festival that is 50 years old. The week-long event includes music, sporting events, and lots of peaches.
250.493.4055
800.663.5052

IDAHO
Idaho International Dance & Music Festival, Rexburg.
Lectures and workshops supplement the dancing, colorfully exhibited by more than 300 participants from a host of countries
208.356.5700

MAINE
Maine Lobster Festival, Rockland.
This five-day event, held at Harbor Park overlooking Penobscot Bay, features all sorts of waterfront recreation, parades, marine exhibits, boat and helicopter rides – and, of course, steamed lobsters.
800.562.2529

NEVADA
Burning Man, Black Rock Desert.
Erupting from life on a stark desert playa in northwestern Nevada, Burning Man rejoices in unconventionality, drawing more than 25,000 people eager to forge a temporary, experimental community where residents will discover self-reliance and will explore radical self-expression.
415.863.5263

PENNSYLVANIA
Musikfest, Bethlehem.
More than 650 free concerts by over 250 national, local and regional groups, ranging from salsa to swing, classical to conga, and folk to funk.
610.332.1300

RHODE ISLAND
Newport JVC Jazz Festival, Newport.
One of the most prestigious jazz events in the U. S., showcasing legendary performers and rising stars.
401.847.3700

SOUTH CAROLINA
Jubilee: Festival of Heritage, Columbia.
This celebration of African-American culture emphasizes traditional art forms, such as basketry, drumming, and story-telling.
803.252.7742 (ext. 25)

VIRGINIA
Old Fiddlers' Convention, Galax.
Musicians from around the world gather to jam and compete in the largest musical convention of its kind in the country.
276.236.8541

SEPTEMBER

BRITISH COLUMBIA
The Fringe – Vancouver's Theatre Festival, Vancouver.
Vancouver hosts an eclectic group of theater, dance, and musical groups from around the world for this 11-day festival modeled after the popular event in Edinburgh, Scotland.
604.257.0350

LOUISIANA
The Original Southwest Louisiana Zydeco Music Festival, Opelousas.
Performers play authentic Creole and Zydeco music in the rural setting where it was born.
337.232.7672

MISSISSIPPI
Mississippi Delta Blues and Heritage Festival, Greenville.
Nationally and internationally known artists perform at one of the South's largest music festivals, dedicated to the plaintive native sound of the Delta.
800.467.3582

NORTH CAROLINA
Mayberry Days, Mount Airy.
For three days each fall, residents of Andy Griffith's real-life hometown celebrate Mayberry, his TV hometown on *The Andy Griffith Show*. Thousands of fans march in the Mayberry Days parade and wait on block-long lines to order pork-chop sandwiches at the Snappy Lunch cafe.
800.286.6193

ONTARIO
Toronto International Film Festival, Toronto.
Established directors and little-known independents alike present their latest dramas, comedies, documentaries, and animated films at one of the world's top-rated film festivals.
416.968.3456

VERMONT
Northeast Kingdom Fall Foliage Festival, Marshfield, Walden, Cabot, Plainfield, Peacham, Barnet, Groton, St. Johnsbury.
Towns throughout Vermont honor the fall foliage with village tours, bazaars, exhibits, and sumptuous church suppers.
800.639.6379

WASHINGTON
Bumbershoot, Seattle.
An old English term for umbrella, this Bumbershoot is a mammoth annual music festival that draws big names of all genres. In spite of its name, sunny skies often bless the festival over Labor Day weekend. Food, crafts, film screenings, and dance performances round out the offerings.
206.281.7788

OCTOBER

ALABAMA
National Shrimp Festival, Gulf Shores.
Four days of beachfront festivities include a parade, music, arts and crafts, and a sumptuous abundance of seafood.
251.968.6904

ARKANSAS
Arkansas Blues & Heritage Festival, Helena.
Some say this Mississippi River town is the birthplace of the blues. They make a strong case by hosting one of the largest blues festivals in the nation every year.
870.338.8798

FLORIDA
Fantasy Fest, Key West.
The Southernmost City pulls out all the stops with Caribbean carnival revelry, Halloween parades, and a touch of wrong-time-of-the-year Mardi Gras.
305.296.1817

GEORGIA
Stone Mountain Highland Games and Scottish Festival, Stone Mountain.
The clans gather for this world-famous festival of all things Scottish – including such traditional Scottish athletic competitions as Tossing the Caber (best described as heaving a telephone pole), Celtic music and dancing, and hearty Highland food.
770.521.0228

NEW MEXICO
Kodak Albuquerque International Balloon Fiesta, Albuquerque.
Over 850 participants gather for the greatest spectacle of its kind in the world. Uniquely shaped balloons and massed sunrise ascensions are featured.
505.842.9918

NOVA SCOTIA
Celtic Colours International Festival, Cape Breton Island.
An international Celtic festival featuring the sounds of local artists together with the burgeoning talents of the global Celtic community. Concerts, dancing, theater, and Celtic-language events make this an exciting ten days.
877.285.2321

OHIO
Pumpkin Show, Circleville.
The state's oldest festival displays more than 100,000 pounds of pumpkin-related products and features three stages of entertainment, contests, and rides.
740.474.7000

NOVEMBER

ALASKA
Alaska Bald Eagle Festival, Haines.
This month the winter population of American bald eagles reaches its peak as some 3,000 eagles congregate around the banks of the Chilkat River, feeding on late-running salmon. This three-day event includes nature tours and educational seminars about the great birds.
907.766.3094

ARKANSAS
World's Championship Duck Calling Contest and Wings Over the Prairie Festival, Stuttgart.
Festivities for the world and state duck calling championships include a duck gumbo cook-off and the Queen Mallard pageant.
870.673.1602

FLORIDA
Florida Pirate Festival, Clearwater
Grab your eye patches and cutlasses, perhaps even your mascara and eyeliner, and practice your "ahrrrs" – then set sail for this family-friendly buccaneer bacchanalia. And remember not to scratch with a hook-hand.
727.518.5341

ILLINOIS
Magnificent Mile Lights Festival, Chicago.
Occurring each year on the Saturday before Thanksgiving, this holiday-season festival of ice-carving demonstrations, strolling carolers, traditional holiday foods, and the unveiling of commercial window displays culminates in a parade on Michigan Avenue and fireworks on the lake. Displays stay up through January.
312.642.3570

MARYLAND
Waterfowl Festival, Easton.
Some 500 artisans exhibit and sell original wildfowl art, carvings, antique decoys and guns, duck stamps and gifts. Also a special sculpture exhibit, seminars, and goose- and duck-calling contests.
410.822.4567

TEXAS
International Chili Championship, Terlingua.
How do you like your chili? Beans or no beans, hotter than a pistol or mildly seasoned? Find out at the granddaddy of chili cook-offs.
888.227.4468

DECEMBER

ARIZONA
Annual Indian Market, Phoenix.
Some 600 Native American artisans from more than 50 tribes demonstrate and sell their works. Activities include music, singing, and dancing.
602.495.0901

BRITISH COLUMBIA
British Columbia Whistler Film Festival, Whistler
Independent international and Canadian films, orbited by media and "industry" glitterati, are a stylishly cool complement to the superb winter sports at this famous resort.
604.935.8035

DISTRICT OF COLUMBIA
National Christmas Tree Lighting/Pageant of Peace, Washington, D.C.
Each year the President lights the the National Christmas Tree on the South Lawn of the White House.
202.619.7222

GEORGIA
Festival of Trees, Atlanta.
Decorated trees and holiday tableaus created by Atlanta's premier artists and designers are the centerpieces of the festival, joined by extravagant gingerbread houses, children's activities, and live entertainment.
404.785.8815

HAWAII
Rip Curl Pipeline Masters, Ehukai Beach Park, Oahu
Held at the North Shore's famous Banzai Pipeline break, this annual showdown of the world's top surfers is the longest running pro surf competition in the U. S.
808.638.7700

NEW MEXICO
Old Town Luminaria Festival, Albuquerque.
An old New Mexican holiday tradition is to set lit candles in paper bags along walkways and rooflines. The illuminated neighborhoods can be admired on foot or from specially provided buses.
800.284.2282

ONTARIO
Winter Festival of Lights, Niagara Falls.
The festival, which begins in late November and runs through early January, includes illumination of Horseshoe Falls and a spectacular fireworks show on New Year's Eve.
800.563.2557

0 Klima-Karten

SUNSHINE

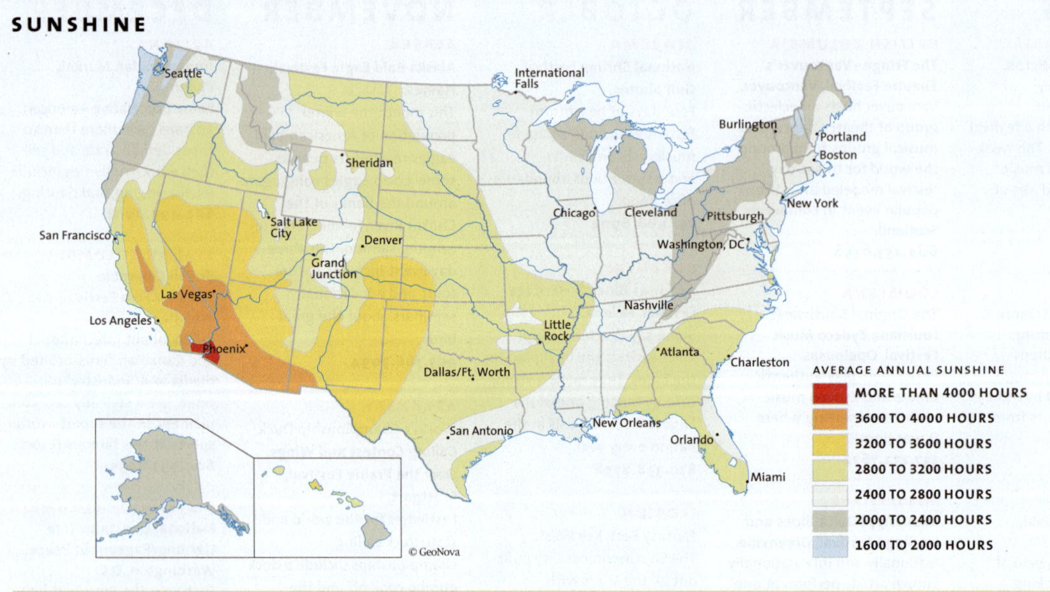

CITY	DAYS OF SUNSHINE
Las Vegas, NV	211.1
Phoenix, AZ	211.0
Los Angeles, CA	186.0
San Francisco, CA	160.3
Grand Junction, CO	136.6
Dallas/Fort Worth, TX	135.5
Salt Lake City, UT	125.0
Little Rock, AR	118.7
Denver, CO	115.2
Atlanta, GA	110.4
New York, NY	106.7
San Antonio, TX	106.1
Nashville, TN	102.9
Charleston, SC	102.3
New Orleans, LA	101.4
Portland, ME	101.3
Boston, MA	98.4
Washington, DC	96.7
Sheridan, WY	95.8
Orlando, FL	89.9
Chicago, IL	83.8
International Falls, MN	76.7
Miami, FL	75.1
Seattle, WA	71.0
Cleveland, OH	66.4
Pittsburgh, PA	58.3
Burlington, VT	57.9

RAINFALL

CITY	DAYS OF RAINFALL
Cleveland, OH	156.0
Burlington, VT	154.0
Pittsburgh, PA	153.3
Seattle, WA	150.4
International Falls, MN	131.3
Miami, FL	129.5
Portland, ME	128.5
Boston, MA	126.5
Chicago, IL	126.3
New York, NY	120.6
Nashville, TN	118.6
Orlando, FL	115.8
Atlanta, GA	115.1
New Orleans, LA	114.5
Charleston, SC	112.9
Washington, DC	112.3
Sheridan, WY	106.8
Little Rock, AR	104.5
Salt Lake City, UT	90.6
Denver, CO	89.1
San Antonio, TX	82.1
Dallas/Fort Worth, TX	78.9
Grand Junction, CO	72.8
San Francisco, CA	62.0
Phoenix, AZ	36.5
Los Angeles, CA	35.2
Las Vegas, NV	26.5

SNOWFALL

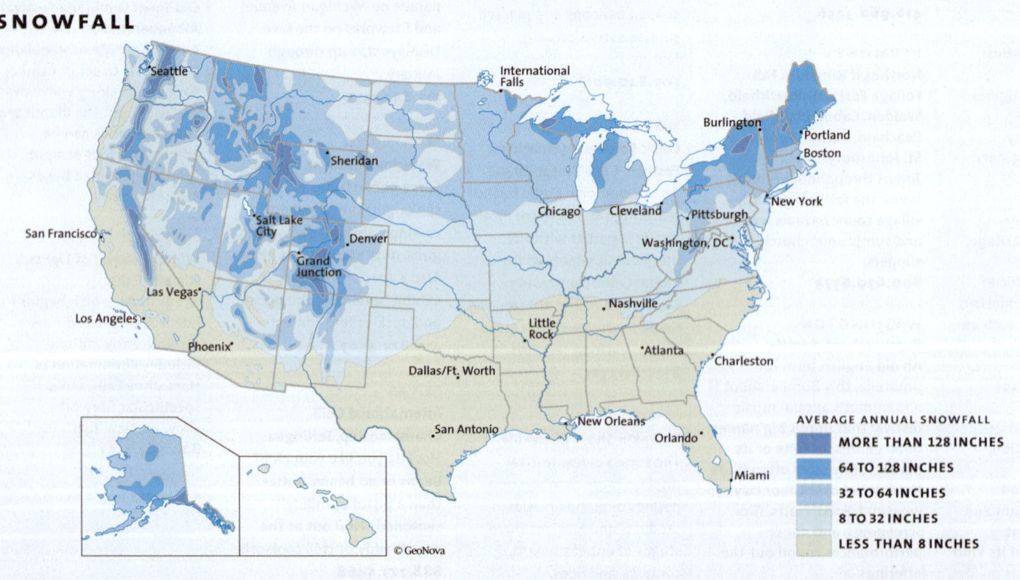

CITY	DAYS OF SNOWFALL
Sheridan, WY	23.6
Burlington, VT	22.0
International Falls, MN	19.5
Cleveland, OH	18.4
Denver, CO	17.9
Salt Lake City, UT	17.8
Portland, ME	17.3
Pittsburgh, PA	12.8
Chicago, IL	11.6
Boston, MA	10.7
Grand Junction, CO	8.7
New York, NY	7.9
Washington, DC	4.6
Nashville, TN	3.5
Seattle, WA	2.4
Little Rock, AR	1.9
Dallas/Fort Worth, TX	1.1
Atlanta, GA	0.6
Las Vegas, NV	0.4
Charleston, SC	0.2
San Antonio, TX	0.2
New Orleans, LA	rare
San Francisco, CA	rare
Los Angeles, CA	0.0
Miami, FL	0.0
Orlando, FL	0.0
Phoenix, AZ	0.0

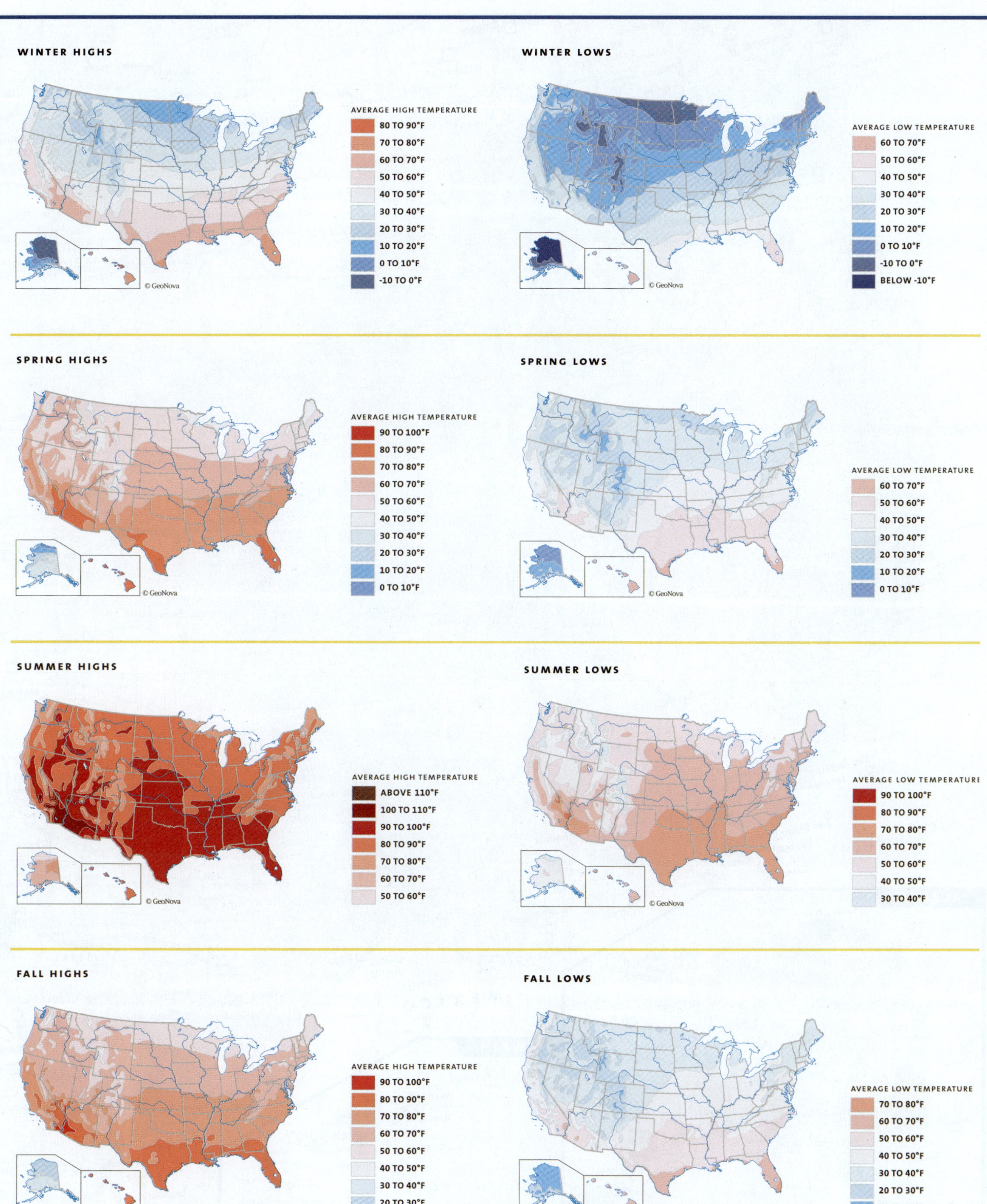
WINTER HIGHS
AVERAGE HIGH TEMPERATURE
80 TO 90°F
70 TO 80°F
60 TO 70°F
50 TO 60°F
40 TO 50°F
30 TO 40°F
20 TO 30°F
10 TO 20°F
0 TO 10°F
-10 TO 0°F
© GeoNova
WINTER LOWS
AVERAGE LOW TEMPERATURE
60 TO 70°F
50 TO 60°F
40 TO 50°F
30 TO 40°F
20 TO 30°F
10 TO 20°F
0 TO 10°F
-10 TO 0°F
BELOW -10°F
© GeoNova
SPRING HIGHS
AVERAGE HIGH TEMPERATURE
90 TO 100°F
80 TO 90°F
70 TO 80°F
60 TO 70°F
50 TO 60°F
40 TO 50°F
30 TO 40°F
20 TO 30°F
10 TO 20°F
0 TO 10°F
© GeoNova
SPRING LOWS
AVERAGE LOW TEMPERATURE
60 TO 70°F
50 TO 60°F
40 TO 50°F
30 TO 40°F
20 TO 30°F
10 TO 20°F
0 TO 10°F
© GeoNova
SUMMER HIGHS
AVERAGE HIGH TEMPERATURE
ABOVE 110°F
100 TO 110°F
90 TO 100°F
80 TO 90°F
70 TO 80°F
60 TO 70°F
50 TO 60°F
© GeoNova
SUMMER LOWS
AVERAGE LOW TEMPERATURE
90 TO 100°F
80 TO 90°F
70 TO 80°F
60 TO 70°F
50 TO 60°F
40 TO 50°F
30 TO 40°F
© GeoNova
FALL HIGHS
AVERAGE HIGH TEMPERATURE
90 TO 100°F
80 TO 90°F
70 TO 80°F
60 TO 70°F
50 TO 60°F
40 TO 50°F
30 TO 40°F
20 TO 30°F
© GeoNova
FALL LOWS
AVERAGE LOW TEMPERATURE
70 TO 80°F
60 TO 70°F
50 TO 60°F
40 TO 50°F
30 TO 40°F
20 TO 30°F
10 TO 20°F
© GeoNova

United States

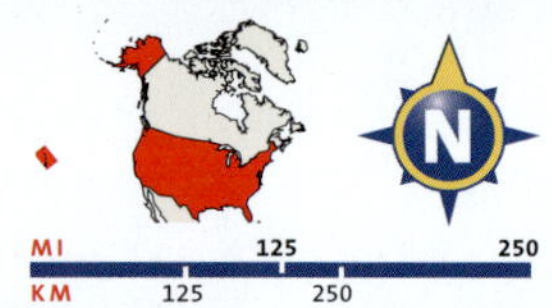

CANADA
ONTARIO
QUÉBEC
NEW BRUNSWICK
MAINE
MINNESOTA
WISCONSIN
MICHIGAN
IOWA
ILLINOIS
INDIANA
OHIO
PENNSYLVANIA
NEW YORK
NEW JERSEY
VT.
N.H.
MASS.
CT.
R.I.
MD.
DE.
WEST VIRGINIA
VIRGINIA
KENTUCKY
TENNESSEE
NORTH CAROLINA
SOUTH CAROLINA
GEORGIA
ALABAMA
MISSISSIPPI
LOUISIANA
ARKANSAS
MISSOURI
FLORIDA
BAHAMAS
OZARK PLATEAU
APPALACHIAN MOUNTAINS
ATLANTIC OCEAN
GULF OF MEXICO
Lake Superior
Lake Michigan
Lake Huron
Lake Erie
Lake Ontario
Chicago
Milwaukee
Detroit
Cleveland
Pittsburgh
Buffalo
Toronto
Ottawa
Montréal
Québec
Boston
Providence
Hartford
New York
Newark
Philadelphia
Baltimore
Washington, DC
Richmond
Norfolk
Virginia Beach
Raleigh
Durham
Greensboro
Winston-Salem
Charlotte
Columbia
Charleston
Savannah
Atlanta
Birmingham
Montgomery
Jacksonville
Tallahassee
Orlando
Tampa
St. Petersburg
Miami
Fort Lauderdale
Nashville
Memphis
Knoxville
Louisville
Lexington
Cincinnati
Columbus
Indianapolis
St. Louis
Kansas City
Minneapolis
St. Paul
Des Moines
Little Rock
Shreveport
Jackson
New Orleans
Baton Rouge
Mobile
Houston
Galveston
Beaumont
Nassau
Key West

Alabama

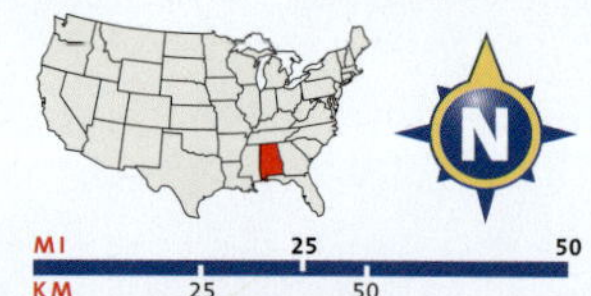

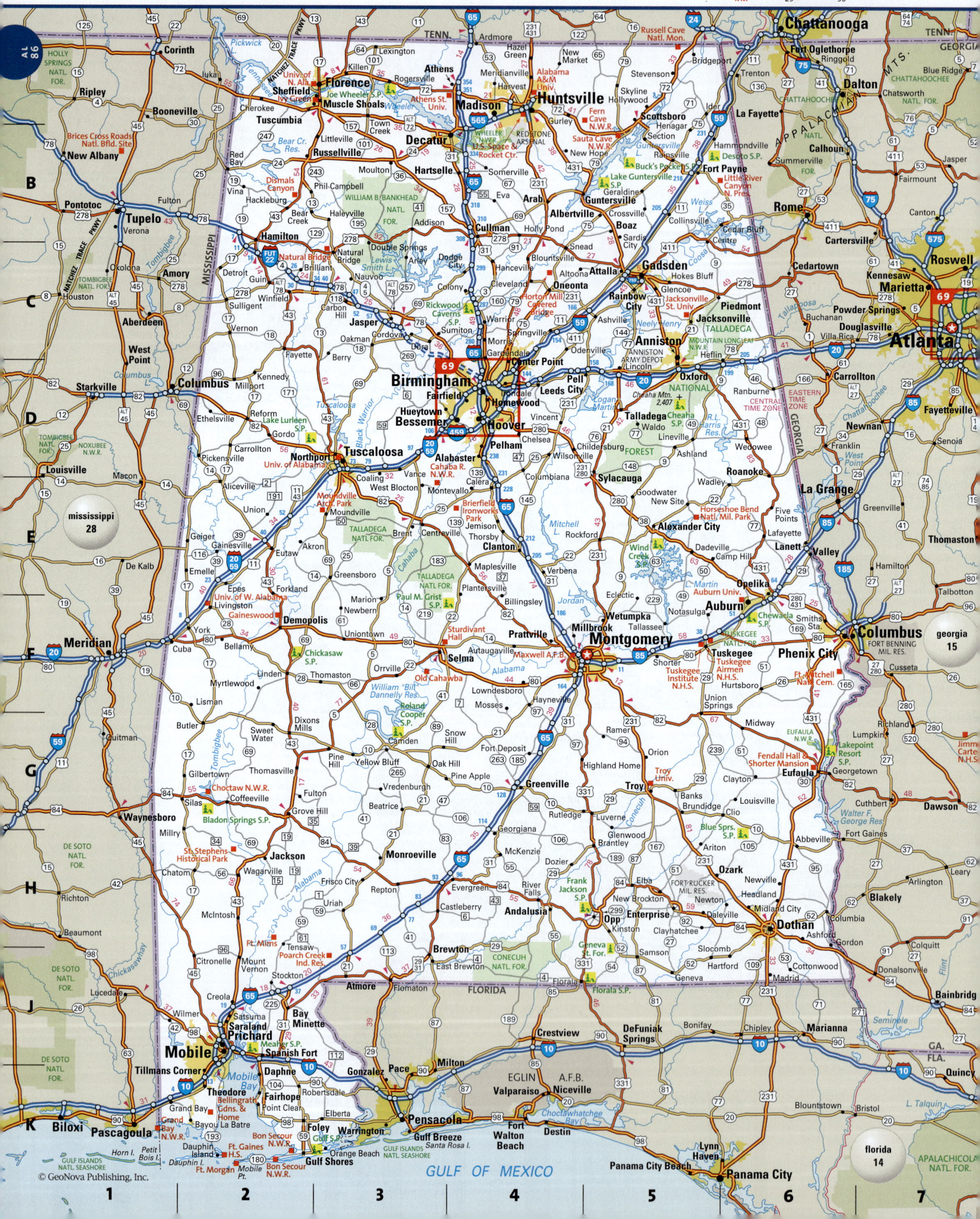

AL 86

Chattanooga
Fort Oglethorpe
Ringgold
Dalton
Chatsworth
Blue Ridge
Rome
Cartersville
Calhoun
Roswell
Marietta
Kennesaw
Powder Springs
Douglasville
Villa Rica
Atlanta
Carrollton
Newnan
Fayetteville
La Grange
West Point
Valley
Lanett
Columbus
Phenix City
Fort Benning Mil. Res.
Cusseta
Richland
Lumpkin
Eufaula
Georgetown
Cuthbert
Dawson
Fort Gaines
Blakely
Colquitt
Donalsonville
Bainbridge
Chattahoochee Natl. For.
Appalachian Mts.
Central Time Zone
Eastern Time Zone
Georgia

Corinth
Iuka
Ripley
Booneville
Tupelo
Pontotoc
New Albany
Brices Cross Roads Natl. Bfld. Site
Fulton
Verona
Okolona
Houston
Amory
Aberdeen
West Point
Starkville
Columbus
Louisville
Macon
Meridian
Quitman
Waynesboro
Lucedale
Biloxi
Pascagoula
Holly Springs Natl. For.
Tombigbee Natl. For.
Noxubee N.W.R.
De Soto Natl. For.
Natchez Trace Pkwy.
Mississippi

Florence
Sheffield
Muscle Shoals
Tuscumbia
Athens
Madison
Huntsville
Decatur
Hartselle
Cullman
Scottsboro
Fort Payne
Guntersville
Albertville
Boaz
Gadsden
Attalla
Oneonta
Jasper
Hamilton
Russellville
Birmingham
Fairfield
Bessemer
Hueytown
Homewood
Hoover
Pelham
Alabaster
Anniston
Oxford
Jacksonville
Talladega
Sylacauga
Tuscaloosa
Northport
Alexander City
Clanton
Prattville
Montgomery
Auburn
Opelika
Tuskegee
Selma
Demopolis
Livingston
Greenville
Troy
Ozark
Enterprise
Dothan
Andalusia
Brewton
Atmore
Monroeville
Jackson
Bay Minette
Saraland
Prichard
Mobile
Daphne
Spanish Fort
Fairhope
Foley
Gulf Shores
Dauphin Island
Tillmans Corner
William B. Bankhead Natl. For.
Talladega Natl. For.
Conecuh Natl. For.
Wheeler N.W.R.
Cheaha Mtn. 2,407
Maxwell A.F.B.
Fort Rucker Mil. Res.
Univ. of Alabama
Auburn Univ.
Troy Univ.
Tennessee
Florida

Crestview
DeFuniak Springs
Marianna
Chipley
Bonifay
Milton
Pace
Gonzalez
Pensacola
Gulf Breeze
Navarre
Fort Walton Beach
Niceville
Valparaiso
Destin
Eglin A.F.B.
Panama City Beach
Panama City
Lynn Haven
Blountstown
Bristol
Quincy
Apalachicola Natl. For.
Gulf Islands Natl. Seashore
Gulf of Mexico

mississippi 28
georgia 15
florida 14

A B C D E F G H J K
1 2 3 4 5 6 7

ALASKA

ARCTIC OCEAN

BEAUFORT SEA

CHUKCHI SEA

BERING SEA

GULF OF ALASKA

PACIFIC OCEAN

Anchorage

Fairbanks

Juneau

Whitehorse

yukon territory 56

northwest territories 56

nunavut 56

british columbia 58

0 100 200 mi
0 100 200 km

HAWAI'IAN ISLANDS

Honolulu

Hilo

PACIFIC OCEAN

0 50 100 mi
0 50 100 km

KAUA'I

Līhu'e

0 5 10 mi
0 5 10 km

HAWAI'I

PACIFIC OCEAN

Hilo

Kailua-Kona

0 10 20 mi
0 10 20 km

O'AHU

PACIFIC OCEAN

Honolulu

Pearl City

0 2 4 6 mi
0 2 4 6 km

MAUI–MOLOKA'I–LĀNA'I

PACIFIC OCEAN

Lahaina

Kahului

Wailuku

0 5 10 15 mi
0 5 10 15 20 km

HI 87
AK 86

1 2 3 4 5 6 7

B C D E F G H J K

Arizona

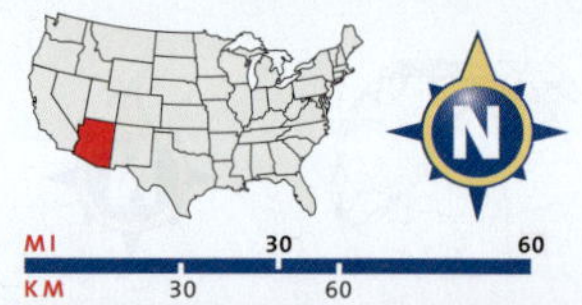
N
MI 30 60
KM 30 60

nevada 32
utah 50
california 8
mexico 68
AZ 86
PAHRANAGAT N.W.R.
PACIFIC TIME ZONE
MOUNTAIN TIME ZONE
St. George
Hurricane
DIXIE NATL. FOR.
ZION NATL. PARK
PAIUTE IND. RES.
GRAND STAIRCASE-ESCALANTE NATL. MON.
GLEN CANYON NATL. REC. AREA
Hovenweep Natl. Mon.
UTE MTN. IND. RES.
Kanab
UTAH
Lake Powell
Rainbow Bridge Natl. Mon.
Navajo Mtn. 10,388
NAVAJO NATION IND. RES.
Mexican Hat
MONUMENT VALLEY
Four Corners Mon.
Mormon Pk. 7,411
Mesquite
Littlefield
Colorado City
Fredonia
KAIBAB IND. RES.
Pipe Spring Natl. Mon.
VERMILION CLIFFS NATL. MON.
Marble Canyon
Glen Canyon Dam
Navajo Bridge
Page
MONUMENT VALLEY NAVAJO TRIBAL PARK
Mexican Water
Teec Nos Pos
Dennehotso
Rock Point
Pastora Pk. 9,412
Shiprock
Mt. Bangs 8,012
SHIVWITS PLATEAU
NEVADA
MOAPA RIVER IND. RES.
Glendale
Jacob Lake
KAIBAB NATL. FOR.
Bitter Springs
Kaibito
Navajo Natl. Mon.
Shonto
Kayenta
Round Rock
Lukachukai
Mt. Trumbull
Mt. Trumbull 8,029
White Mesa Natural Bridge
NAVAJO NATION IND. RES.
Rough Rock
Tsaile
Many Farms
Cow Springs
Nellis A.F.B.
LAKE MEAD NATL. REC. AREA
Las Vegas
Henderson
Hoover Dam
Boulder City
GRAND CANYON-PARASHANT NATL. MON.
GRAND CANYON NATL. PARK
House Rock Buffalo Ranch
Pt. Imperial 8,803
North Rim
Supai
HAVASUPAI IND. RES.
Grand Canyon
Tusayan Ruin and Mus.
Tusayan
Tonalea
Tuba City
Moenkopi
HOPI
Pinon
Chinle
CANYON DE CHELLY NATL. MON.
White House Ruins
Sawmill
Grand Canyon Skywalk
Meadview
LAKE MEAD NATL. REC. AREA
Joshua Tree Forest
Natural Bridge
KAIBAB NATL. FOR.
Cameron
PAINTED DESERT
IND. RES.
Kykotsmovi
Hotevilla
Hopi Cultural Center
Polacca
Second Mesa
Keams Canyon
Fort Defiance
Window Rock
Hubbell Trading Post Natl. Hist. Site
Ganado
St. Michaels
HUALAPAI IND. RES.
Red L.
Dolan Springs
Mt. Tipton 7,148
Truxton
Peach Springs
Grand Canyon Caverns
Gray Mountain
Little Colorado
WUPATKI NATL. MON.
Grand Falls
Humphreys Pk. 12,633
Sunset Crater Volcano Natl. Mon.
Bidahochi
Lupton
Mohave
LAKE MEAD N.R.A.
Hackberry
Valentine
Seligman
Ash Fork
Williams
Parks
KAIBAB NATL. FOR.
Flagstaff
Leupp
Chambers
Sanders
Laughlin
Bullhead City
Kingman
Hualapai Pk. 8,417
Pine Springs
Bill Williams Mtn. 9,256
Bellemont
CAMP NAVAJO
Mountainaire
Walnut Canyon Natl. Mon.
Meteor Crater Natural Landmark
Winslow
Leupp Corner
Homolovi Ruins S.P.
Joseph City
Painted Desert Visitor Ctr.
PETRIFIED FOREST NATL. PARK
Holbrook
Sun Valley
ZUNI IND. RES.
FORT MOJAVE IND. RES.
Mohave Valley
Needles
Yucca
HAVASU
Topock
COCONINO
Oak Creek Canyon Slide Rock S.P.
Munds Park
Mormon L.
Mormon Lake
Paulden
Sedona
Tuzigoot Natl. Mon.
Red Rock S.P.
Hide Creek Mtn. 7,272
Wikieup
Chino Valley
Jerome
Clarkdale
Cottonwood
Jerome S.H.P.
PRESCOTT NATL. FOR.
Happy Jack
Prescott
Prescott Valley
Lake Montezuma
Montezuma Castle Natl. Mon.
Fort Verde S.H.P.
Camp Verde
Heber
SITGREAVES NATL. FOR.
Snowflake
Taylor
Clay Springs
Fool Hollow Lake Rec. Area
St. Johns
Concho
Lyman Lake S.P.
L. Havasu
Lake Havasu City
CHEMEHUEVI IND. RES.
London Bridge
Lake Havasu S.P.
Cattail Cove S.P.
Bagdad
Skull Valley
Kirkland
Kirkland Junction
Dewey
Mayer
Wilhoit
Arcosanti
Strawberry
Pine
Towers Mtn. 7,528
Wagoner
Yarnell
Alamo L.
Alamo Lake S.P.
Bill Williams
Parker Dam
Buckskin Mountain S.P.
Parker
Vidal Junction
Congress
AGUA FRIA NATL. MON.
Tonto Natural Bridge S.P.
Star Valley
Payson
Show Low
Pinetop-Lakeside
Springerville
Eagar
FORT APACHE IND. RES.
Young
Rye
Black Canyon City
Mazatzal Pk. 7,888
TONTO
Cibecue
Carrizo
McNary
Greer
Nutrioso
Alpine
Mt. Baldy 11,403
Whiteriver
Fort Apache
COLORADO RIVER IND. RES.
Poston
Bouse
Aquila
Forepaugh
Wickenburg
New River
Cave Creek
Carefree
Aztec Pk. 7,694
APACHE NATL. FOR.
Salome
Wenden
Morristown
Wittmann
Pioneer Ariz. Living Hist. Mus.
Pleasant
FORT MCDOWELL I.R.
Theodore Roosevelt L.
Roosevelt
Salt River Canyon
Blythe
Quartzsite
Brenda
Hope
Ehrenberg
Sun City
Glendale
Fountain Hills
Tonto Natl. Mon.
TONTO NATL. FOREST
Scottsdale
Mesa
Lost Dutchman S.P.
Apache Jct.
Miami
Globe
San Carlos
SAN CARLOS IND. RES.
Maple Pk. 8,294
Tonopah
Palo Verde
Buckeye
Phoenix
Tempe
Chandler
Komatke
Superior
Boyce Thompson Arboretum S.P.
Peridot
CIBOLA N.W.R.
MOUNTAIN TIME ZONE
Palm Canyon
KOFA N.W.R.
YUMA
Castle Dome Pk. 3,788
Imperial N.W.R.
GILA RIVER IND. RES.
Sun Lakes
Florence Junction
Painted Rocks Petroglyph Site
Hyder
SONORAN DESERT
Maricopa
MARICOPA (AK-CHIN) I.R.
Ak-Chin
Sacaton
Florence
Kearny
Hayden
Winkelman
San Carlos L.
Bylas
Fort Thomas
Morenci
Clifton
GILA BOX RIPARIAN NATL. CONS. AREA
Guthrie
Casa Grande Ruins Natl. Mon.
Casa Grande
Coolidge
Dudleyville
CORONADO
Pima
Safford
Martinez Lake
PROVING GROUND
Sentinel
Gila Bend
Dateland
Paloma
Table Mtn. 6,158
Thatcher
Mt. Graham 10,713
Roper Lake S.P.
Swift Trail Junction
Duncan
Franklin
Fort Yuma Ind. Res.
Dome
Wellton
Tacna
Mohawk
NATL. MON.
Table Top Mtn. 4,373
Arizona City
Eloy
Picacho
Picacho Peak S.P.
Biosphere 2
Oracle
Mammoth
CORONADO NATL. FOR.
Somerton
Yuma
Cocopah Ind. Res.
San Luis
BARRY M. GOLDWATER AIR FORCE RANGE
YUMA DESERT
Kaka
Red Rock
North Komelik
Marana
Catalina
Catalina S.P.
Oracle S.P.
San Manuel
Mt. Lemmon 9,157
Bonita
Cochise Visitor Ctr. & Chiricahua Natl. Mon.
FOR. Regional Mus.
San Luis Río Colorado
CABEZA PRIETA NATL. WILDLIFE REFUGE
Ajo
Why
Hickiwan
Santa Rosa
TOHONO O'ODHAM NATION
IRONWOOD FOREST NATL. MON.
Cortaro
SAGUARO NATL. PARK
Oro Valley
South Tucson
Tucson
Cascabel
Willcox
Bowie
San Simon
U.S. MEXICO
Quijotoa
Schuchk
Three Points
Mission San Xavier del Bac
TOHONO O'ODHAM (SAN XAVIER) IND. RES.
Vail
Colossal Cave
Dos Cabezas
Cochise
Fort Bowie Natl. Hist. Site
CHIRICAHUA NATL. MON.
Cochise Head 8,109
ORGAN PIPE CACTUS NATL. MON.
Pisinimo
Haivana Nakya
IND. RES.
Kitt Peak Natl. Observatory
Sahuarita
Green Valley
Kartchner Caverns S.P.
Benson
St. David
Dragoon
CORONADO N.F.
DESIERTO DE ALTAR
Lukeville
Sonoyta
Ali Chuk
Sells
Continental
LAS CIENEGAS N.C.A.
SAN PEDRO RIPARIAN N.C.A.
Sunizona
Chiricahua Pk. 9,796
Golfo de Santa Clara
Baboquivari Pk. 7,730
BUENOS AIRES N.W.R.
Amado
Mt. Wrightson 9,453
Tubac Presidio S.H.P.
FORT HUACHUCA MIL. RES.
Huachuca City
Tombstone
Tombstone Courthouse S.H.P.
Elfrida
McNeal
Apache
SONORA
San Miguel
Tumacacori
Tumacacori Natl. Hist. Park
Rio Rico
Patagonia
Patagonia Lake S.P.
Sierra Vista
Lavender Pit/Queen Mine
Bisbee
Pirtleville
Naco
Douglas
San Bernardino N.W.R.
Quitovac
Sasabe
CORONADO NATL. FOR.
Nogales
CORONADO NATL. MEM.
Agua Prieta
Puerto Peñasco
San Felipe
GULF OF CALIFORNIA
NEW MEXICO
CALIF.
B C D E F G H J K
1 2 3 4 5 6 7

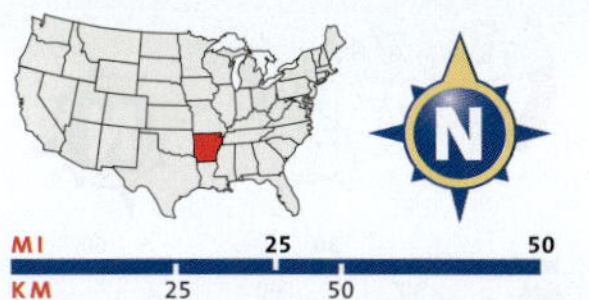

missouri 29

tennessee 20

mississippi 28

louisiana 23

texas 48

AR 86

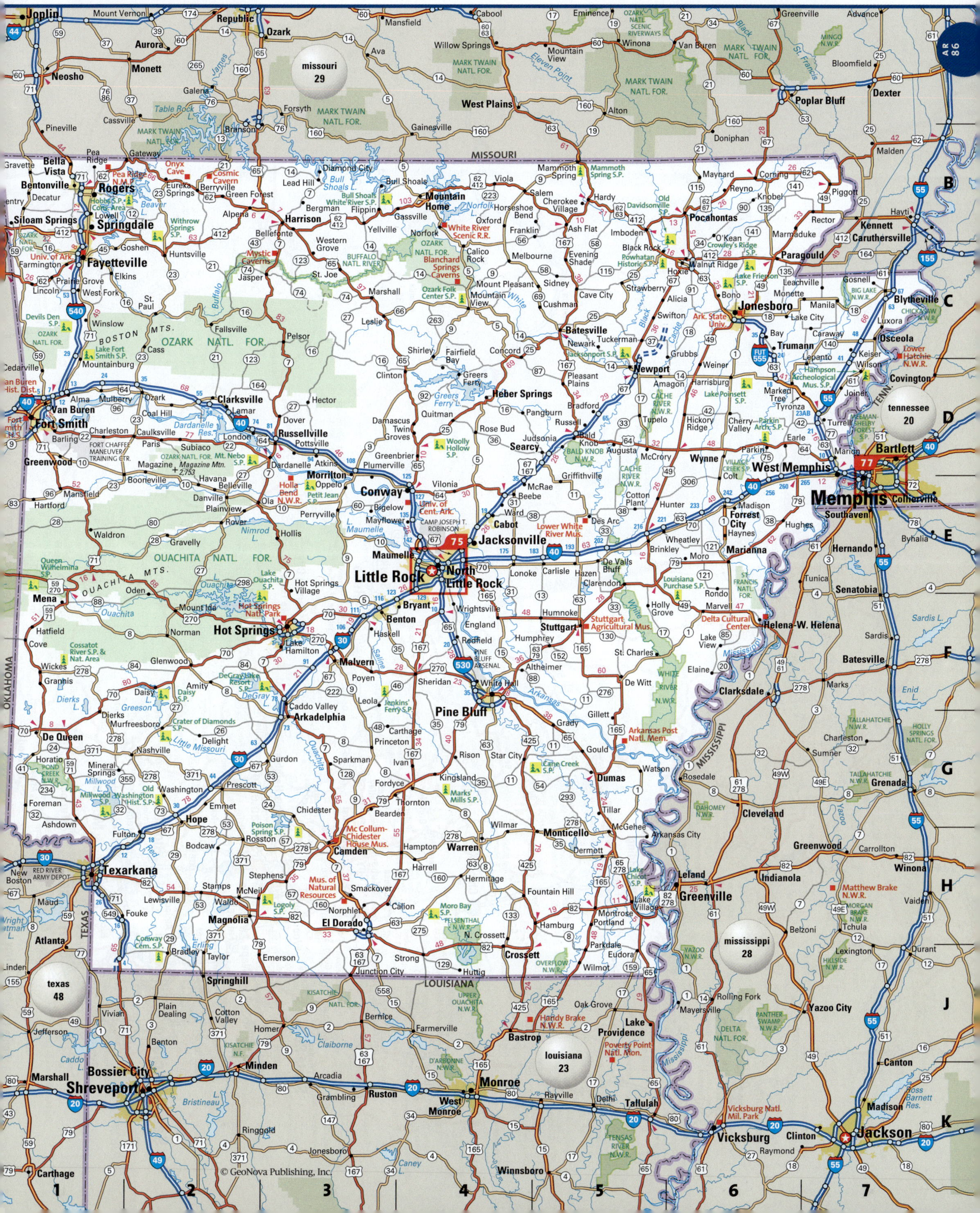

California

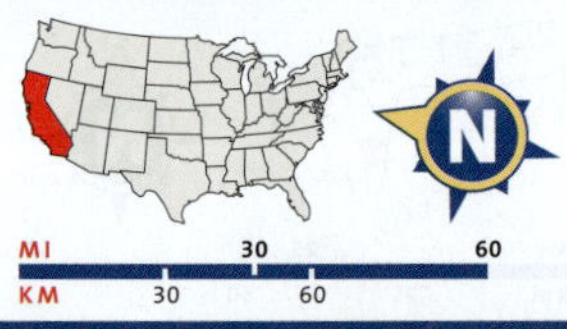

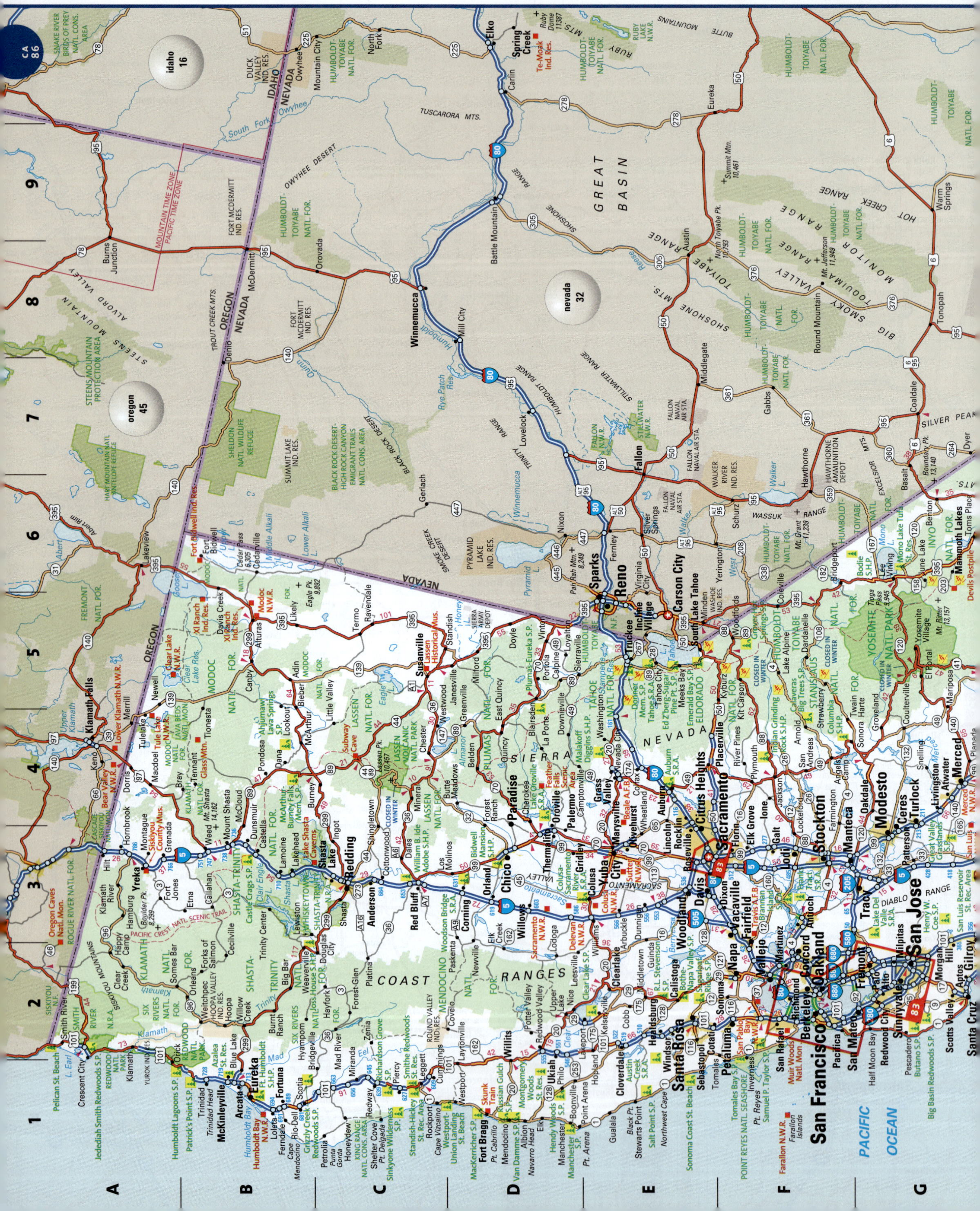

TRAVEL NOTE: California has started numbering freeway exits using a mileage-based numbering system (shown here). Full implementation is expected to take several years.
Los Angeles
San Diego
Las Vegas
Bakersfield
Fresno
Santa Barbara
Long Beach
Tijuana
Mexicali
Yuma
MOJAVE DESERT
PACIFIC OCEAN
NEVADA
ARIZ.
BAJA CALIF.
arizona 6
mexico 68
CA 86
© GeoNova Publishing, Inc.

Colorado

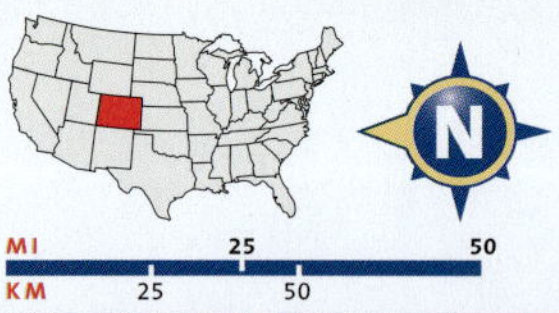

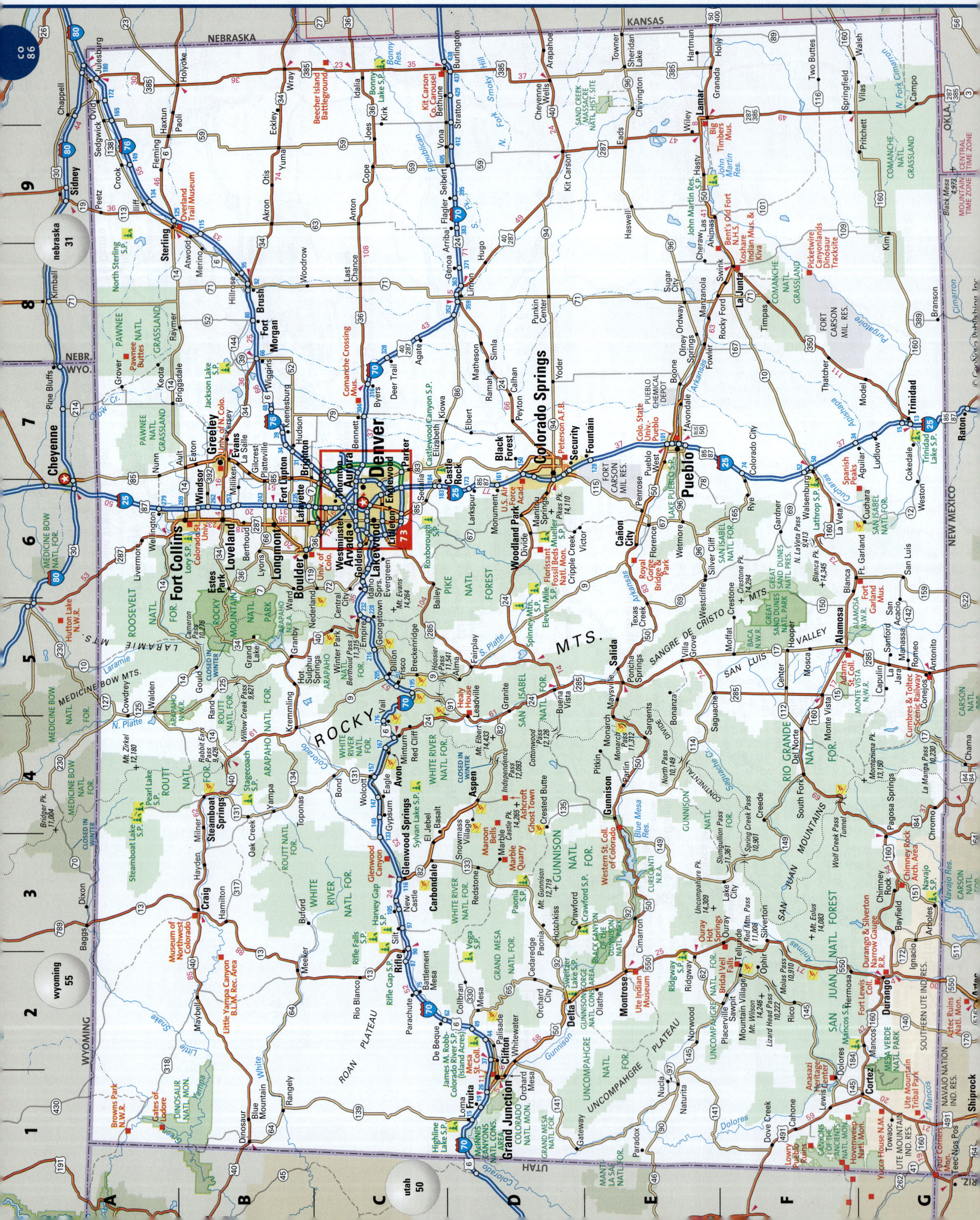

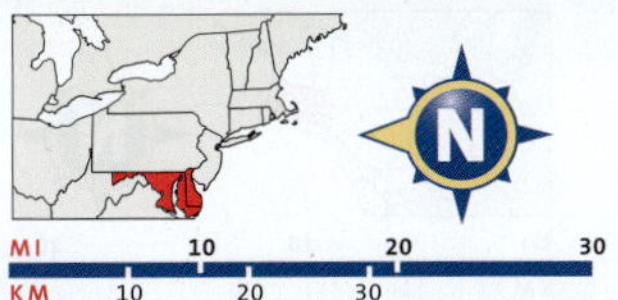

ATLANTIC OCEAN

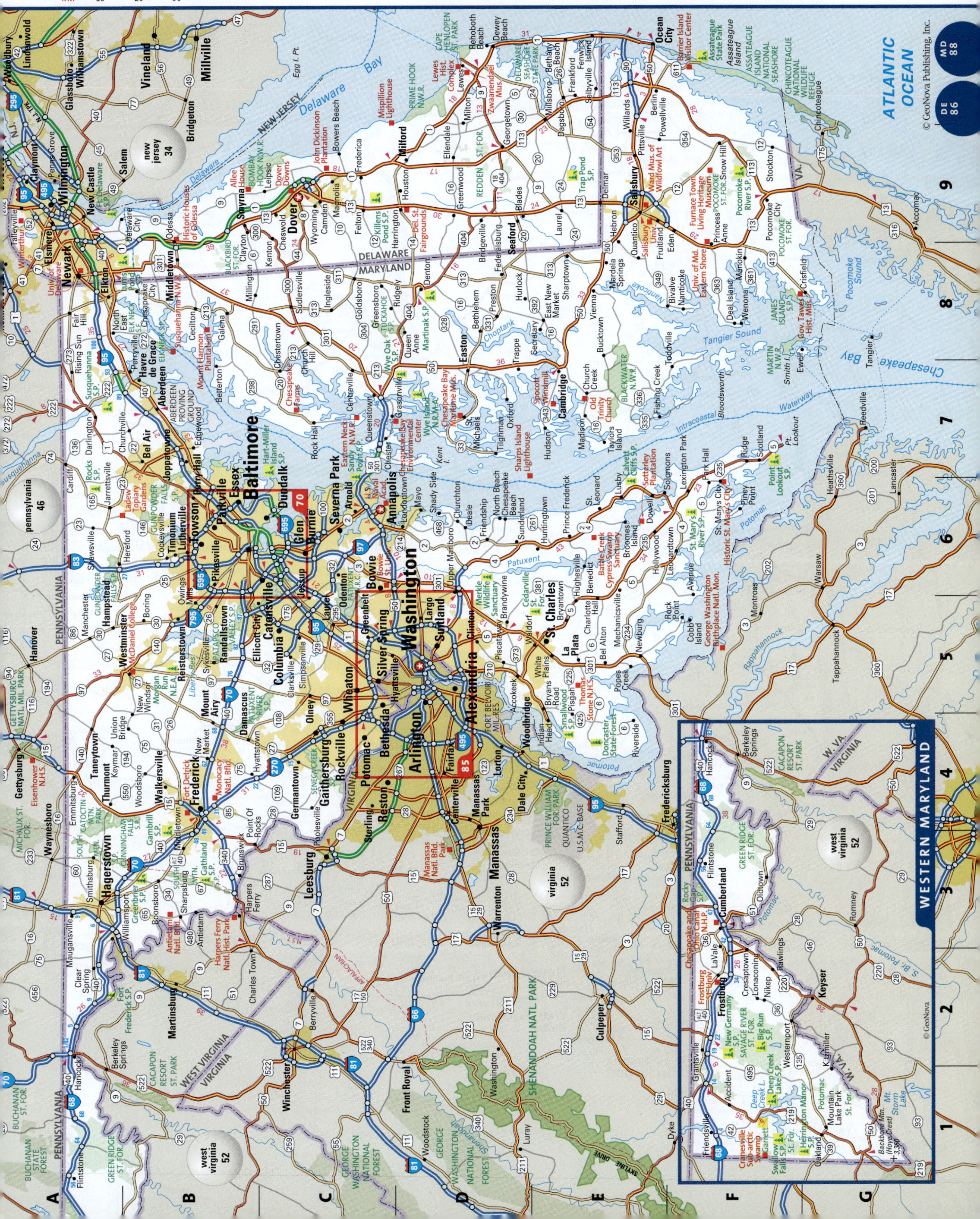

WESTERN MARYLAND

DE 86

MD 88

Conn., Mass. & Rhode Island

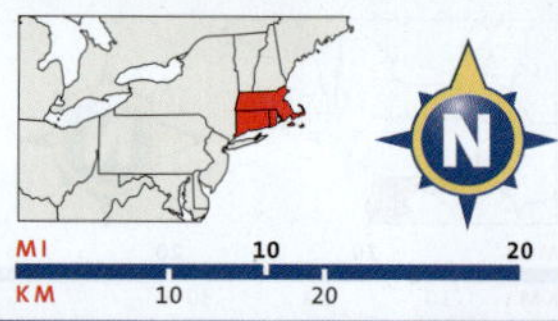

vermont 33

new hampshire 33

new york 36

RI 91

MA 88

CT 86

VERMONT

NEW HAMPSHIRE

MASSACHUSETTS

CONNECTICUT

NEW YORK

TACONIC RANGE

THE BERKSHIRES

Long Island Sound

Block Island Sound

Long Island

Quabbin Res.

Albany

Troy

Pittsfield

North Adams

Bennington

Brattleboro

Greenfield

Northampton

Amherst

Holyoke

Springfield

Chicopee

Westfield

Worcester

Fitchburg

Leominster

Gardner

Torrington

Hartford

West Hartford

Wethersfield

Newington

East Hartford

Manchester

Vernon

Enfield

Bristol

New Britain

Southington

Middletown

Meriden

Waterbury

Naugatuck

Danbury

Shelton

New Haven

West Haven

East Haven

Milford

Stratford

Bridgeport

Fairfield

Norwalk

Stamford

Greenwich

White Plains

Port Chester

Norwich

New London

Groton

Willimantic

Plainfield

Putnam

Storrs

1 2 3 4 5 6 7

B C D E F G H J K

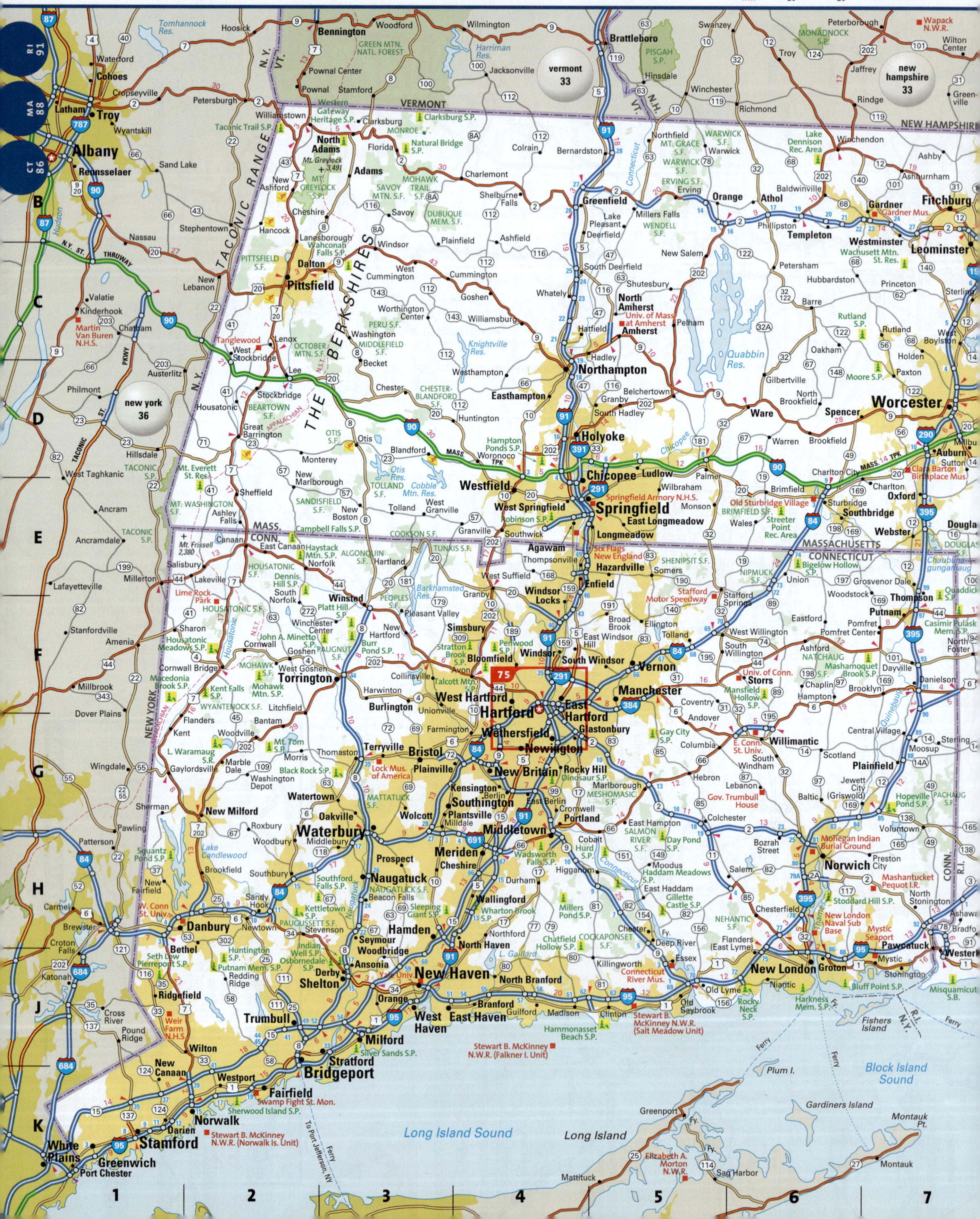

ATLANTIC OCEAN
Massachusetts Bay
Cape Cod Bay
Buzzards Bay
Nantucket Sound
Vineyard Sound
Rhode Island Sound
Muskeget Channel
CAPE COD
Boston
Providence
Worcester
Lowell
Lawrence
Haverhill
Newburyport
Gloucester
Salem
Lynn
Cambridge
Quincy
Brockton
Plymouth
Taunton
Fall River
New Bedford
Newport
Warwick
Cranston
Pawtucket
Woonsocket
Nashua
Hyannis
Falmouth
Provincetown
Chatham
Martha's Vineyard
Nantucket Island
Elizabeth Is.
Block Island
Monomoy Island
CAPE COD NATIONAL SEASHORE
Ferry

Florida

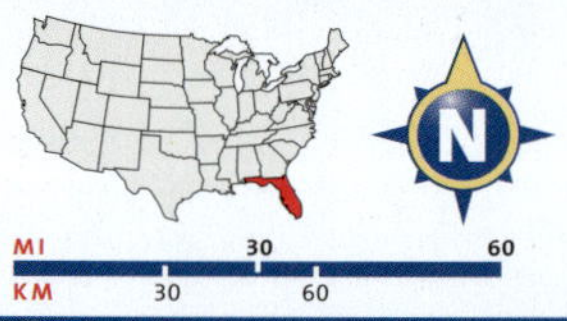

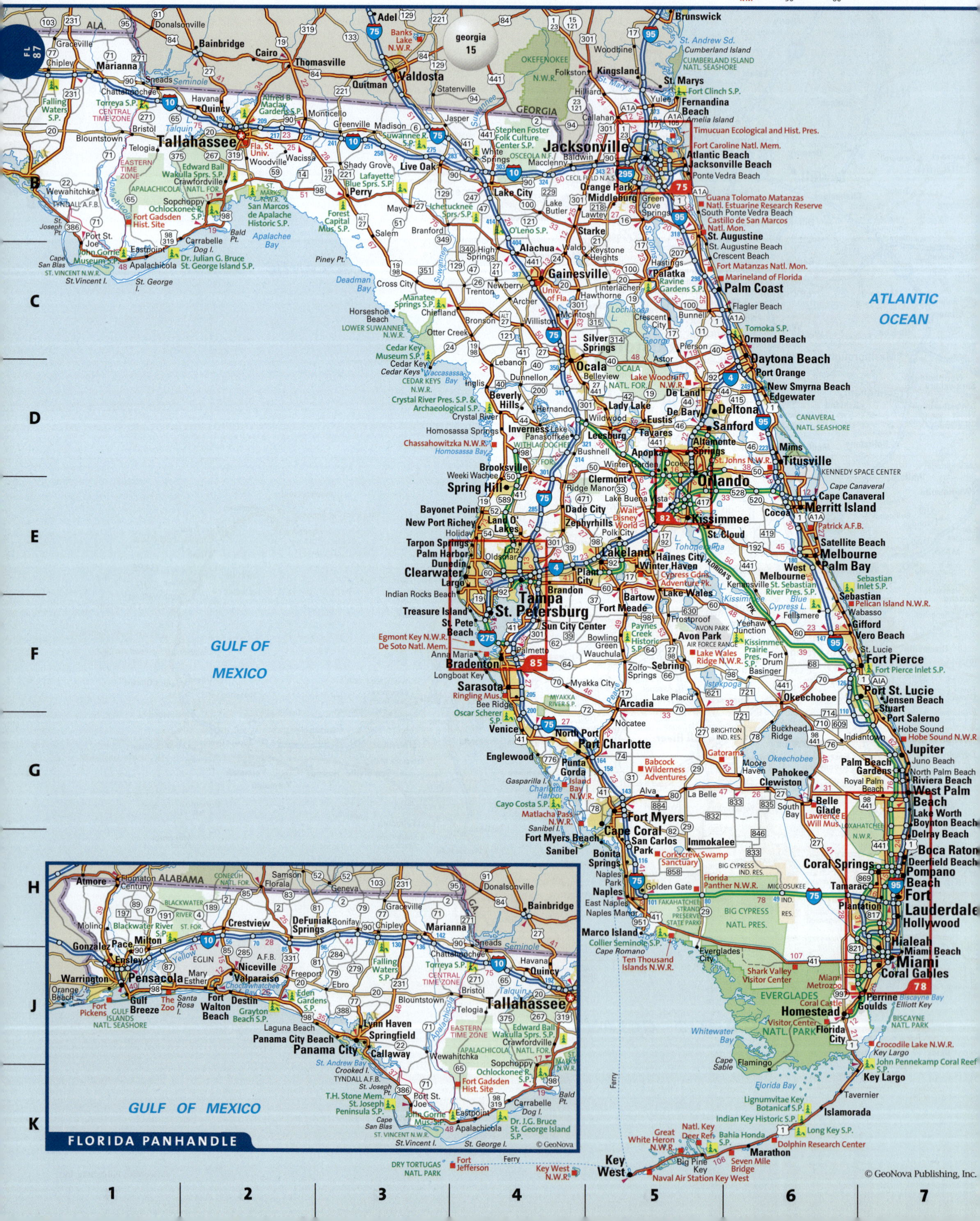

ATLANTIC OCEAN

GULF OF MEXICO

FLORIDA PANHANDLE

GULF OF MEXICO

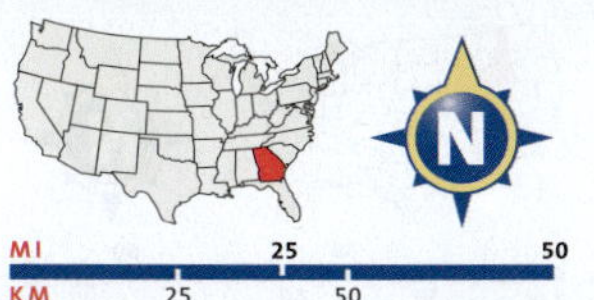

Chattanooga
Dalton
Rome
Cartersville
Marietta
Roswell
Gainesville
Athens
Atlanta
Carrollton
Newnan
LaGrange
Griffin
Columbus
Phenix City
Macon
Warner Robins
Milledgeville
Augusta
North Augusta
Aiken
Dublin
Statesboro
Savannah
Hinesville
Americus
Albany
Tifton
Valdosta
Thomasville
Waycross
Brunswick
St. Simons Island
Jekyll Island
Kingsland
St. Marys
Jacksonville
Tallahassee
Dothan
Auburn
Opelika
Greenville
Spartanburg
Anderson
Rock Hill
Columbia
Orangeburg
CHATTAHOOCHEE NATL. FOR.
OCONEE NATL. FOR.
SUMTER NATL. FOR.
OKEFENOKEE N.W.R.
OSCEOLA NATL. FOR.
APALACHICOLA NATL. FOR.
FORT BENNING MIL. RES.
FORT STEWART MIL. RES.
U.S. DEPT. OF ENERGY SAVANNAH RIVER SITE
ATLANTIC OCEAN
ALABAMA
FLORIDA
TENN.
N.C.
S.C.
south carolina 38
alabama 4
florida 14
GA 87
CENTRAL TIME ZONE
EASTERN TIME ZONE
1 2 3 4 5 6 7
A B C D E F G H J K

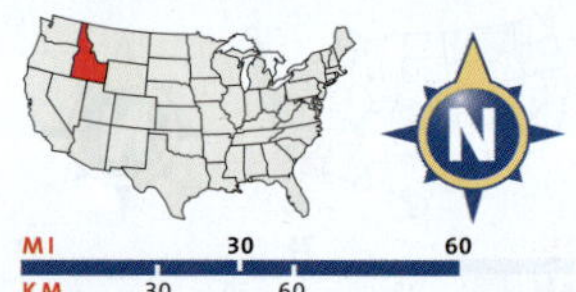
N
MI 30 60
KM 30 60

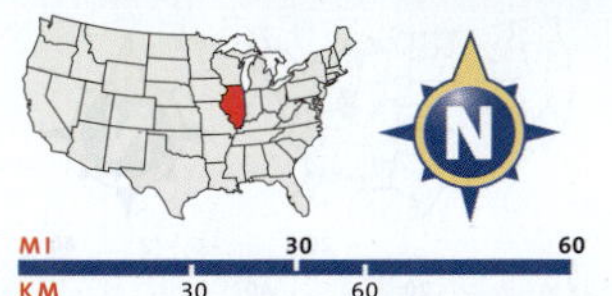

LAKE MICHIGAN

iowa 19

missouri 29

indiana 18

kentucky 20

IL 87

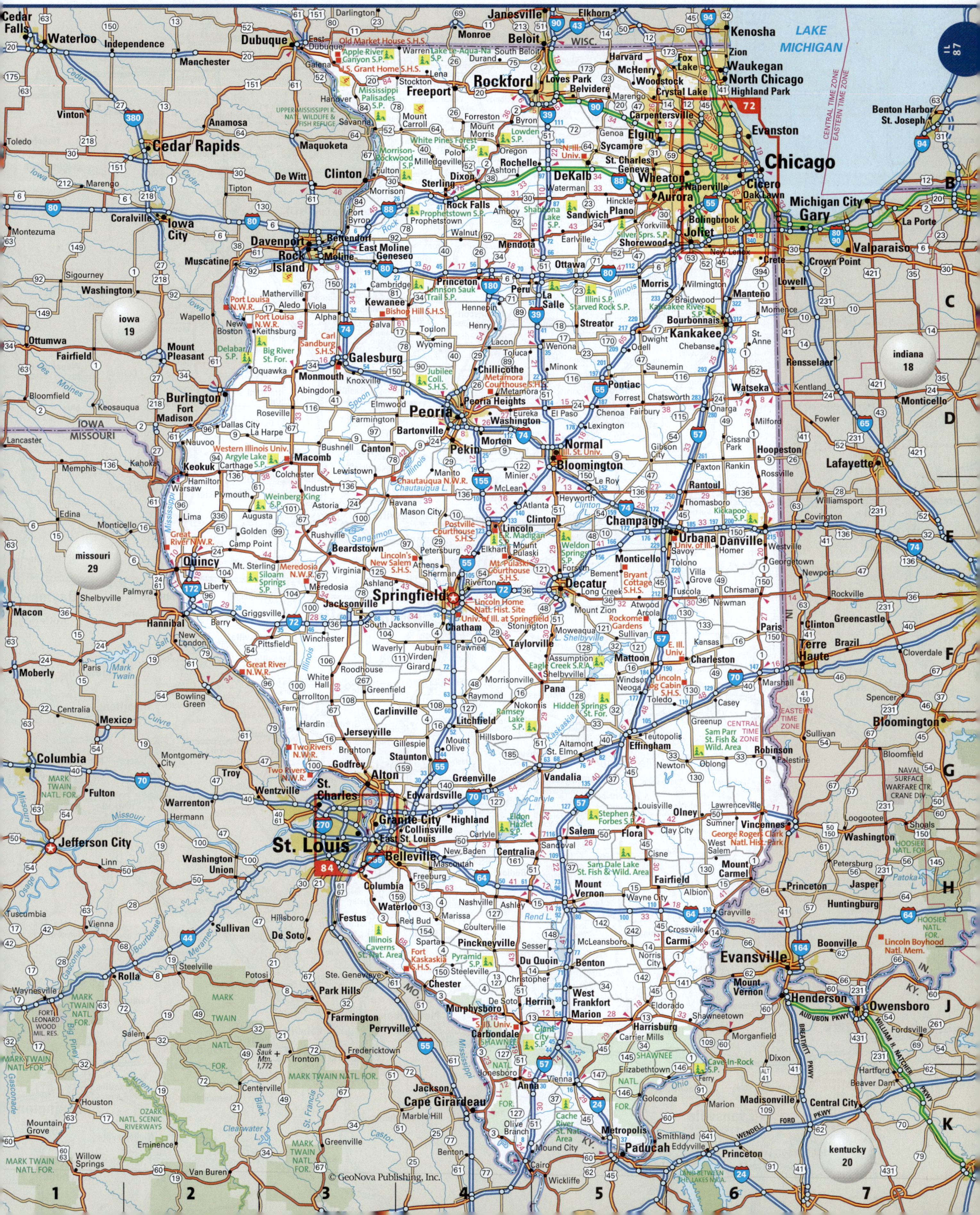

Indiana

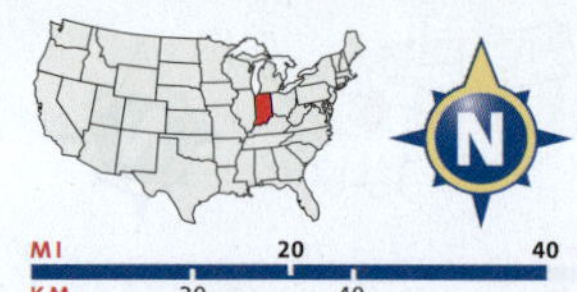

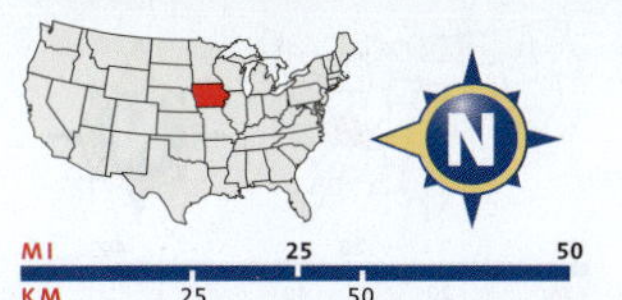

wisconsin 54
illinois 17
minnesota 25
missouri 29
nebraska 31
south dakota 41
IA 87

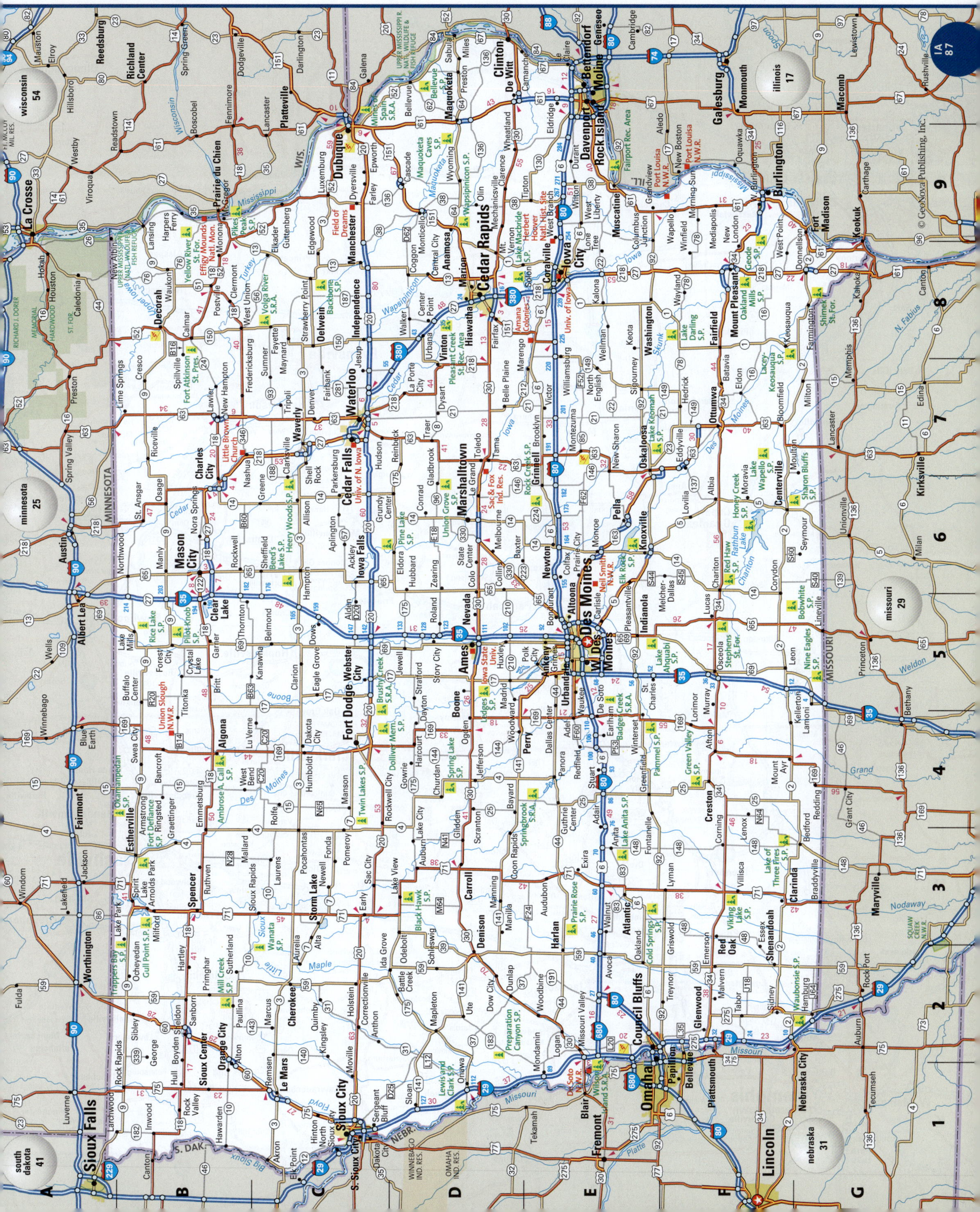

Kentucky & Tennessee

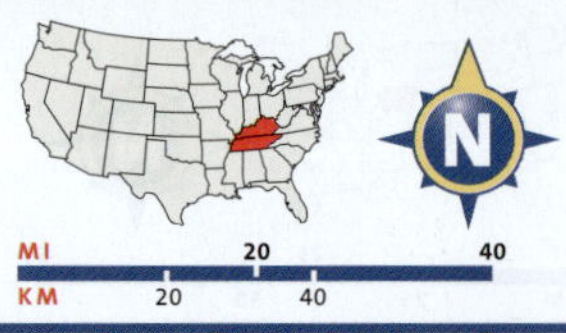

Cincinnati
Covington
Louisville
Lexington
Frankfort
Richmond
Knoxville
Chattanooga
Cleveland
Oak Ridge
Huntington
Charleston
Ashland
Asheville
Kingsport
Bristol
Johnson City
Spartanburg
ohio 42
west virginia 52
virginia 52
north carolina 38
south carolina 38
DANIEL BOONE NATL. FOR.
GREAT SMOKY MOUNTAINS NATL. PARK
APPALACHIAN MTS.
CHEROKEE NATL. FOR.
JEFFERSON NATL. FOR.
PISGAH NATL. FOR.
NANTAHALA NATL. FOR.
WAYNE NATL. FOR.
EASTERN TIME ZONE
CENTRAL TIME ZONE
TN 91
KY 88

Kansas

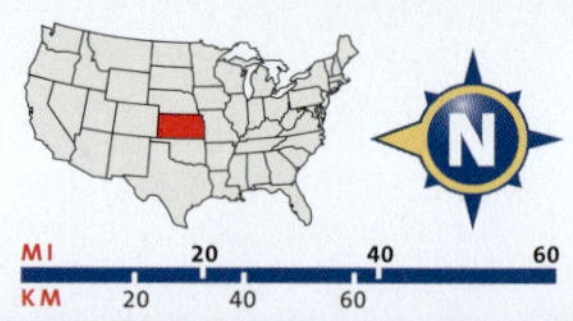

MI 25 50
KM 25 50

LA 88

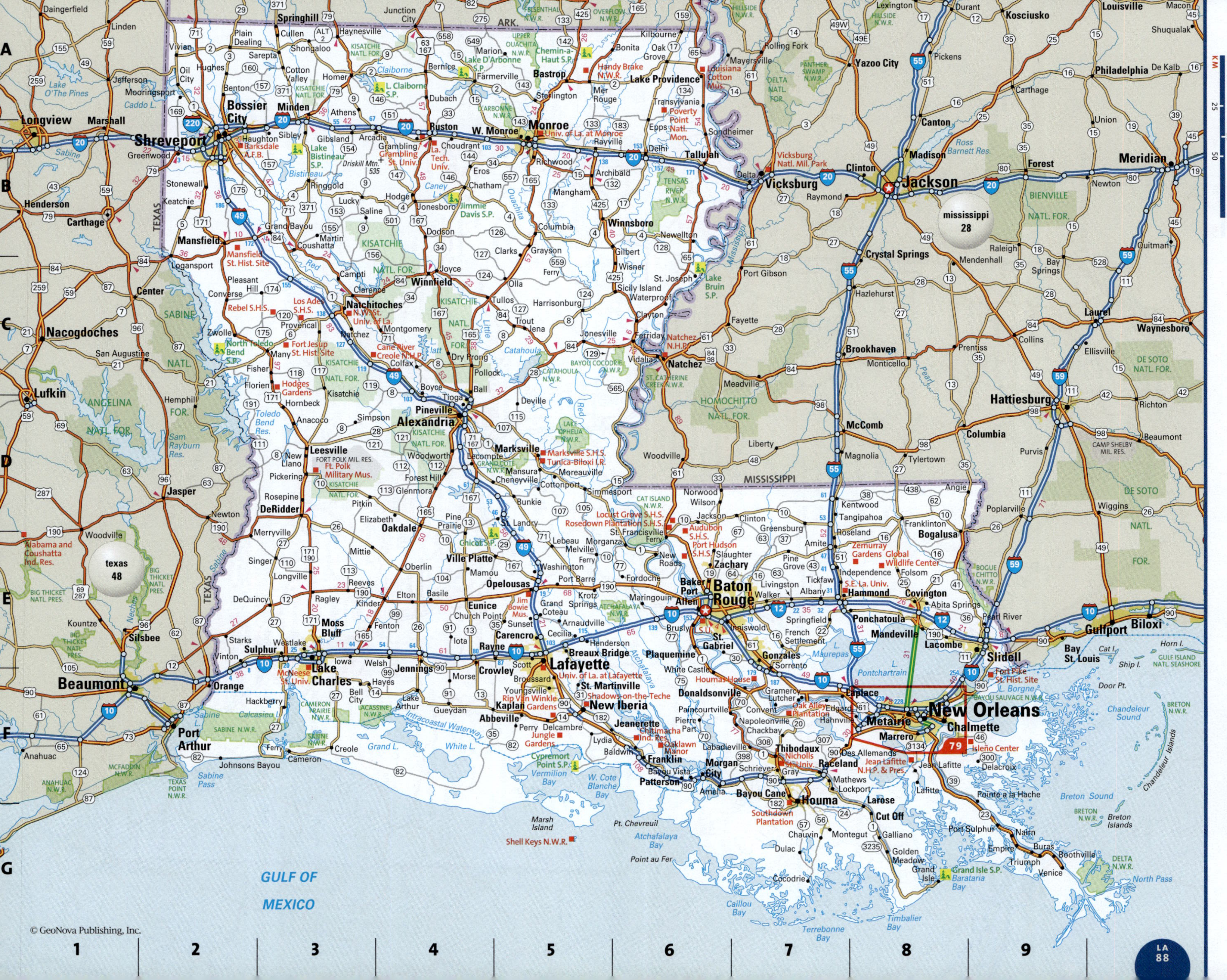

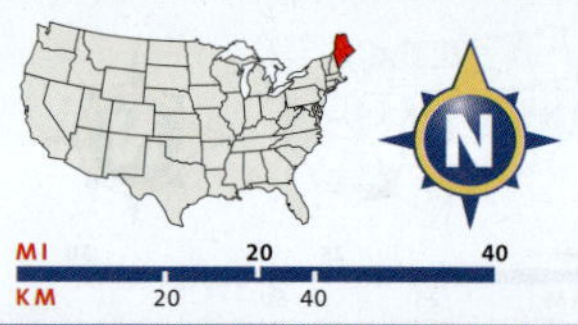

ME 88

québec 64

new brunswick 66

new hampshire 33

ST. LAWRENCE

APPALACHIAN

MOUNTAINS

CANADA
U.S.

QUÉBEC

NEW BRUNSWICK

EASTERN TIME ZONE

ATLANTIC TIME ZONE

Baie-St-Paul

Mont-Carmel

St-Jean-Port-Joli

Beaupré

Montmagny

Charlesbourg

Québec

Lévis

Charny

St-Pamphile

St-Marcel

Ste-Marie

Lac-Etchemin

Beauceville

St-Georges

Thetford Mines

La Guadeloupe

Disraeli

Beaulac

Stornoway

Lac Mégantic

Gould

Scotstown

Edmundston

Madawaska

Grand Isle

Fort Kent

St. John

St. Francis

Dickey

Eagle Lake

Winterville

Soldier Pond

Van Buren

St-Léonard

Grand Falls/Grand Sault

Hamlin

New Sweden

Caribou

Limestone

Fort Fairfield

Washburn

Presque Isle

Portage

Mapleton

Ashland

Masardis

Mars Hill

Bridgewater

Florenceville

Monticello

Littleton

Houlton

Woodstock

Nashwaak Bridge

Fredericton

Oromocto

Smyrna Mills

Oakfield

Linneus

Island Falls

Patten

Sherman Mills

Haynesville

North Amity

Orient

Danforth

Macwahoc

Reed

Medway

East Millinocket

Millinocket

Norcross

Grindstone

Mattawamkeag

Brookton

Vanceboro

Thomaston Corner

Welsford

Topsfield

Springfield

Lee

Lincoln

Winn

Waite

Princeton

St. Stephen

Calais

St. Andrews

Blacks Harbour

Grand Lake Stream

Woodland (Baileyville)

Alexander

Burlington

Howland

Passadumkeag

Olamon

Old Town

Orono

Great Pond

Bangor

Brewer

East Holden

Hampden

Amherst

Aurora

Wesley

Perry

Pembroke

Dennysville

Eastport

Lubec

Whiting

Cutler

East Machias

Machias

Northfield

Jonesboro

Deblois

Waltham

Green Lake

Ellsworth

Franklin

Cherryfield

Harrington

Columbia Falls

Jonesport

Milbridge

Steuben

Gouldsboro

Winter Harbor

Bar Harbor

Trenton

Northeast Harbor

Southwest Harbor

Bass Harbor

Frenchboro

Stonington

Deer Isle

Sedgwick

Blue Hill

Castine

Bucksport

Orland

Searsport

Belfast

Frankfort

Winterport

Dixmont

Unity

Liberty

Searsmont

Lincolnville

Camden

Rockland

North Haven

Vinalhaven

Thomaston

Warren

Waldoboro

Union

Jefferson

Washington

Damariscotta

Wiscasset

Bath

Brunswick

Boothbay Harbor

New Harbor

Port Clyde

Monhegan

Popham Beach

Freeport

Yarmouth

Falmouth

Portland

Cape Elizabeth

Westbrook

Gray

Windham

Standish

Old Orchard Beach

Saco

Biddeford

Kennebunk

Kennebunkport

Sanford

Alfred

Springvale

Rochester

Berwick

North Berwick

Ogunquit

York Beach

York Harbor

York Vil.

Kittery

Portsmouth

Dover

Durham

Northwood

Augusta

Hallowell

Gardiner

Winthrop

Lewiston

Auburn

Mechanic Falls

Turner

Greene

Richmond

Lisbon Falls

Waterville

Winslow

Fairfield

Clinton

Skowhegan

Norridgewock

Pittsfield

Newport

Hartland

Canaan

Madison

Anson

North Anson

Solon

Bingham

Athens

Harmony

Dexter

Corinna

East Corinth

Kenduskeag

Hermon

Bradford

Lagrange

Milo

Dover-Foxcroft

Guilford

Monson

Brownville Junction

Greenville

Rockwood

Kokadjo

Lily Bay

Jackman

Long Pond

Moosehead

The Forks

Caratunk

Lake Parlin

Eustis

Stratton

Carrabassett

Kingfield

Rangeley

Oquossoc

Phillips

Salem

Strong

Farmington

Weld

Wilton

Livermore Falls

Livermore

Dixfield

Canton

Mexico

Rumford

Byron

Andover

Upton

Wilsons Mills

Newry

Bethel

Bryant Pond

Gilead

Berlin

North Waterford

Norway

South Paris

Harrison

Bridgton

Lovell

Fryeburg

Naples

Casco

Sebago

Hiram

Cornish

West Ossipee

Ossipee

Limerick

Hollis Center

Shapleigh

Chesuncook Village

Pittston Farm

Seboomook

North East Carry

Clayton Lake

Oxbow

Belgrade

Hinckley

New Sharon

Mont-Carmel

St-Quentin

ALLAGASH WILDERNESS WATERWAY

RESTRICTED ROADS

BAXTER STATE PARK

Mt. Katahdin 5,268

White Cap Mtn. 3,644

Sugarloaf Mtn. 4,237

Saddleback Mtn. 4,116

Snow Mtn. 3,948

Mt. Cabot 4,160

Mt. Washington 6,288

WHITE MTN. NATL. FOR.

WHITE MTS.

APPALACHIAN N.S.T.

Aroostook N.W.R.

Aroostook S.P.

Tri-Cultural Mus.

Ft. Kent St. Hist. Site

Acadian Village

Lumberman's Mus.

Katahdin Iron Works S.H.S.

Little Wilson Falls

Peaks-Kenny S.P.

Penobscot Ind. Res.

Sunkhaze Meadows N.W.R.

Univ. of Maine

Indian Township Ind. Res.

St. Croix Island Intl. Hist. Site

Passamaquoddy Pleasant Point Ind. Res.

Roosevelt Campobello Intl. Park

W. Quoddy Head Lighthouse

Quoddy Head S.P.

Cobscook Bay S.P.

Moosehorn N.W.R.

Fort O'Brien S.H.S.

Cross I. N.W.R.

Roque Bluffs S.P.

Petit Manan N.W.R.

Lamoine S.P.

Hulls Cove Vis. Ctr.

Acadia Natl. Park

Bass Harbor Head Lighthouse

Swan Lake S.P.

Fort Knox S.H.S.

Penobscot Marine Mus.

Fort Point S.H.S.

Camden Hills S.P.

Montpelier

Reversing Falls

Ft. Edgecomb S.H.S.

Maine Maritime Mus.

Colonial Pemaquid S.H.S.

Lighthouse & Fisherman's Museum

Seal Island N.W.R.

Ft. Popham S.H.S.

Desert of Maine

Eagle I. S.H.S.

Portland Head Lighthouse

Biddeford Pool

Rachel Carson N.W.R.

Cape Neddick Lighthouse

Vaughn Woods S.P.

Fort McClary S.H.P.

Sebago L. S.P.

Songo Lock

Snow Falls Gorge

Maine State Mus.

L. George S.P.

Ft. Halifax S.H.S.

Piazza Rock

Rangeley L. S.P.

Grafton Notch S.P.

Lily Bay S.P.

Moosehead L.

Chesuncook L.

Chamberlain L.

Churchill L.

Munsungan L.

Grand L. Seboeis

Grand L. Matagamon

Millinocket L.

Pemadumcook L.

Seboeis L.

Sebec L.

Flagstaff L.

Aziscohos L.

Mooselookmeguntic L.

Richardson Lakes

Umbagog L.

Sebago L.

Lake Winnipesaukee

Piscataquis

Kennebec

Penobscot

Aroostook

St. John

Mattawamkeag

Baskahegan L.

Grand L.

W. Grand L.

Nicatous L.

Big L.

Squa Pan L.

Magaguadavic L.

Oromocto L.

Miramichi

Chaudière

Casco Bay

Penobscot Bay

Grand Manan Island

Grand Manan Channel

North Head

Grand Harbour

BAY OF FUNDY

GULF OF MAINE

ATLANTIC OCEAN

To Yarmouth, N.S. (Seasonal)

MAINE TPK.

1 2 3 4 5 6 7

B C D E F G H J K

© GeoNova Publishing, Inc.

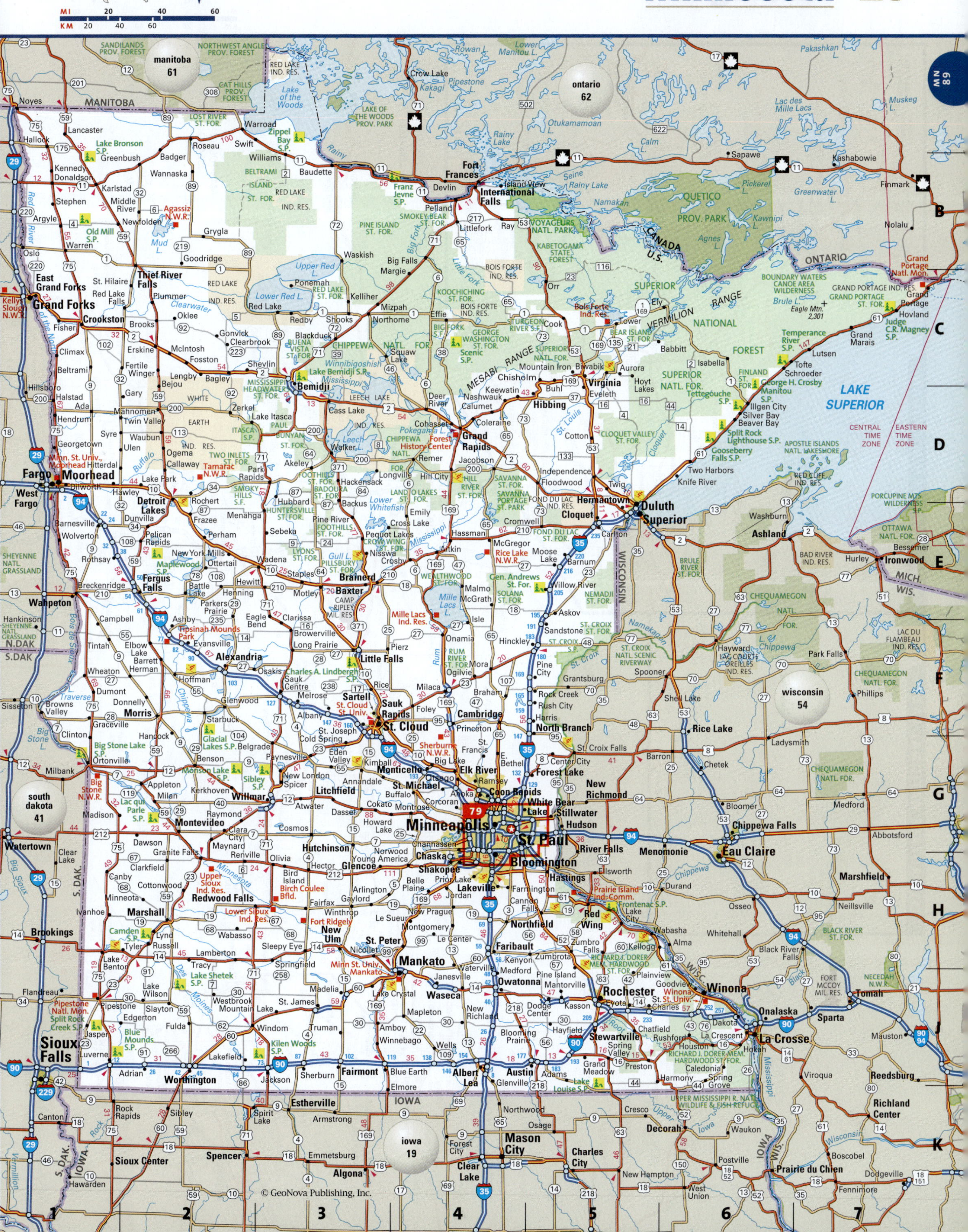
MI 20 40 60
KM 20 40 60
manitoba 61
ontario 62
wisconsin 54
south dakota 41
iowa 19
MN 89
MANITOBA
ONTARIO
CANADA
U.S.
WISCONSIN
S. DAK.
N. DAK
S.DAK
IOWA
MICH.
WIS.
LAKE SUPERIOR
CENTRAL TIME ZONE
EASTERN TIME ZONE
Lake of the Woods
Rainy Lake
Upper Red L.
Lower Red L.
Mille Lacs Lake
Leech Lake
Lake Winnibigoshish
QUETICO PROV. PARK
VOYAGEURS NATL. PARK
SUPERIOR NATL. FOR.
SUPERIOR NATIONAL FOREST
CHIPPEWA NATL. FOR.
CHEQUAMEGON NATL. FOR.
MESABI RANGE
VERMILION RANGE
BOUNDARY WATERS CANOE AREA WILDERNESS
RED LAKE IND. RES.
BOIS FORTE IND. RES.
LEECH LAKE IND. RES.
Mille Lacs Ind. Res.
GRAND PORTAGE IND. RES.
Grand Portage Natl. Mon.
Pipestone Natl. Mon.
Eagle Mtn. 2,301
International Falls
Fort Frances
Baudette
Warroad
Roseau
Thief River Falls
East Grand Forks
Grand Forks
Crookston
Bemidji
Grand Rapids
Hibbing
Virginia
Ely
Grand Marais
Two Harbors
Duluth
Superior
Cloquet
Fargo
Moorhead
Detroit Lakes
Fergus Falls
Wahpeton
Alexandria
Brainerd
Baxter
Little Falls
St. Cloud
Sauk Rapids
Willmar
Montevideo
Hutchinson
Minneapolis
St. Paul
Bloomington
Lakeville
Shakopee
Hastings
Red Wing
Northfield
Faribault
Owatonna
Mankato
New Ulm
St. Peter
Marshall
Worthington
Sioux Falls
Fairmont
Albert Lea
Austin
Rochester
Winona
La Crosse
Eau Claire
Chippewa Falls
Mason City
Watertown
Brookings
Ashland
Hayward
Rice Lake
Menomonie
Spencer
Sioux Center
Estherville
Algona
Decorah
Wisconsin
Mississippi
© GeoNova Publishing, Inc.
A B C D E F G H J K
1 2 3 4 5 6 7

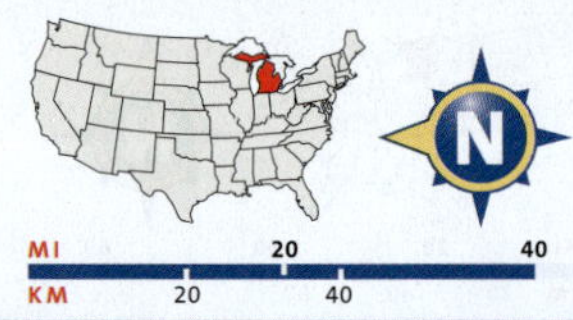

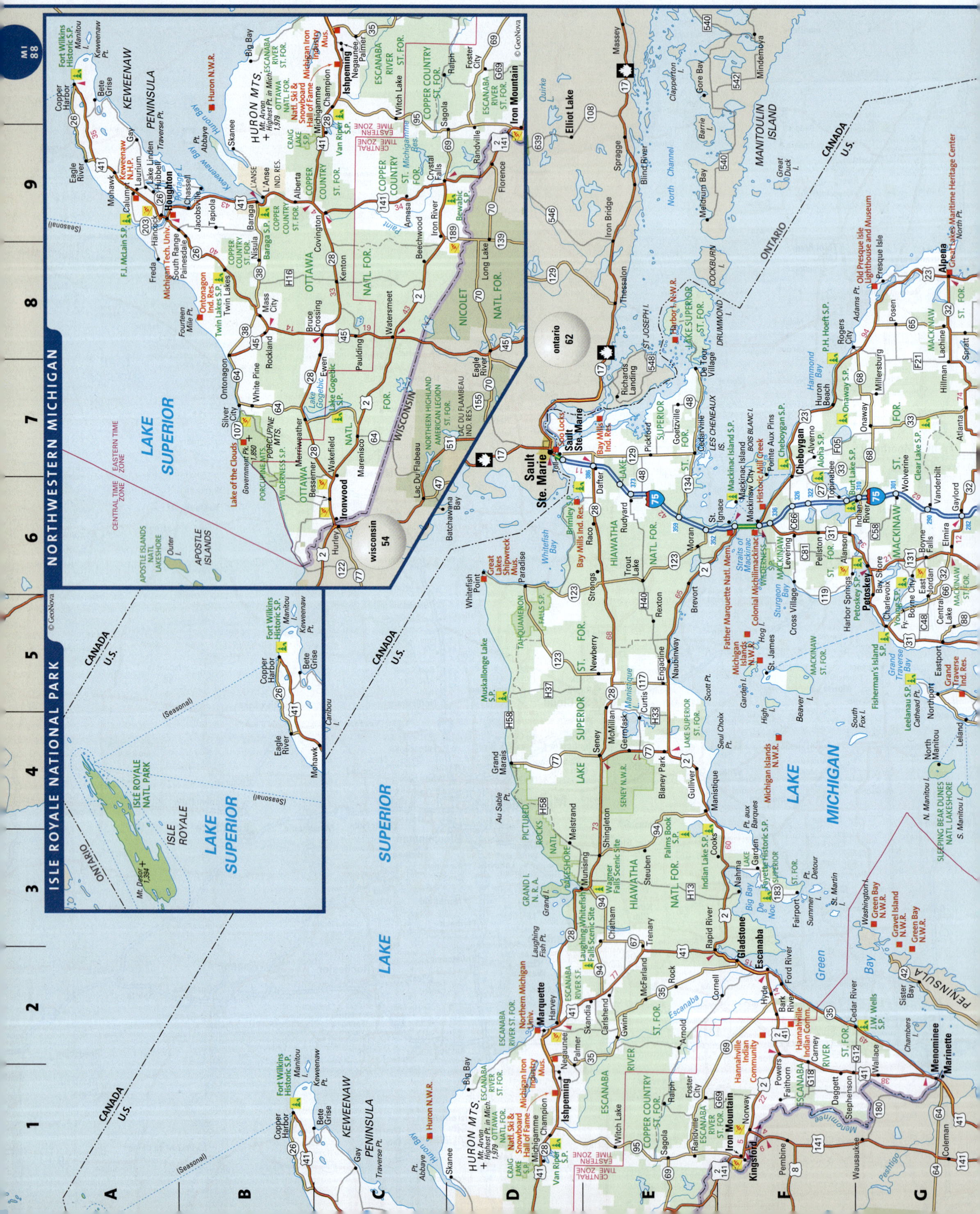

MI 88

NORTHWESTERN MICHIGAN

LAKE SUPERIOR

KEWEENAW PENINSULA

Copper Harbor · Eagle River · Mohawk · Calumet · Laurium · Lake Linden · Hubbell · Houghton · Hancock · South Range · Painesdale · Chassell · Jacobsville · Tapiola · Baraga · L'Anse · Skanee · Big Bay · Alberta · Covington · Kenton · Nisula · Mass City · Twin Lakes · Ontonagon · Rockland · White Pine · Silver City · Bergland · Bruce Crossing · Ewen · Paulding · Watersmeet · Marenisco · Wakefield · Bessemer · Ironwood · Hurley · Lac Du Flambeau · Eagle River · Long Lake · Florence · Iron River · Crystal Falls · Amasa · Sagola · Randville · Iron Mountain · Foster City · Ralph · Witch Lake · Champion · Michigamme · Ishpeming · Negaunee · Palmer

HURON MTS · + Mt. Arvon Highest Pt. in Mich. 1,979

PORCUPINE MTS. · Lake of the Clouds · Government Pk. 1,850

OTTAWA NATL. FOR. · COPPER COUNTRY ST. FOR. · ESCANABA RIVER ST. FOR. · NICOLET NATL. FOR. · NORTHERN HIGHLAND AMERICAN LEGION ST. FOR. · LAC DU FLAMBEAU IND. RES.

APOSTLE ISLANDS NATL. LAKESHORE · APOSTLE ISLANDS · Outer I.

CENTRAL TIME ZONE · EASTERN TIME ZONE

WISCONSIN

wisconsin 54

© GeoNova

ISLE ROYALE NATIONAL PARK

ISLE ROYALE NATL PARK · ISLE ROYALE · Mt. Desor 1,394 · LAKE SUPERIOR · ONTARIO · CANADA · U.S. · (Seasonal) · Copper Harbor · Eagle River · Mohawk · Caribou I.

© GeoNova

LAKE SUPERIOR · CANADA · U.S. · ONTARIO · ontario 62

Sault Ste. Marie · Elliot Lake · Massey · Spragge · Blind River · Iron Bridge · Thessalon · Richards Landing · Batchawana Bay · North Channel · MANITOULIN ISLAND · ST. JOSEPH I. · DRUMMOND I. · COCKBURN I. · Gore Bay · Mindemoya

Whitefish Point · Paradise · Grand Marais · Newberry · Seney · McMillan · Germfask · Curtis · Engadine · Naubinway · Rexton · Trout Lake · Strongs · Raco · Brimley · Dafter · Rudyard · Pickford · Cedarville · Hessel · De Tour Village · Goetzville · St. Ignace · Moran · Brevort · Mackinaw City · Mackinac Island · Cheboygan · Alverno · Onaway · Rogers City · Posen · Alpena · Hillman · Atlanta · Vanderbilt · Gaylord · Wolverine · Indian River · Topinabee · Pellston · Levering · Alanson · Petoskey · Harbor Springs · Boyne City · Boyne Falls · Charlevoix · East Jordan · Elmira · Central Lake · Eastport · Northport · Leland · Cross Village · Beaver I. · St. James

Munising · Melstrand · Shingleton · Wetmore · Chatham · Trenary · Steuben · Manistique · Gulliver · Blaney Park · Cooks · Nahma · Garden · Fairport · Rapid River · Gladstone · Escanaba · Wells · Cornell · Bark River · Hyde · Ford River · Harris · Powers · Carney · Stephenson · Daggett · Wallace · Cedar River · Menominee · Marinette · Wausaukee · Coleman · Pembine · Kingsford · Norway · Vulcan · Iron Mountain · Randville · Sagola · Foster City · Ralph · Witch Lake · Gwinn · McFarland · Rock · Arnold · Carlshend · Skandia · Harvey · Marquette · Negaunee · Ishpeming · Palmer · Champion · Michigamme · Big Bay · Skanee

PICTURED ROCKS NATL. LAKESHORE · GRAND I. N.R.A. · HIAWATHA NATL. FOR. · LAKE SUPERIOR ST. FOR. · SENEY N.W.R. · MACKINAW ST. FOR. · ESCANABA RIVER ST. FOR. · COPPER COUNTRY ST. FOR. · SLEEPING BEAR DUNES NATL. LAKESHORE

LAKE MICHIGAN · Green Bay · Big Bay De Noc · Straits of Mackinac · Grand Traverse Bay

PENINSULA · CANADA · U.S.

LAKE HURON
LAKE MICHIGAN
LAKE ERIE
Saginaw Bay
Green Bay
Detroit
Windsor
Lansing
Grand Rapids
Flint
Saginaw
Bay City
Ann Arbor
Kalamazoo
Battle Creek
Jackson
Toledo
Chicago
Milwaukee
Green Bay
Manitowoc
Sheboygan
Racine
Kenosha
Gary
South Bend
Muskegon
Holland
Traverse City
Cadillac
Midland
Port Huron
Sarnia
ontario 62
ohio 42
indiana 18
wisconsin 54
CENTRAL TIME ZONE
EASTERN TIME ZONE
© GeoNova Publishing, Inc.
MI 88

Mississippi

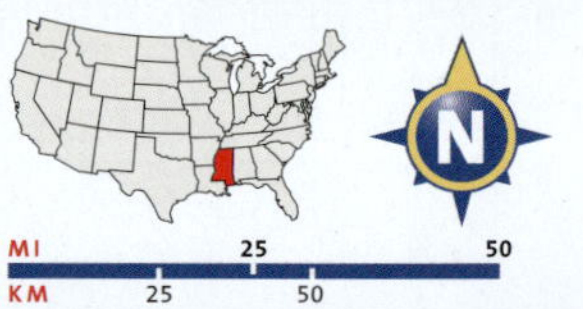

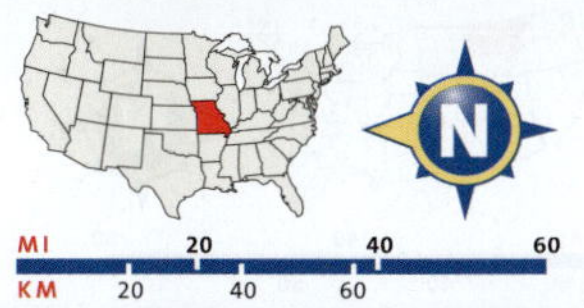

illinois 17
kentucky 20
tennessee 20
arkansas 7
kansas 22
oklahoma 44
nebraska 31
MO 89

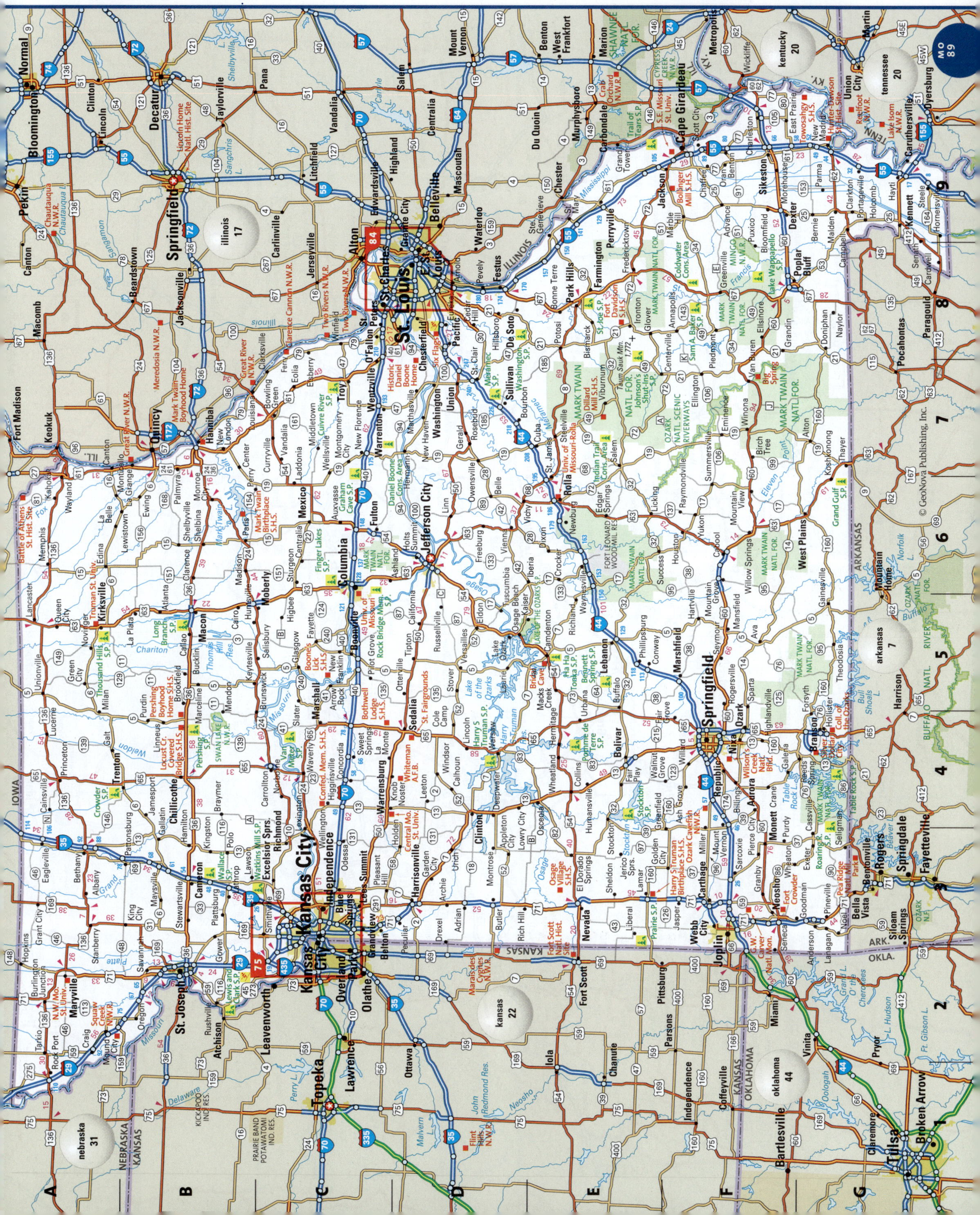

Montana

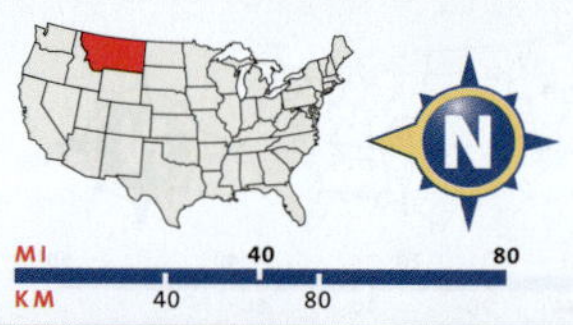

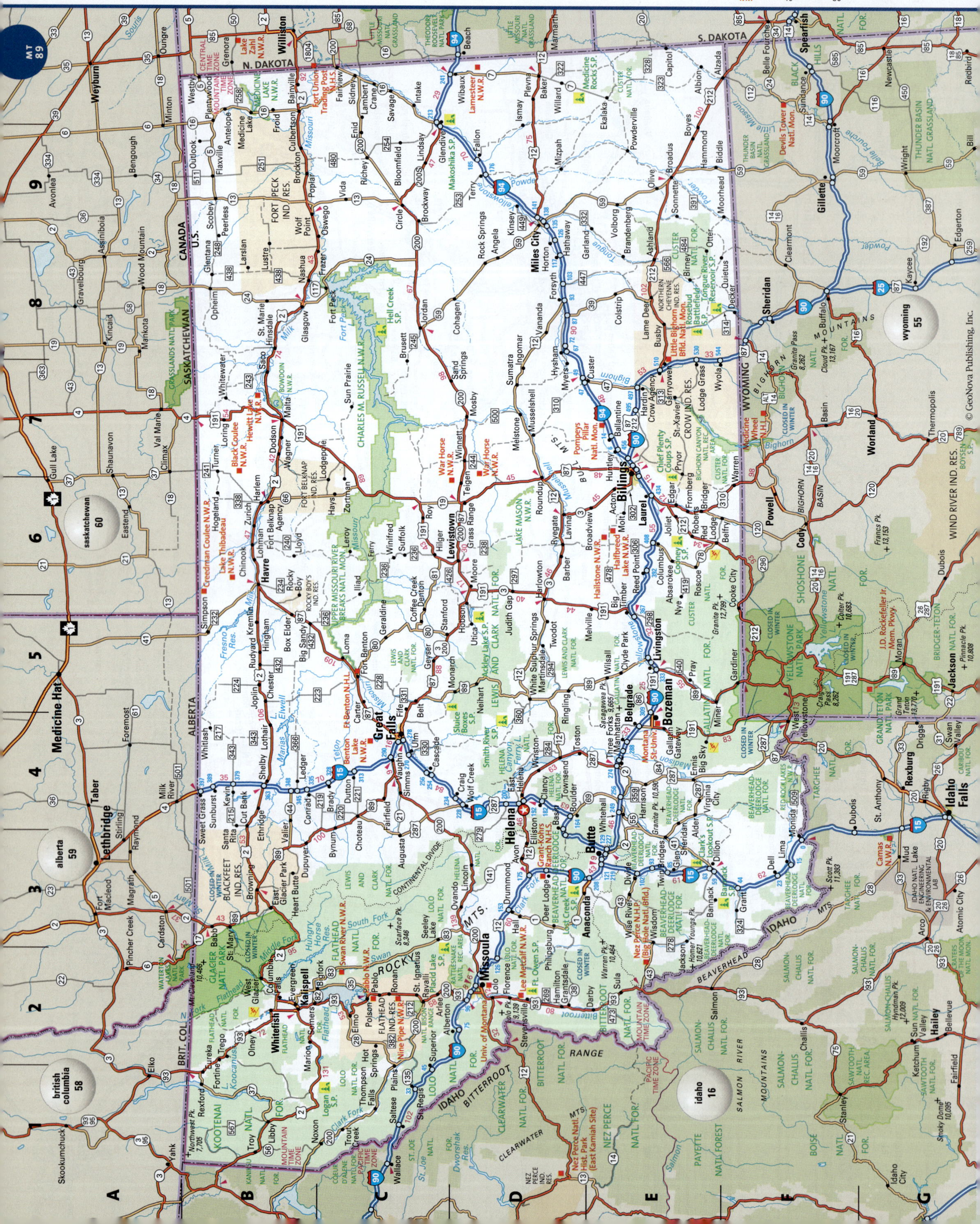

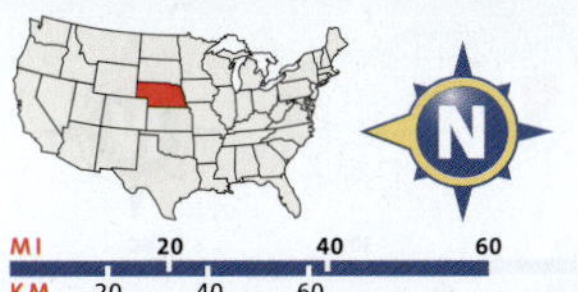
N
MI 20 40 60
KM 20 40 60

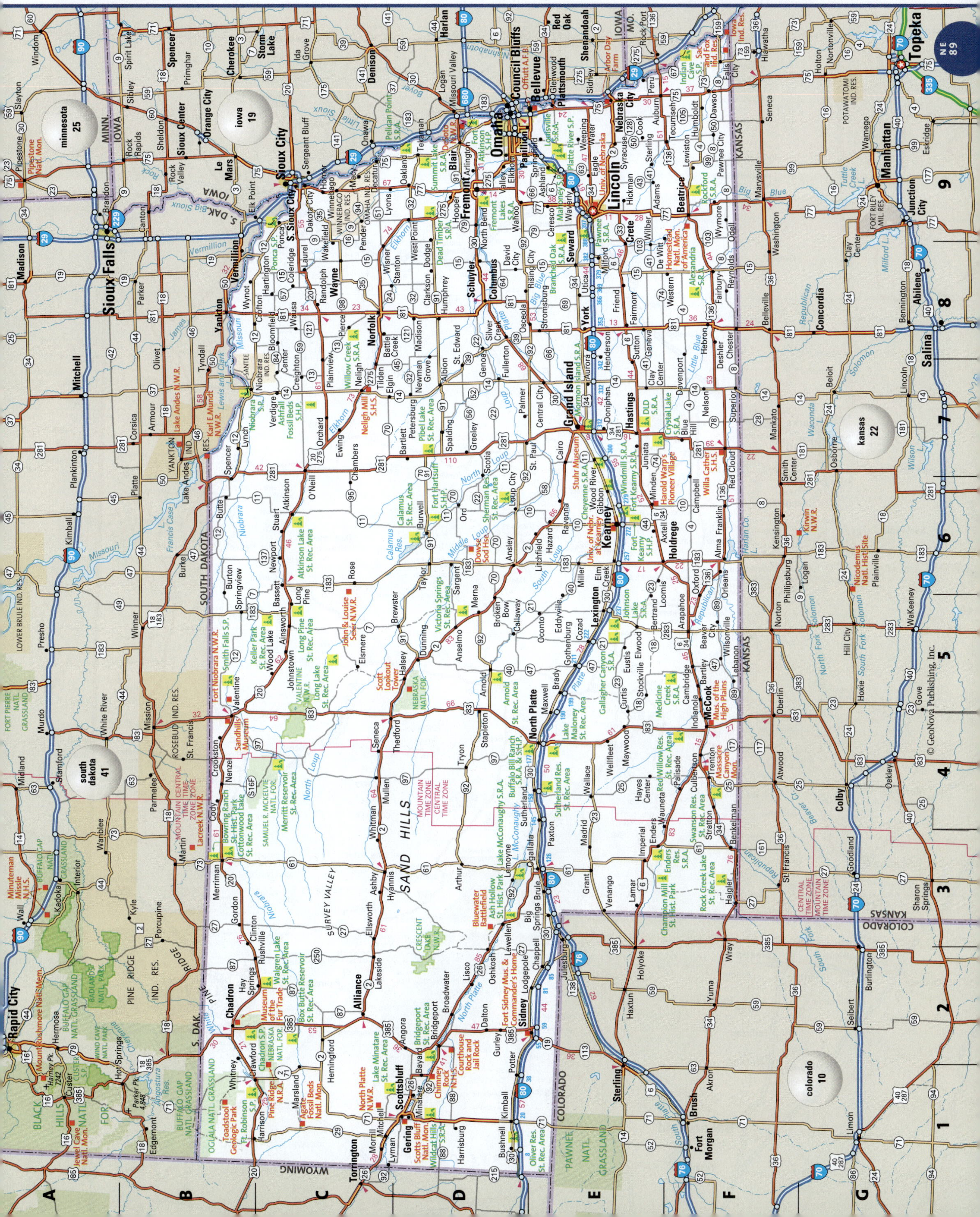

Nevada

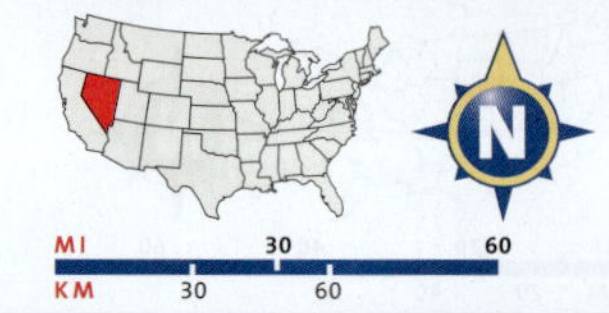

MI
30
60
KM
30
60
N

NV
89
OREGON
IDAHO
UTAH
ARIZONA
CALIFORNIA
GREAT BASIN
Denio
McDermitt
Owyhee
Jackpot
Jarbidge
Orovada
Paradise Valley
Winnemucca
Golconda
Battle Mountain
Carlin
Elko
Spring Creek
Wells
Oasis
West Wendover
Lovelock
Nixon
Wadsworth
Sparks
Reno
Fernley
Fallon
Carson City
Incline Village
Truckee
South Lake Tahoe
Minden
Gardnerville
Yerington
Hawthorne
Mina
Tonopah
Goldfield
Austin
Eureka
Ely
McGill
Baker
Pioche
Caliente
Panaca
Alamo
Rachel
Beatty
Pahrump
Indian Springs
Mesquite
Overton
North Las Vegas
Las Vegas
Henderson
Boulder City
Searchlight
Laughlin
Bullhead City
Kingman
St. George
Bishop
Mammoth Lakes
Fresno
Bakersfield
Death Valley
Great Basin N.P.
Lake Tahoe
Pyramid L.
Walker Lake S.R.A.
Nellis Air Force Range Complex
Nevada Test Site
Lake Mead Natl. Rec. Area
MOJAVE DESERT
PACIFIC TIME ZONE
MOUNTAIN TIME ZONE

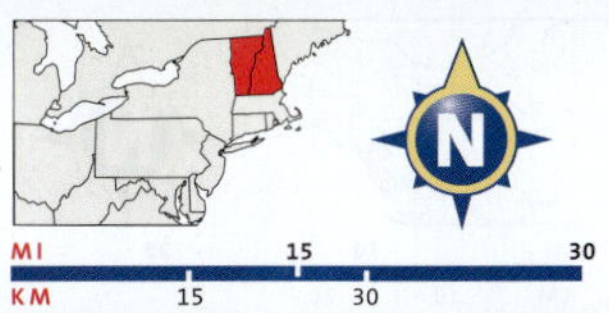

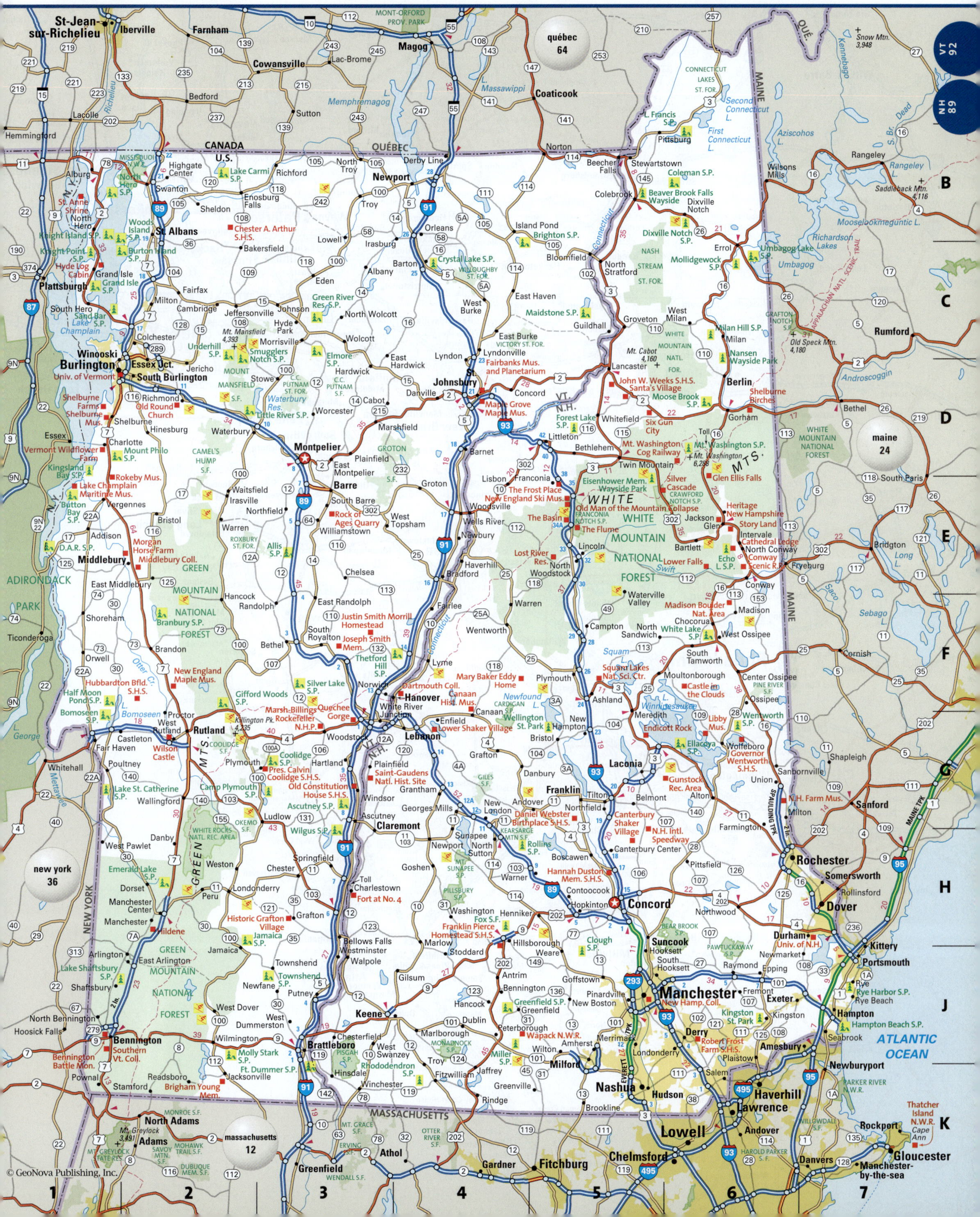

CANADA
U.S.
QUÉBEC
MAINE
NEW YORK
MASSACHUSETTS
ATLANTIC OCEAN
WHITE MOUNTAIN NATIONAL FOREST
GREEN MOUNTAIN NATIONAL FOREST
WHITE MTS.
GREEN MTS.

québec 64
maine 24
new york 36
massachusetts 12
VT 92
NH 89

Burlington
Montpelier
Barre
Rutland
Bennington
Brattleboro
St. Johnsbury
Concord
Manchester
Nashua
Portsmouth
Keene
Lebanon
Laconia
Dover
Rochester
Berlin
Lowell

New Jersey

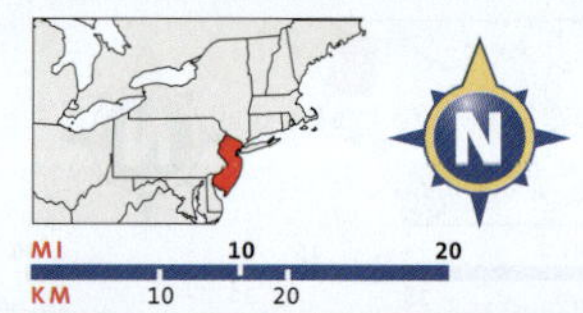

NJ 89
new york 36
pennsylvania 46
maryland 11
delaware 11

ATLANTIC OCEAN

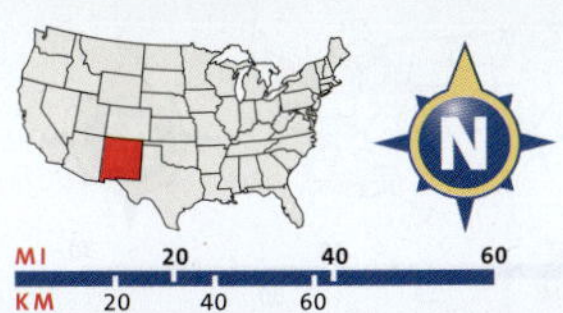

Colorado
Cortez
Durango
Pagosa Springs
Alamosa
Trinidad
Navajo Nation Ind. Res.
Mesa Verde Natl. Park
Ute Mountain Ind. Res.
Southern Ute Ind. Res.
San Juan Natl. For.
Rio Grande Natl. For.
Wolf Creek Pass Tunnel
Monte Vista N.W.R.
San Isabel Natl. For.
Fort Carson Mil. Res.
Comanche Natl. Grassland
Kim
Four Corners Mon.
colorado 10
oklahoma 44
texas 48
mexico 68
Shiprock
Farmington
Aztec
Bloomfield
Kirtland
Flora Vista
Cedar Hill
Aztec Ruins Natl. Mon.
Salmon Ruins & Heritage Park
Navajo Lake S.P.
Angel Peak B.L.M. Rec. Area
Dulce
Lumberton
Chama
Cumbres and Toltec Scenic Railroad
Heron Lake S.P.
El Vado Lake S.P.
Jicarilla Apache Ind. Res.
Carson Natl. For.
Tierra Amarilla
Tres Piedras
Costilla
Questa
Red River
Wheeler Pk. 13,161
Taos Pueblo
Taos
Ranchos de Taos
Eagle Nest
Angel Fire
Cimarron
Cimarron Canyon S.P.
Raton
Sugarite Canyon S.P.
Capulin Volcano Natl. Mon.
Capulin
Folsom
Des Moines
Clayton Lake S.P.
Kiowa Natl. Grassland
Clayton
Maxwell
Maxwell N.W.R.
Springer
Philmont Boy Scout Ranch
Abbott
Gladstone
Grenville
Texline
Felt
Black Mesa 4,973
Navajo Nation Ind. Res.
Sanostee
Newcomb
Naschitti
Tsaile
Canyon de Chelly Natl. Mon.
Blanco Trading Post
Nageezi
Lindrith
Gavilan
Echo Amphitheater
Abiquiu Res.
Abiquiu
El Rito
Ojo Caliente
Peñasco
Picuris Pueblo
Chaco Culture N.H.P.
Pueblo Bonito Ruins
Continental Divide
Cuba
Regina
Youngsville
Santa Fe Natl. For.
Ohkay Owingeh Pueblo
Española
Santa Clara Pueblo
Valles Caldera Natl. Pres.
San Ildefonso Pueblo
Los Alamos
Chimayo
Santa Cruz
Pojoaque
Nambe Pueblo
Santa Fe Baldy 12,622
Sangre de Cristo Mts.
Cerro Vista 11,939
Ocate
Guadalupita
Mora
Fort Union Natl. Mon.
Wagon Mound
Levy
Watrous
Roy
Bueyeros
Sedan
Amistad
Mosquero
Nara Visa
Navajo
Tohatchi
Coyote Canyon
Window Rock
Crownpoint
Torreon
Jemez Springs
Jemez St. Mon.
White Rock
Bandelier Natl. Mon.
Tesuque
Santa Fe
Sapello
Storrie Lake S.P.
Las Vegas
Las Vegas N.W.R.
Romeroville
Los Montoyas
Trementina
Conchas Lake S.P.
Conchas Dam
Ute Lake S.P.
Logan
Tucumcari
Tucumcari Hist. Mus.
Yah-Tah-Hey
Church Rock
Gallup
Manuelito
Thoreau
Prewitt
Ambrosia Lake
San Mateo
Mt. Taylor 11,301
Zia Pueblo
Jemez Pueblo
Cochiti Pueblo
Santo Domingo Pueblo
San Felipe Pueblo
Kasha-Katuwe Tent Rocks N.M.
La Cienega
San Ysidro
Bernalillo
Rio Rancho
Alameda
Petroglyph Natl. Mon.
Albuquerque
Cibola Natl. For.
Madrid
Galisteo
Lamy
Pecos
Pecos Natl. Hist. Park
Ribera
Villanueva
Villanueva S.P.
Serafina
Dilia
Santa Rosa Lake S.P.
Newkirk
Cuervo
San Jon
Caprock Amphitheater
Quay
Sanders
Zuni Pueblo
Zuni Ind. Res.
Ramah
El Morro
El Morro Natl. Mon.
Bluewater
Milan
Grants
Bandera Crater & Ice Caves
San Rafael
El Malpais Natl. Mon.
El Malpais Natl. Cons. Area
Cebolleta Pk. 8,762
Laguna
Paguate
Casa Blanca
Acoma Pueblo
Mesita
Enchanted Mesa
Isleta Pueblo
Padillas
Edgewood
Kirtland A.F.B.
Moriarty
Stanley
Clines Corners
White Lakes
Miera
Bosque Farms
Los Lunas
Valencia
Tajique
Estancia
Los Chavez
Manzano Pk. 10,098
Belen
Quarai
Abo
Mountainair
Willard
Encino
Vaughn
Santa Rosa
Pastura
Puerto de Luna
Site of Coronado's Bridge
Sumner L.
Sumner Lake S.P.
Fort Sumner
Taiban
Grave of Billy the Kid
Bosque Redondo Mem. at Ft. Sumner St. Mon.
House
Field
Grady
Melrose
Clovis
Cannon A.F.B.
Texico
Oasis S.P.
Floyd
Portales
Eastern New Mexico Univ.
Elida
Dora
Grulla N.W.R.
Causey
Fence Lake
Alamo
Navajo Nation Ind. Res.
Quemado
Pie Town
Alegres Mtn. 10,244
Datil Well B.L.M. Rec. Area
Datil
Magdalena
Sevilleta N.W.R.
Bernardo
La Joya
San Acacia
Lemitar
Gran Quivira
Salinas Pueblo Missions Natl. Mon.
Gallinas Pk. 8,615
Claunch
Corona
Duran
Ramon
Eagar
Apache Natl. For.
Aragon
Old Horse Springs
National Radio Astronomy Observatory VLA Telescope
Kelly Ghost Town
South Baldy 10,783
Socorro
San Antonio
Bingham
Bosque del Apache N.W.R.
Mt. Withington 10,115
Valley of Fires B.L.M. Rec. Area
Ancho
Alpine
Luna
Apache Creek
Reserve
Ft. Craig Hist. Site
'Trinity Site' Site of World's First Atomic Bomb
Carrizozo
Lincoln
Capitan
Arabela
Lincoln St. Mon.
Hondo
Bitter Lake N.W.R.
Roswell
Bottomless Lakes S.P.
Elkins
Milnesand
Llano Estacado
Gila Natl. For.
Alma
Black Mtn. 9,250
Whitewater Baldy 10,890
The Catwalk
Gila Cliff Dwellings Natl. Mon.
Pleasanton
Mule Creek
Black Range
Monticello
Cuchillo
Reeds Pk. 10,011
Williamsburg
Elephant Butte Res.
Elephant Butte Lake S.P.
Truth or Consequences
Jornada del Muerto
Oscuro
White Sands Missile Range
Nogal
Three Rivers Petroglyph B.L.M. Rec. Site
Sierra Blanca 11,973
Ruidoso
Ruidoso Downs
Hubbard Mus. of the American West
Mescalero
Mescalero Ind. Res.
Midway
Dexter
Hagerman
Plains
Caprock
Tatum
Buckhorn
Cliff
Silver City
Santa Clara
Bayard
Hurley
Mangas Springs
Tyrone
W. New Mex. Univ.
Hillsboro
Caballo Res.
Caballo
Caballo Lake S.P.
Arrey
Tularosa
White Sands Space Harbor
La Luz
N. Mex. Mus. of Space History
Cloudcroft
Alamogordo
Holloman A.F.B.
White Sands Natl. Mon.
San Andres Mts.
San Andres N.W.R.
San Andres Pk. 8,239
Alamo Pk. 9,700
Sunspot Solar Observatory
Elk
Mayhill
Oliver Lee Memorial S.P.
Lake Arthur
Artesia
Hope
Loco Hills
Maljamar
Lovington
Humble City
Hobbs
Duncan
Burro Pk. 8,035
White Signal
San Lorenzo
City of Rocks S.P.
Salem
Hatch
Nutt
Leasburg Dam S.P.
Radium Springs
Dona Aña
Organ
Pinon
Seven Rivers
Brantley Lake S.P.
Carlsbad
Arkansas Junction
Nadine
Eunice
Lordsburg
Shakespeare Ghost Town
Separ
Deming
Rockhound S.P.
Las Cruces
University Park
Organ Mts. B.L.M. Rec. Area
Mesilla
Vado
Orogrande
Fort Bliss Mil. Res.
Guadalupe Mts.
Sitting Bull Falls
Loving
Malaga
Whites City
Carlsbad Caverns Natl. Park
Jal
Animas
Playas
Hachita
Rodeo
Animas Pk. 8,532
Coronado Natl. For.
Columbus
Pancho Villa S.P.
Anthony
Chaparral
Sunland Park
El Paso
Guadalupe Mts. Natl. Park
Guadalupe Pk. 8,751
Nickel Creek
Salt Basin
Kermit
Mentone
Chihuahua
Ciudad Juárez
Socorro
Hueco Mts.
Fabens
Mountain Time Zone
Central Time Zone
Cloverdale Ghost Town
U.S.
Mexico
Sonora
Nogales
Ascensión
Guadalupe
McNary
Sierra Blanca 6,890
Sierra Blanca
Van Horn
Pecos
Balmorhea
Rio Grande
Arizona
Utah
Texas
Okla.
NM 90

© GeoNova Publishing, Inc.

1 2 3 4 5 6 7
B C D E F G H J K

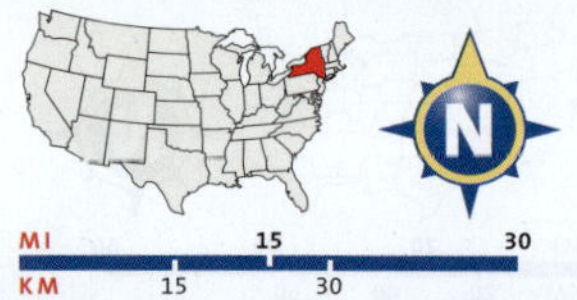

NY 90

SOUTHERN NEW YORK

connecticut 12

new jersey 34

ontario 62

pennsylvania 46

Torrington, Hartford, West Hartford, New Britain, Bristol, Waterbury, Meriden, Middletown, Norwich, Willimantic, New London, Danbury, New Haven, West Haven, Bridgeport, Milford, Norwalk, Stamford, Greenwich, Poughkeepsie, New Paltz, Newburgh, Middletown, Monticello, Port Jervis, White Plains, Yonkers, New Rochelle, Paterson, Paramus, Passaic, Newark, Elizabeth, Plainfield, New York, Hempstead, Hicksville, Levittown, Brentwood, Huntington Station, Central Islip, Patchogue, Riverhead, Southampton, East Hampton, Montauk

Long Island Sound, LONG ISLAND, ATLANTIC OCEAN, FIRE ISLAND NATL. SEASHORE, DELAWARE WATER GAP NATL. REC. AREA

Toronto, Mississauga, Oakville, Milton, Burlington, Hamilton, St. Catharines, Niagara Falls, Welland, Buffalo, Cheektowaga, North Tonawanda, West Seneca, Lockport, Batavia, Rochester, Irondequoit, Greece, Henrietta, Geneva, Canandaigua, Seneca Falls, Waterloo, Hornell, Bath, Corning, Elmira, Olean, Salamanca, Jamestown, Dunkirk, Erie, Bradford, Warren

LAKE ONTARIO, LAKE ERIE, CANADA, U.S., ONTARIO, PENNSYLVANIA, ALLEGHENY NATL. REC. AREA, FINGER LAKES NATL. FOR.

© GeoNova

A B C D E F G H J K

1 2 3 4 5 6 7

ontario
62
vermont
33
massachusetts
12
connecticut
12
QUÉBEC
CANADA
U.S.
ONTARIO
PENNSYLVANIA
VERMONT
MASS.
CONN.
ADIRONDACK PARK
ADIRONDACK MOUNTAINS
CATSKILL PARK
CATSKILL MTS.
FORT DRUM MIL. RES.
ONONDAGA IND. RES.
Kingston
Cornwall
Massena
Ogdensburg
Potsdam
Canton
Malone
Plattsburgh
Burlington
Watertown
Oswego
Syracuse
Rome
Utica
Herkimer
Auburn
Ithaca
Cortland
Norwich
Binghamton
Oneonta
Saratoga Springs
Glens Falls
Schenectady
Albany
Troy
Amsterdam
Kingston
Hudson
Pittsfield
Bennington
Middlebury
Lake Placid
Saranac Lake
Tupper Lake
Old Forge
Mt. Marcy 5,344
Slide Mtn. 4,204
© GeoNova Publishing, Inc.
B
C
D
E
F
G
H
J
K
8
9
10
11
12
13
14

North & South Carolina

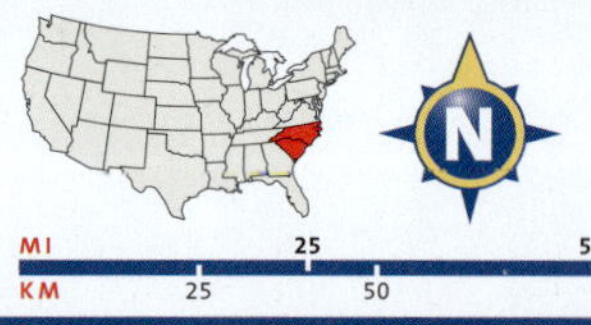

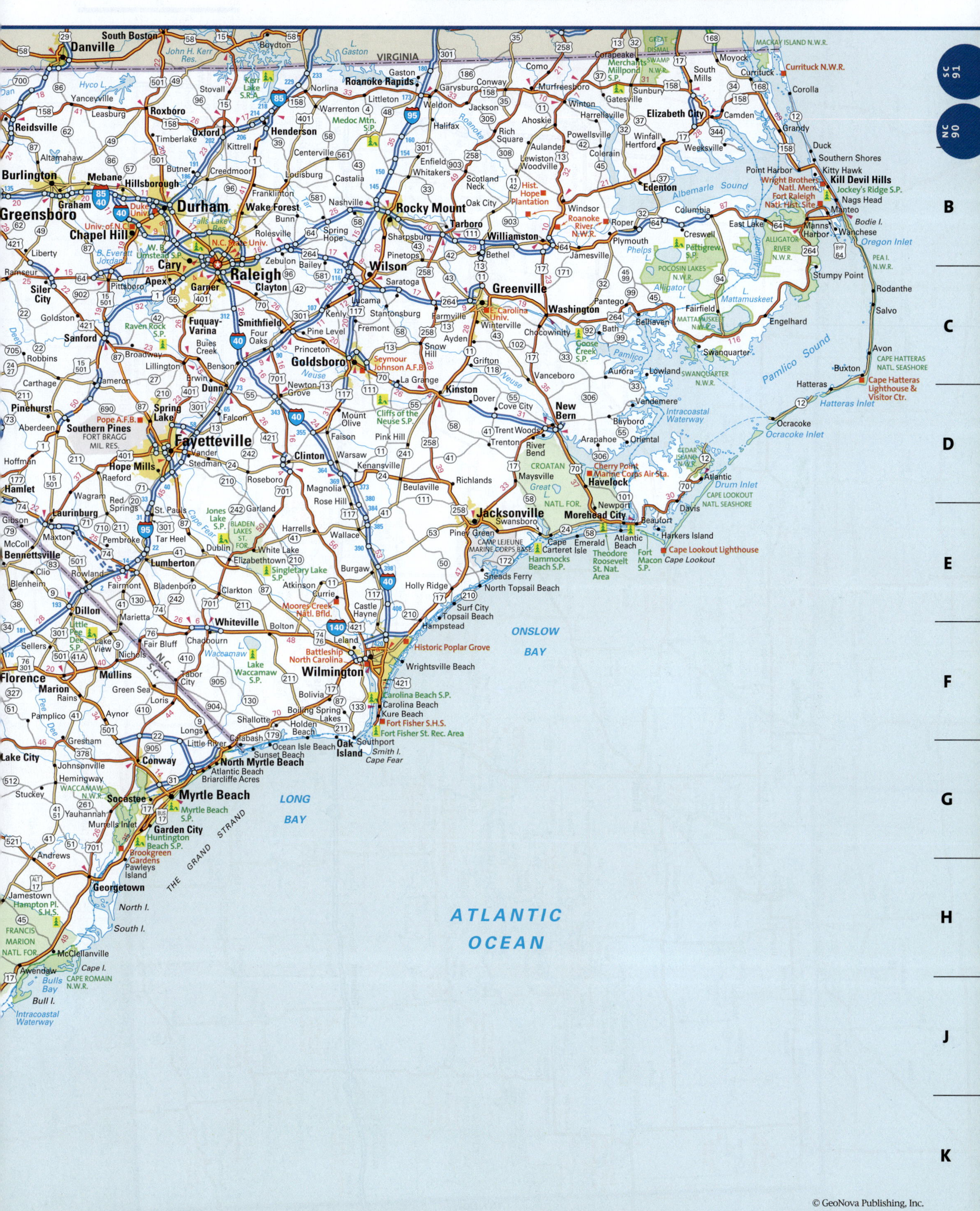

VIRGINIA
SC 91
NC 90
Danville
South Boston
Boydton
Roanoke Rapids
Weldon
Gaston
Garysburg
Conway
Murfreesboro
Como
Corapeake
Moyock
Currituck
Currituck N.W.R.
Corolla
Mackay Island N.W.R.
Great Dismal Swamp N.W.R.
Merchants Millpond S.P.
South Mills
Elizabeth City
Camden
Grandy
Duck
Southern Shores
Kitty Hawk
Kill Devil Hills
Wright Brothers Natl. Mem.
Jockey's Ridge S.P.
Nags Head
Fort Raleigh Natl. Hist. Site
Manteo
Manns Harbor
Wanchese
Bodie I.
Oregon Inlet
Pea I. N.W.R.
Rodanthe
Salvo
Avon
Cape Hatteras Natl. Seashore
Buxton
Cape Hatteras Lighthouse & Visitor Ctr.
Hatteras
Hatteras Inlet
Ocracoke
Ocracoke Inlet
Pamlico Sound
Albemarle Sound
Edenton
Hertford
Winfall
Weeksville
Point Harbor
Columbia
East Lake
Alligator River N.W.R.
Pettigrew S.P.
Pocosin Lakes N.W.R.
Mattamuskeet
Fairfield
Engelhard
Swanquarter
Swanquarter N.W.R.
Stumpy Point
Yanceyville
Leasburg
Roxboro
Reidsville
Oxford
Henderson
Kerr Lake S.R.A.
John H. Kerr Res.
Warrenton
Littleton
Medoc Mtn. S.P.
Norlina
Halifax
Enfield
Whitakers
Scotland Neck
Rich Square
Jackson
Ahoskie
Aulander
Lewiston Woodville
Winton
Harrellsville
Powellsville
Colerain
Gatesville
Sunbury
Windsor
Hist. Hope Plantation
Roanoke River N.W.R.
Roper
Plymouth
Creswell
Jamesville
Williamston
Bethel
Tarboro
Rocky Mount
Oak City
Nashville
Castalia
Louisburg
Centerville
Franklinton
Wake Forest
Creedmoor
Butner
Kittrell
Burlington
Mebane
Hillsborough
Graham
Greensboro
Durham
Duke Univ.
Chapel Hill
Univ. of N.C.
Falls Lake Res.
N.C. State Univ.
Raleigh
Cary
Apex
Garner
Rolesville
Bunn
Zebulon
Bailey
Wilson
Spring Hope
Sharpsburg
Pinetops
Saratoga
Greenville
E. Carolina Univ.
Winterville
Washington
Chocowinity
Goose Creek S.P.
Bath
Pantego
Belhaven
Aurora
Lowland
Vandemere
Bayboro
Oriental
Arapahoe
Intracoastal Waterway
Cedar Island N.W.R.
Atlantic
Drum Inlet
Cape Lookout Natl. Seashore
Davis
Harkers Island
Beaufort
Cape Lookout Lighthouse
Cape Lookout
Fort Macon S.P.
Atlantic Beach
Morehead City
Newport
Havelock
Cherry Point Marine Corps Air Sta.
Croatan Natl. For.
New Bern
River Bend
Trent Woods
Trenton
Maysville
Cove City
Dover
Vanceboro
Grifton
Kinston
La Grange
Ayden
Farmville
Snow Hill
Stantonsburg
Fremont
Lucama
Kenly
Pine Level
Princeton
Smithfield
Four Oaks
Selma
Clayton
Fuquay-Varina
Holly Springs
Siler City
Pittsboro
Liberty
Ramseur
B. Everett Jordan L.
Goldston
Sanford
Raven Rock S.P.
Broadway
Lillington
Buies Creek
Erwin
Dunn
Benson
Newton Grove
Goldsboro
Seymour Johnson A.F.B.
Mount Olive
Cliffs of the Neuse S.P.
Pink Hill
Faison
Warsaw
Kenansville
Beulaville
Richlands
Jacksonville
Swansboro
Camp Lejeune Marine Corps Base
Piney Green
Cape Carteret
Emerald Isle
Hammocks Beach S.P.
Theodore Roosevelt St. Nat. Area
Sneads Ferry
North Topsail Beach
Holly Ridge
Surf City
Topsail Beach
Hampstead
Onslow Bay
Historic Poplar Grove
Wrightsville Beach
Wilmington
Battleship North Carolina
Leland
Castle Hayne
Moores Creek Natl. Bfld.
Currie
Atkinson
Burgaw
Wallace
Rose Hill
Magnolia
Harrells
Clinton
Roseboro
Garland
Salemburg
Falcon
Spring Lake
Fayetteville
Pope A.F.B.
Southern Pines
Fort Bragg Mil. Res.
Aberdeen
Pinehurst
Carthage
Robbins
Cameron
Hope Mills
Raeford
Vander
Stedman
Hoffman
Hamlet
Wagram
Red Springs
St. Pauls
Laurinburg
Maxton
Pembroke
Lumberton
Tar Heel
Dublin
Jones Lake S.P.
Bladen Lakes St. For.
White Lake
Elizabethtown
Singletary Lake S.P.
Clarkton
Bladenboro
Fairmont
Rowland
Marietta
Whiteville
Bolton
Chadbourn
Lake Waccamaw
Lake Waccamaw S.P.
Tabor City
Fair Bluff
Nichols
Lake View
Dillon
Little Pee Dee S.P.
Sellers
Bennettsville
McColl
Gibson
Clio
Blenheim
Florence
Marion
Mullins
Rains
Green Sea
Loris
Aynor
Pamplico
Gresham
Lake City
Johnsonville
Hemingway
Stuckey
Waccamaw N.W.R.
Conway
Longs
Little River
Calabash
Sunset Beach
Ocean Isle Beach
Shallotte
Holden Beach
Bolivia
Boiling Spring Lakes
Oak Island
Southport
Smith I.
Cape Fear
Carolina Beach S.P.
Carolina Beach
Kure Beach
Fort Fisher S.H.S.
Fort Fisher St. Rec. Area
North Myrtle Beach
Atlantic Beach
Briarcliffe Acres
Socastee
Myrtle Beach
Myrtle Beach S.P.
Murrells Inlet
Garden City
Huntington Beach S.P.
Brookgreen Gardens
Pawleys Island
The Grand Strand
Long Bay
Yauhannah
Andrews
Georgetown
Hampton Pl. S.H.S.
North I.
South I.
Francis Marion Natl. For.
McClellanville
Awendaw
Cape I.
Cape Romain N.W.R.
Bulls Bay
Bull I.
Intracoastal Waterway
N.C.
S.C.
Atlantic Ocean
B
C
D
E
F
G
H
J
K
8
9
10
11
12
13
14

North Dakota

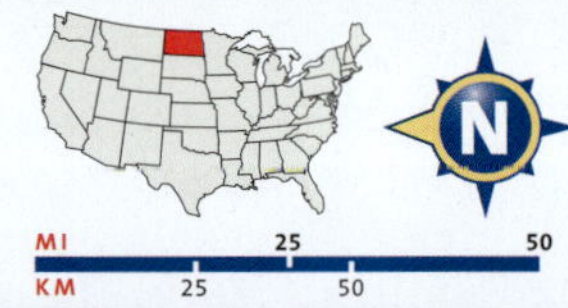

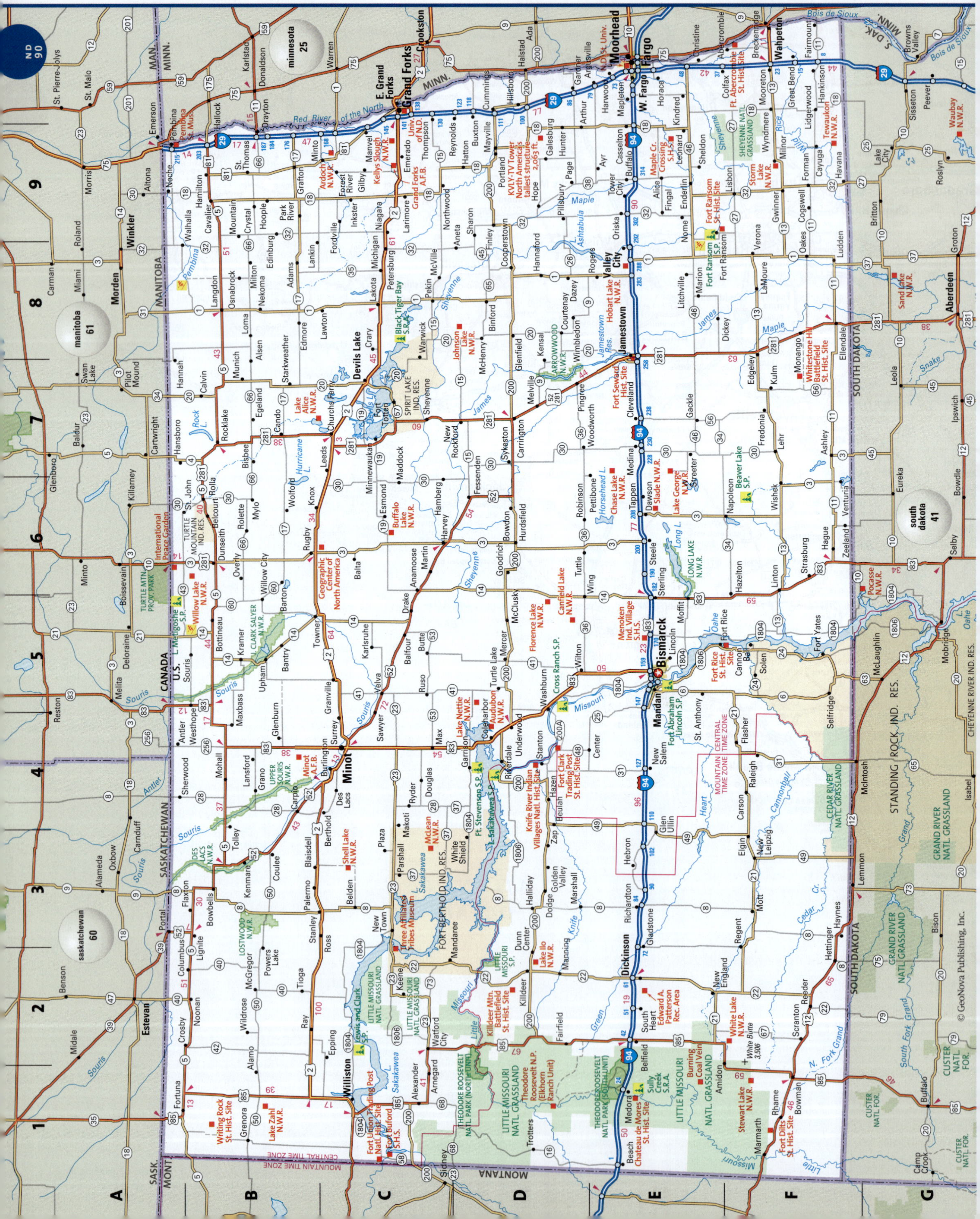

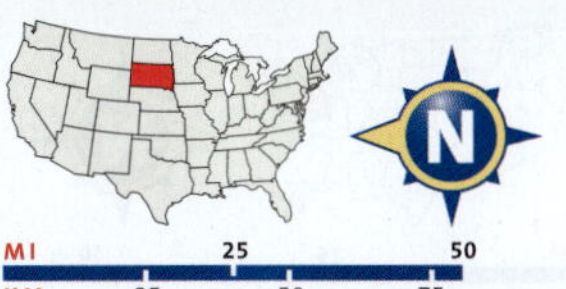
N
MI 25 50
KM 25 50 75

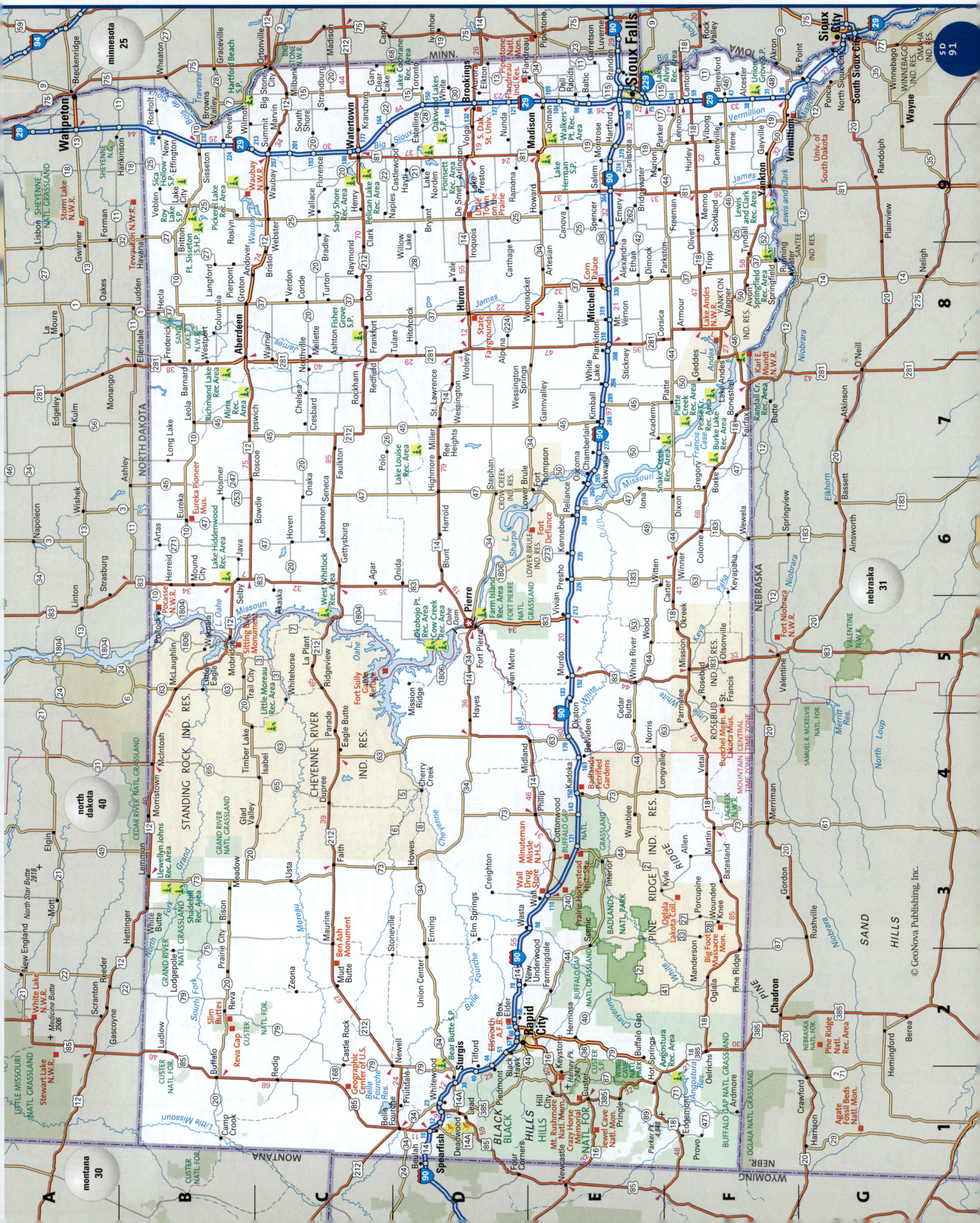

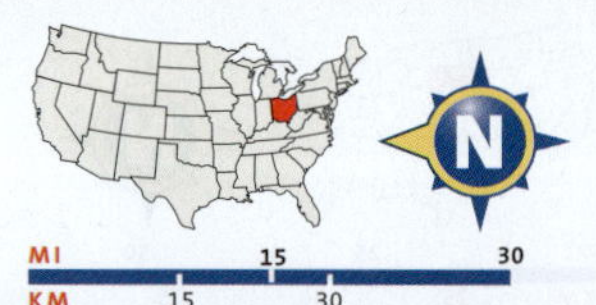

N
MI 15 30
KM 15 30

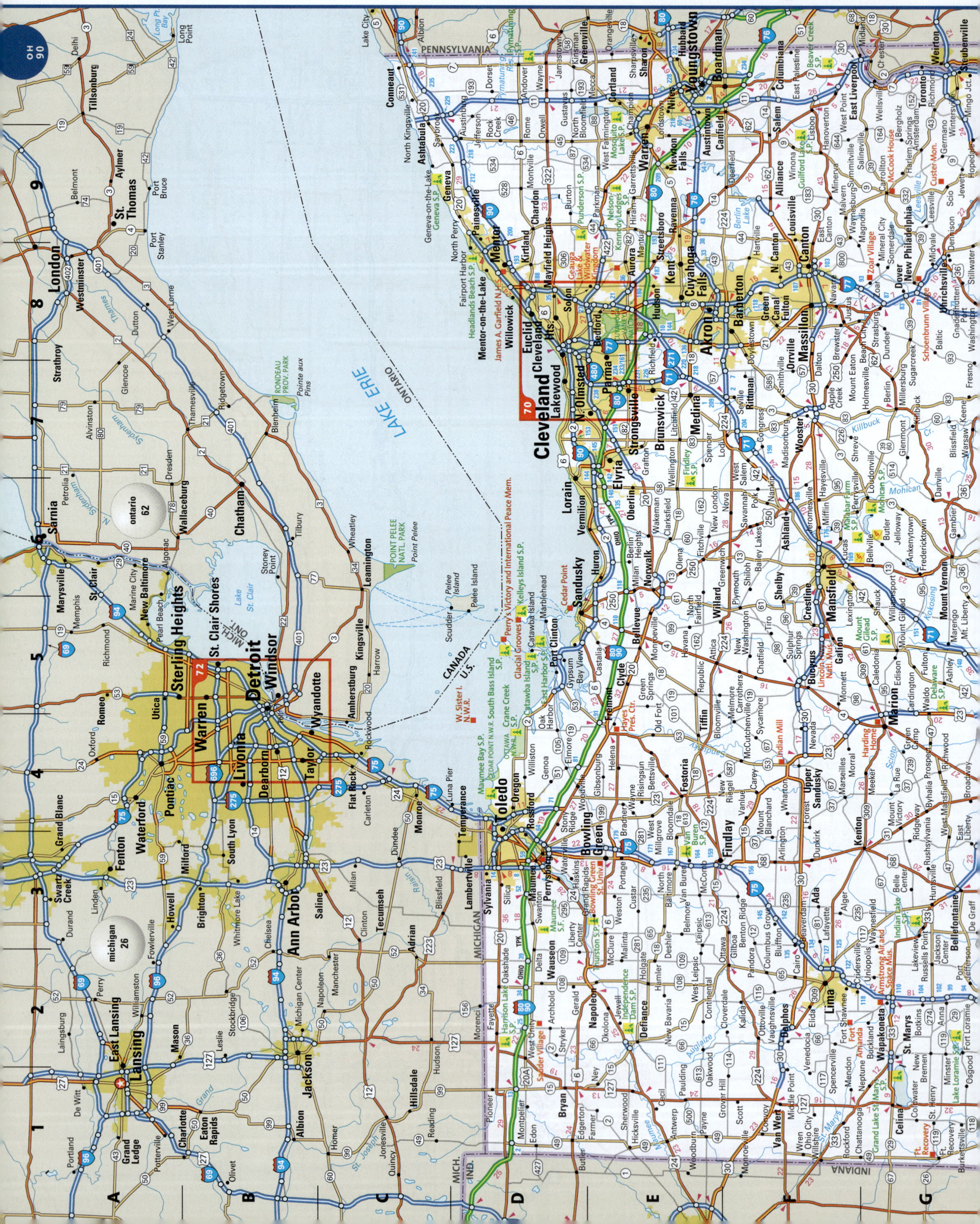

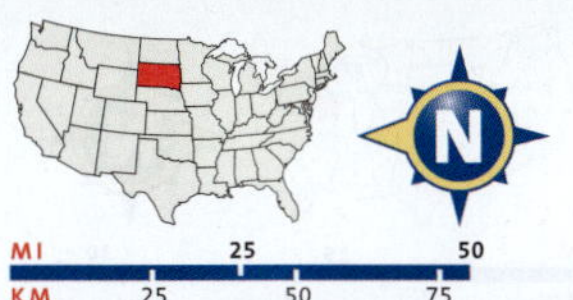

N
MI 25 50
KM 25 50 75

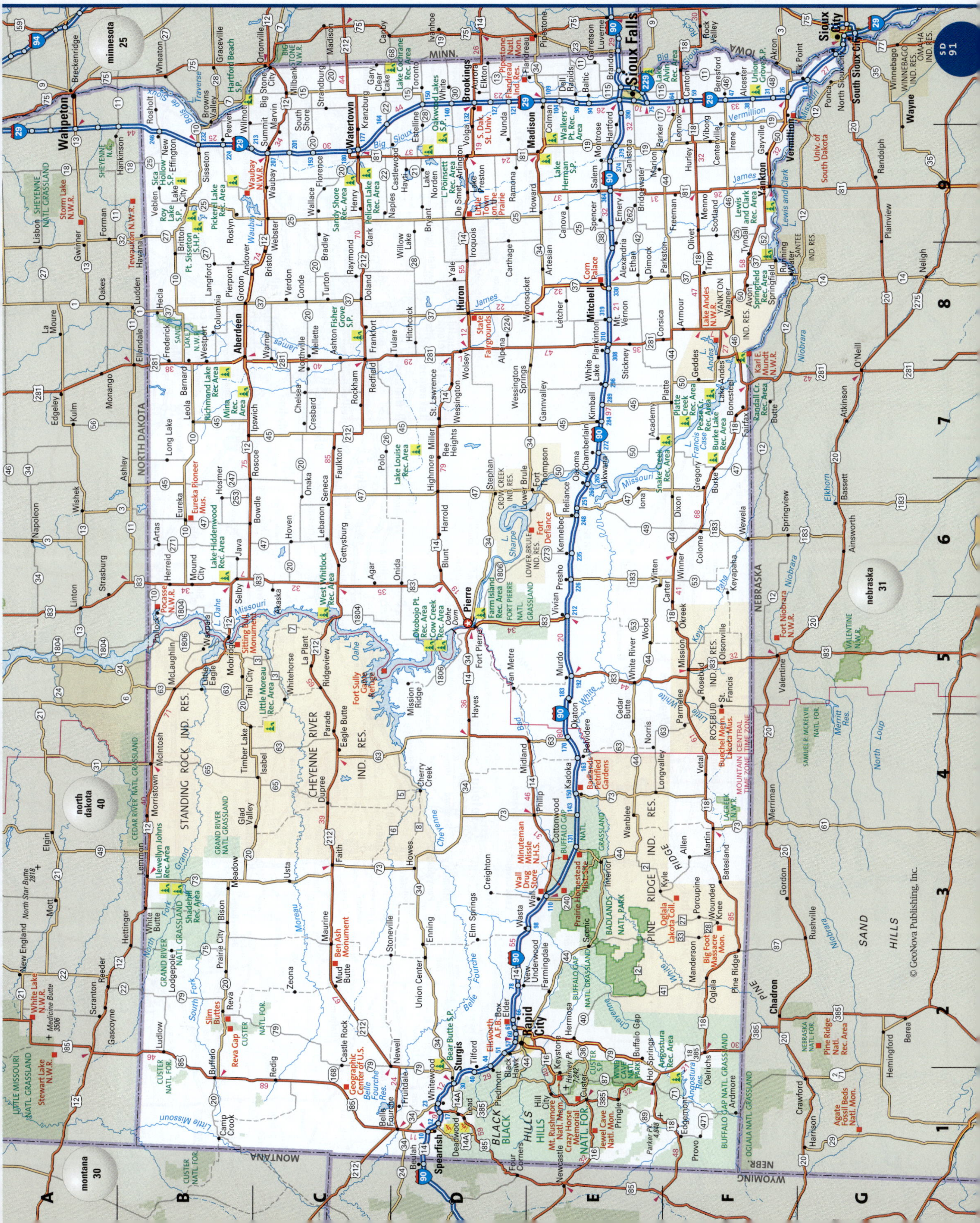

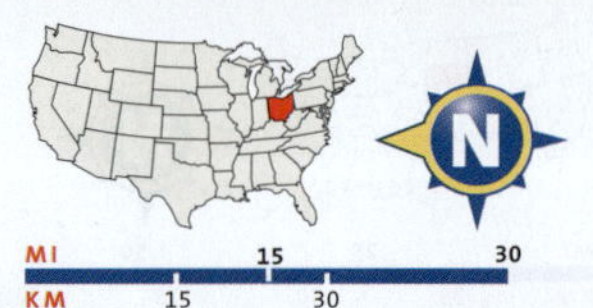
MI 15 30
KM 15 30
N

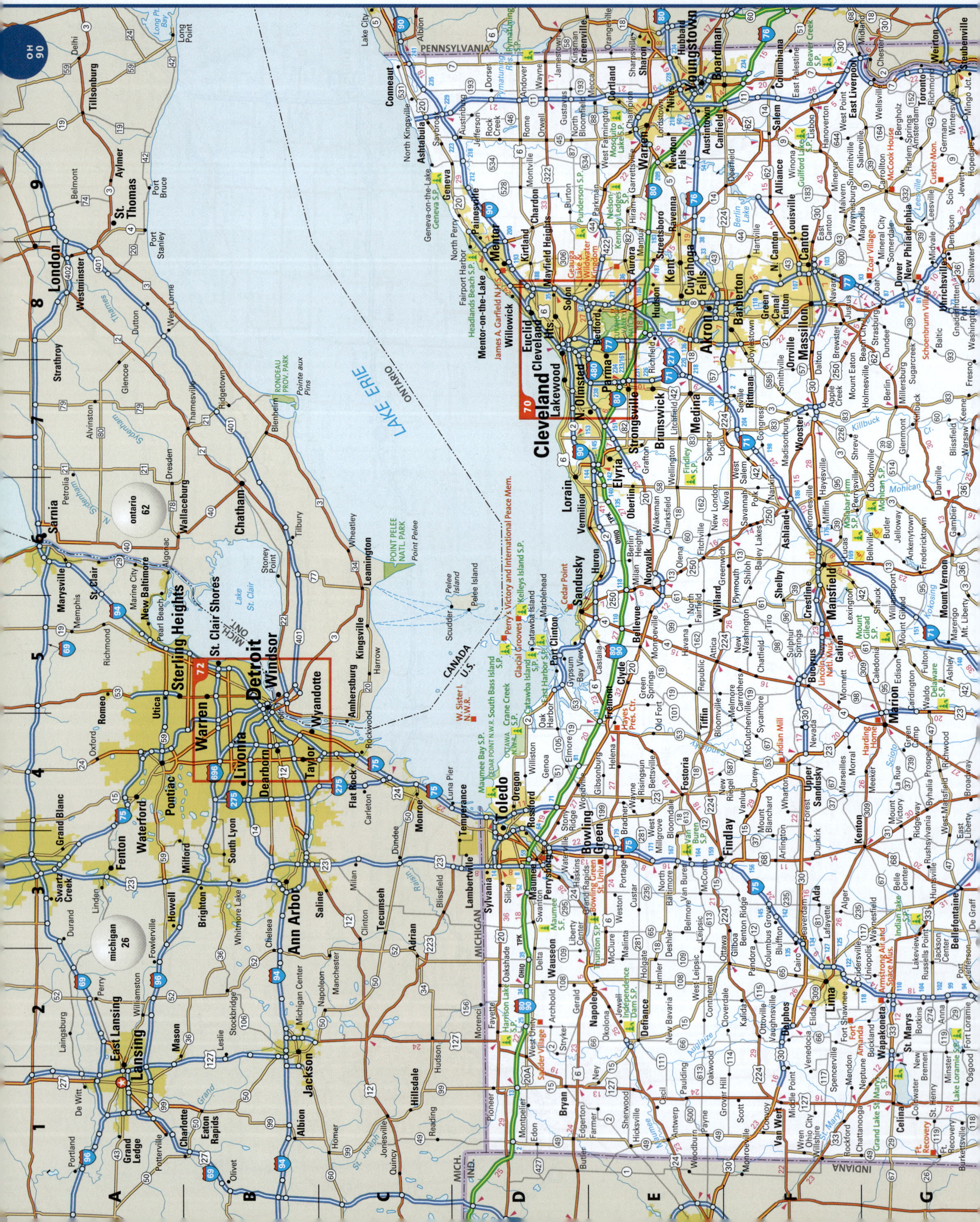

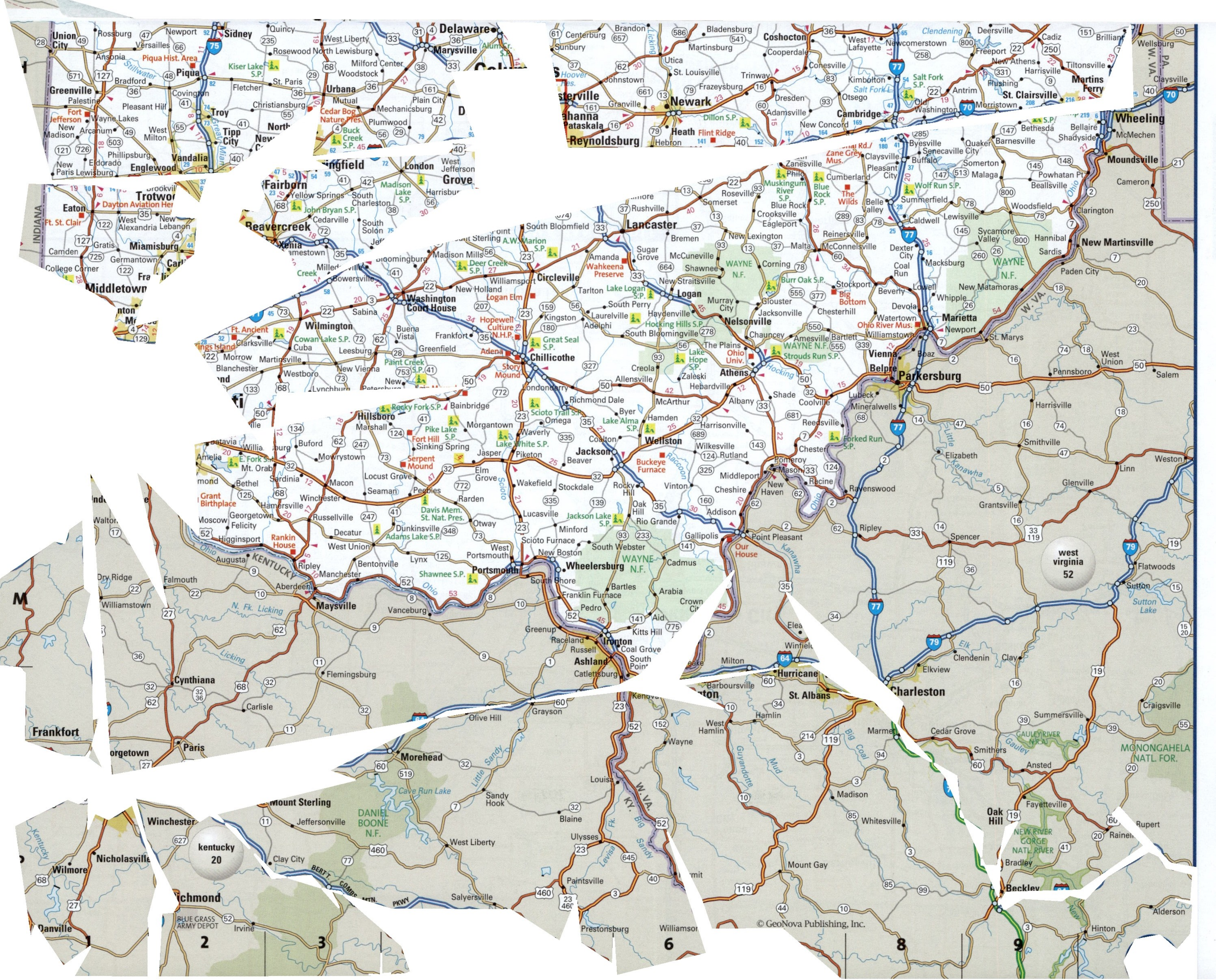

Wheeling
Moundsville
New Martinsville
Parkersburg
Marietta
Athens
Charleston
Huntington
Ashland
Portsmouth
Chillicothe
Lancaster
Circleville
Newark
Cambridge
Zanesville
Jackson
Gallipolis
Point Pleasant
Ironton
Maysville
Hillsboro
Wilmington
Washington Court House
Delaware
Marysville
Urbana
Sidney
Piqua
Troy
Greenville
Xenia
Beavercreek
Middletown
Miamisburg
Fairborn
London
Logan
Nelsonville
Wellston
Ravenswood
Ripley
Spencer
Beckley
Fayetteville
Oak Hill
Morehead
Mount Sterling
Winchester
Paris
Cynthiana
Frankfort
Nicholasville
Wilmore
Danville
West Virginia 52
Kentucky 20
WAYNE N.F.
DANIEL BOONE N.F.
MONONGAHELA NATL. FOR.
© GeoNova Publishing, Inc.

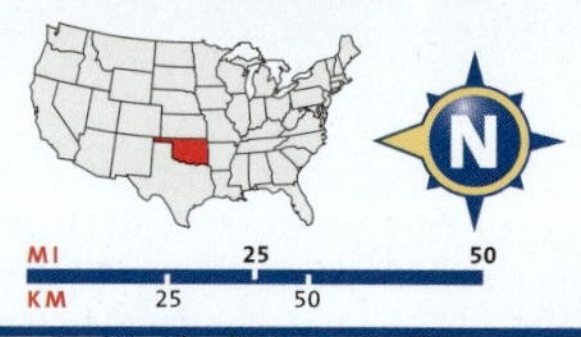
N
MI 25 50
KM 25 50

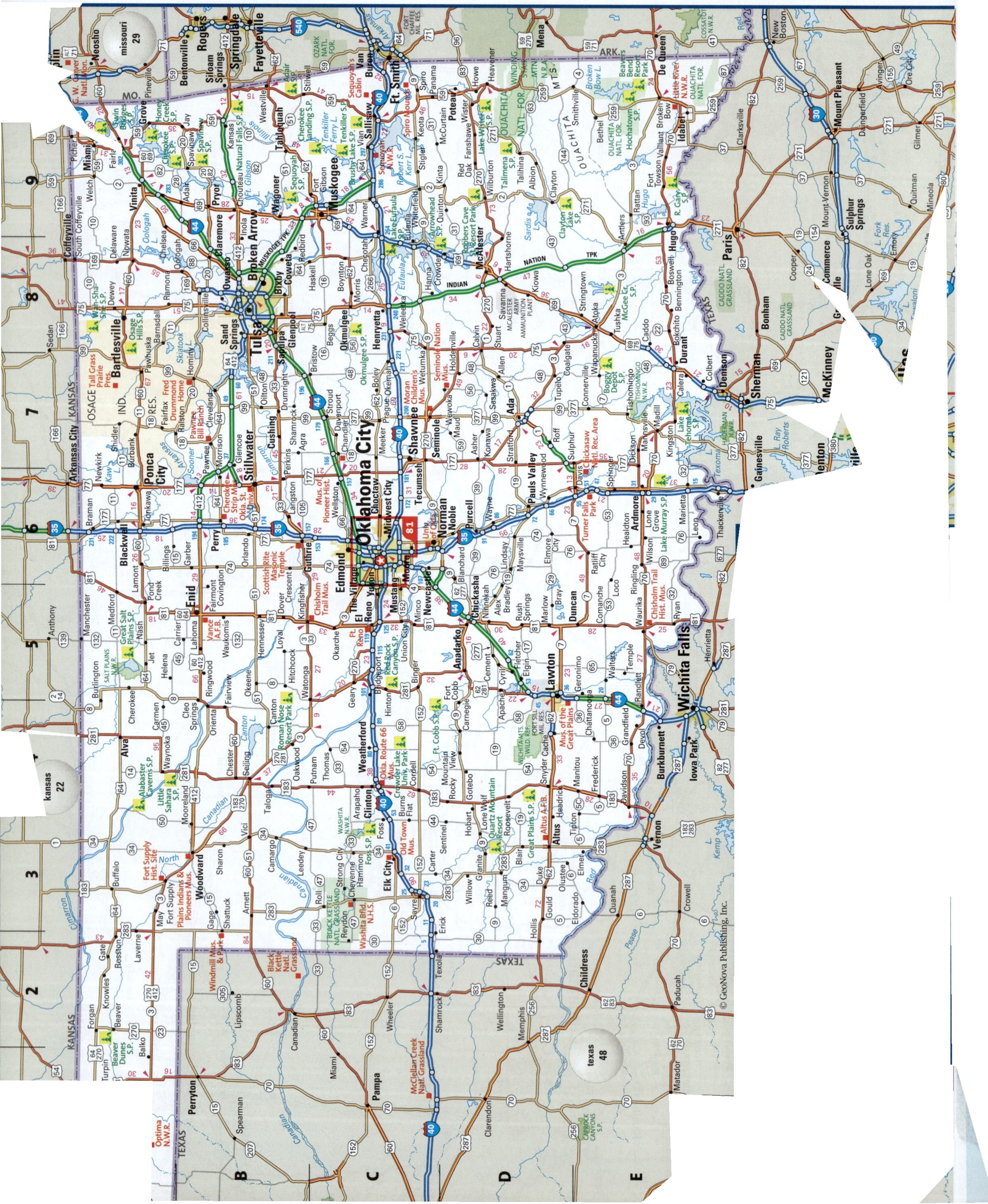

MI 20 40 60
KM 20 40 60
N
Portland
Salem
Eugene
Springfield
Corvallis
Albany
Bend
Medford
Klamath Falls
Pendleton
La Grande
Baker City
Ontario
Burns
The Dalles
Hood River
Astoria
Newport
Coos Bay
Roseburg
Grants Pass
Ashland
Vancouver
Walla Walla
Pasco
Kennewick
Richland
Caldwell
Nampa
Lakeview
Redmond
Prineville
Madras
Hermiston
Longview
Kelso
Florence
McMinnville
Tillamook
Seaside
Brookings
Crescent City
PACIFIC
OCEAN
CASCADE
CALAPOOYA MTS.
BLUE MTS.
WALLOWA MTS.
STEENS MOUNTAIN
PUEBLO MTS.
TROUT CREEK MTS.
KLAMATH MTS.
OWYHEE MTS.
HELLS CANYON
ALVORD DESERT
HORSE HEAVEN HILLS
YAKAMA IND. RES.
WARM SPRINGS IND. RES.
UMATILLA IND. RES.
NEZ PERCE IND. RES.
FORT MCDERMITT IND. RES.
CRATER LAKE NATL. PARK
MALHEUR N.W.R.
HART MOUNTAIN NATL. ANTELOPE REFUGE
SHELDON NATL. WILDLIFE REFUGE
OCHOCO NATL. FOR.
MALHEUR NATL. FOR.
UMATILLA NATL. FOR.
WALLOWA-WHITMAN NATL. FOR.
WILLAMETTE NATL. FOR.
DESCHUTES NATL. FOR.
FREMONT
WINEMA
UMPQUA
SIUSLAW NATL. FOR.
MOUNT HOOD
GIFFORD PINCHOT
SISKIYOU NATL. FOR.
OREGON DUNES NATL. REC. AREA
COLUMBIA RIVER GORGE NATL. SCENIC AREA
WASHINGTON
IDAHO
NEVADA
CALIFORNIA
washington 51
idaho 16
nevada 32
california 8
PACIFIC TIME ZONE MOUNTAIN TIME ZONE
PACIFIC CREST N.S.T.
A
B
C
D
E
F
G
1
2
3
4
5
6
7
8
9
OR 91
© GeoNova Publishing, Inc.

Pennsylvania

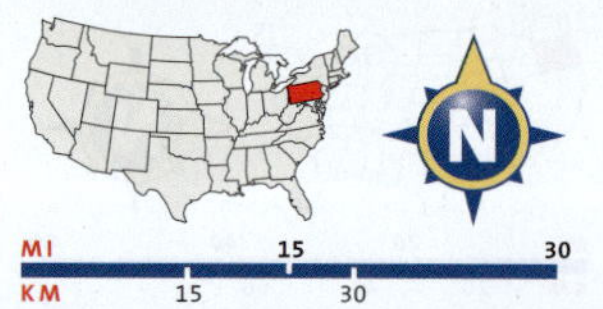

PA 91

ohio 42

west virginia 52

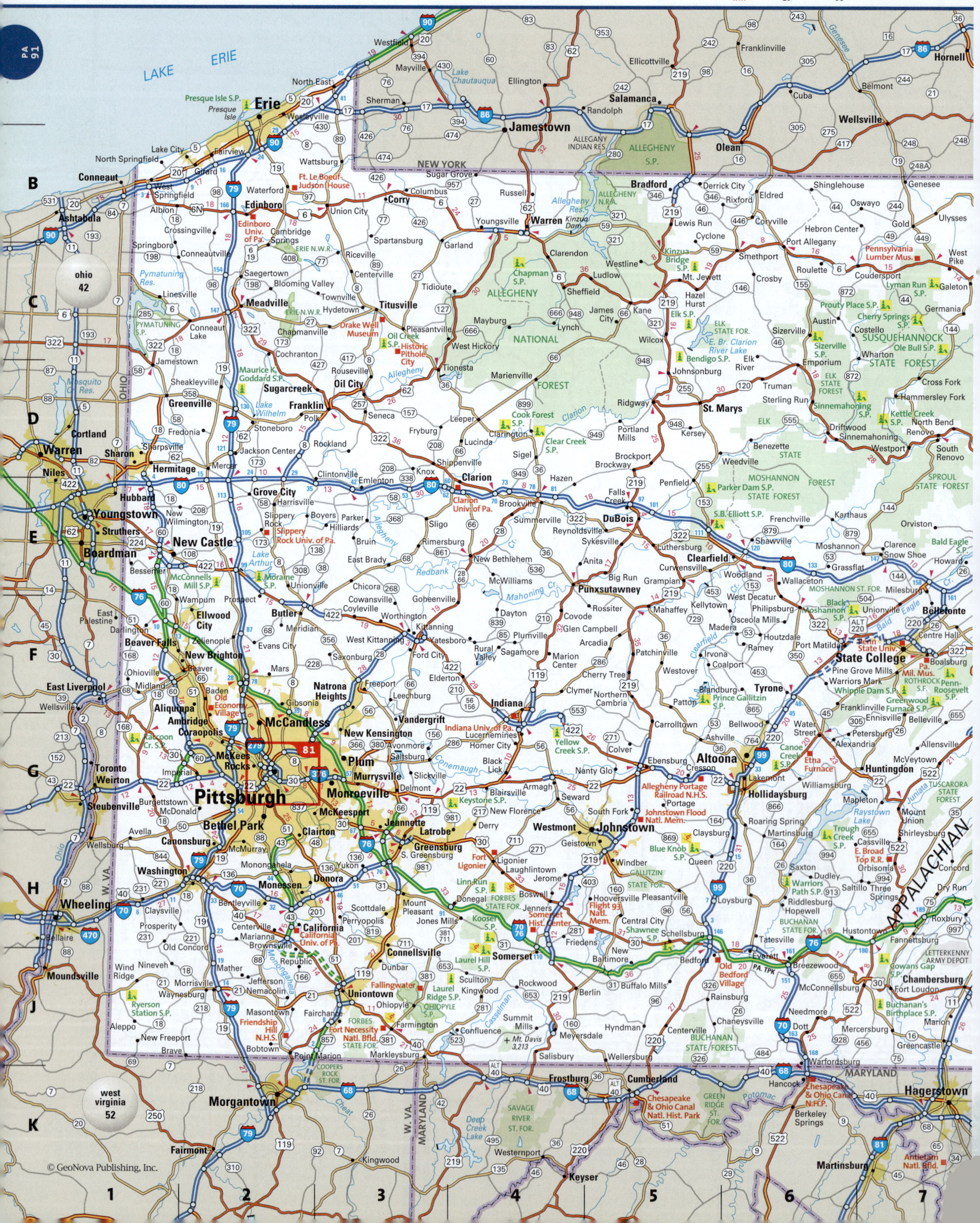

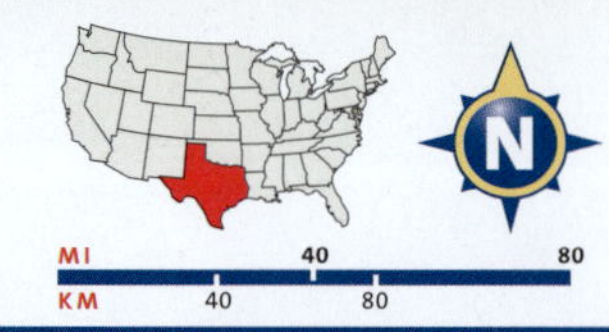

TX 91

TEXAS PANHANDLE

OKLAHOMA
Wichita Falls
Sherman
Denison
Paris
Texarkana
Denton
McKinney
Lewisville
Plano
Grapevine
Irving
Ft. Worth
Dallas
Arlington
Abilene
Sweetwater
Weatherford
Cleburne
Waxahachie
Terrell
Longview
Marshall
Shreveport
Tyler
Kilgore
Athens
Corsicana
Palestine
Nacogdoches
Lufkin
Jacksonville
Henderson
Carthage
Natchitoches
San Angelo
Brownwood
Coleman
Stephenville
Waco
Temple
Killeen
Copperas Cove
Belton
Bryan
College Station
Huntsville
Georgetown
Round Rock
Austin
Cedar Park
San Marcos
New Braunfels
San Antonio
Seguin
Kerrville
Fredericksburg
Brenham
Conroe
The Woodlands
Houston
Pasadena
Baytown
Beaumont
Port Arthur
Orange
Lake Charles
Galveston
Texas City
Sugar Land
Victoria
Port Lavaca
Beeville
Corpus Christi
Kingsville
Laredo
Nuevo Laredo
Zapata
Edinburg
McAllen
Mission
Harlingen
Brownsville
Matamoros
Reynosa
Monterrey
Sabinas Hidalgo
Piedras Negras
Eagle Pass
Uvalde
Del Rio
EDWARDS PLATEAU
GULF OF MEXICO
PADRE ISLAND NATL. SEASHORE
MEXICO
U.S.
ARKANSAS
LOUISIANA
TAMAULIPAS
NUEVO LEÓN
arkansas 7
louisiana 23
TX 91
B
C
D
E
F
G
H
J
K
8
9
10
11
12
13
14
© GeoNova Publishing, Inc.

Utah

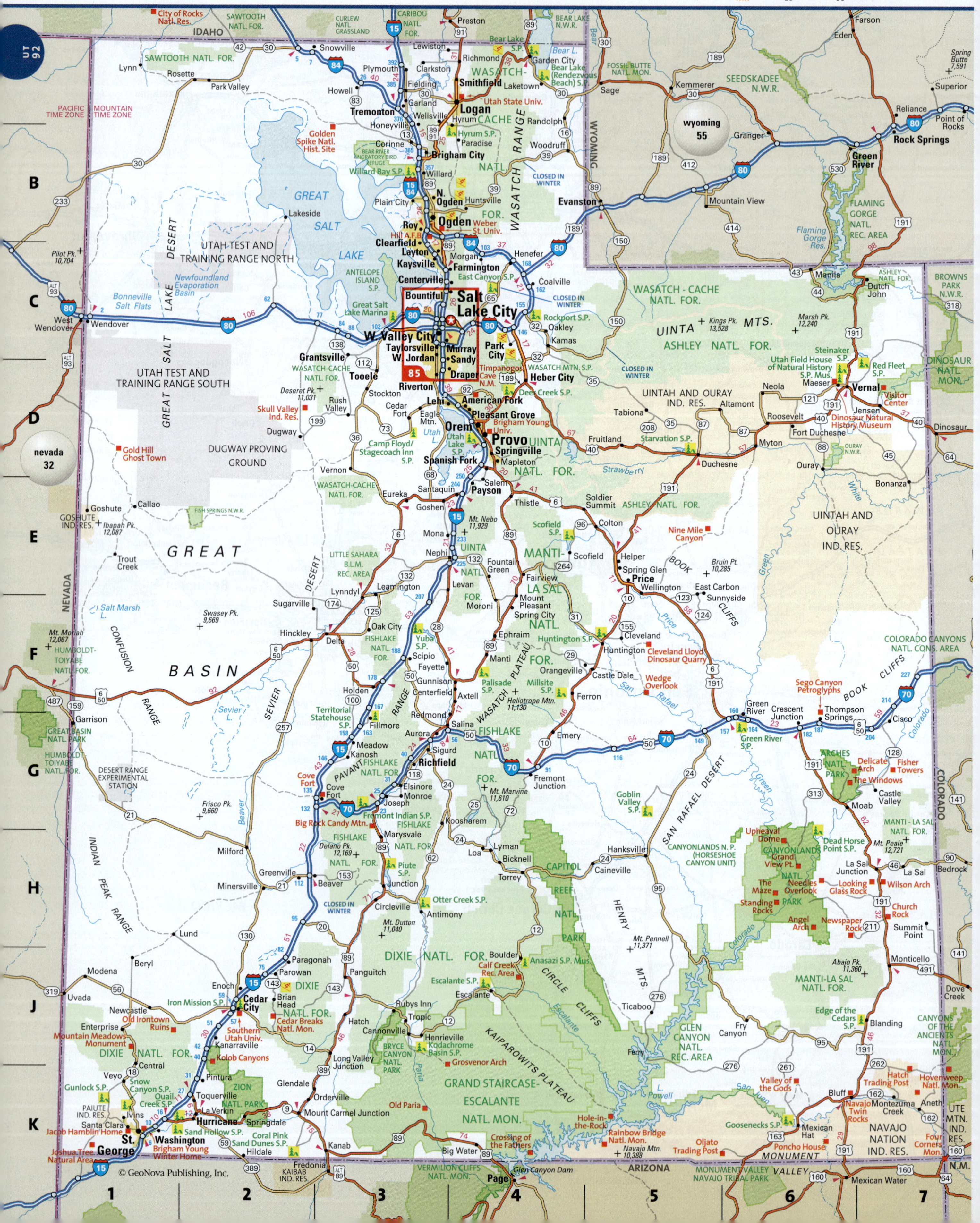

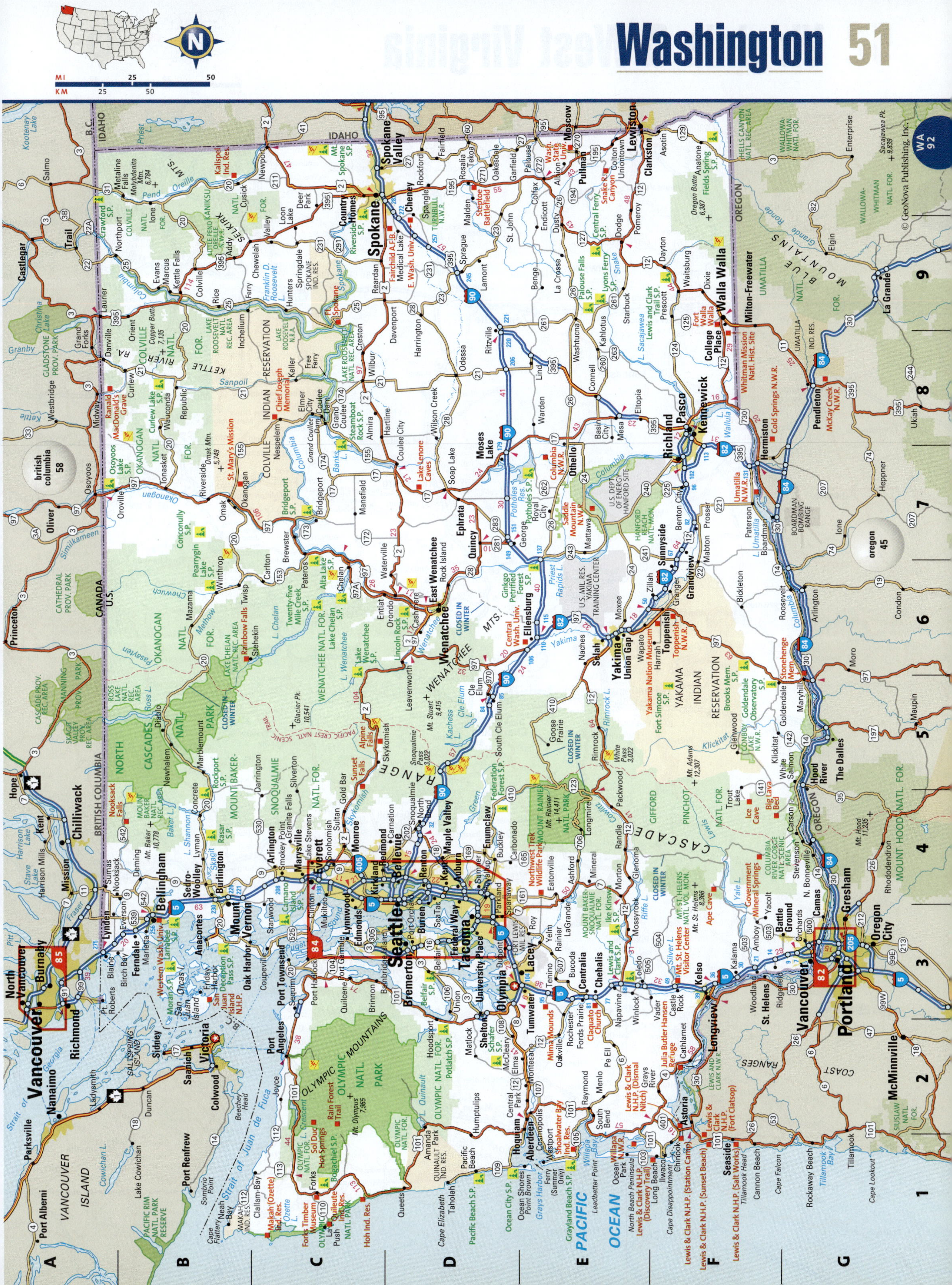

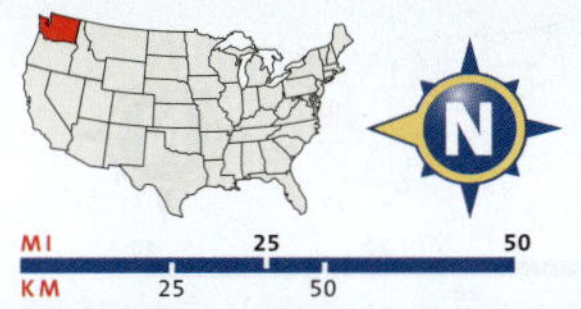
N
MI 25 50
KM 25 50

Virginia & West Virginia

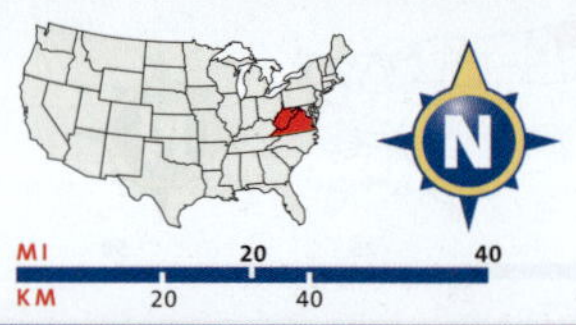

WV 92
VA 92

WV 92
VA 92
pennsylvania 46
maryland 11
new jersey 34
delaware 11
Allentown
Bethlehem
Indiana
Altoona
Johnstown
Harrisburg
Lebanon
Reading
Trenton
Princeton
Norristown
Philadelphia
York
Lancaster
Gettysburg
Chambersburg
Wilmington
Newark
Hagerstown
Frederick
Baltimore
Washington
Arlington
Alexandria
Annapolis
Dover
Vineland
Millville
Cumberland
Martinsburg
Winchester
Leesburg
Manassas
Harrisonburg
Staunton
Waynesboro
Charlottesville
Fredericksburg
Richmond
Petersburg
Lynchburg
Hampton
Newport News
Norfolk
Portsmouth
Virginia Beach
Chesapeake
Suffolk
Salisbury
Chesapeake Bay
ATLANTIC
OCEAN
Delaware Bay
PA.
MD.
DEL.
W.VA.
VA.
N.C.
© GeoNova Publishing, Inc.
B
C
D
E
F
G
H
J
K
8
9
10
11
12
13
14

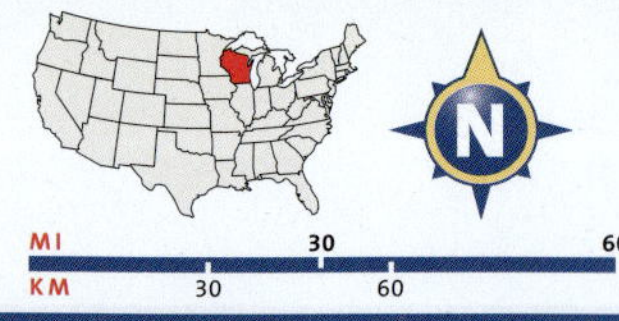

MI 30 60
KM 30 60
N

LAKE SUPERIOR
CENTRAL TIME ZONE
EASTERN TIME ZONE
KEWEENAW PENINSULA
LAKE SUPERIOR
LAKE MICHIGAN
APOSTLE ISLANDS NATL. LAKESHORE
CLOQUET VALLEY ST. FOR.
Two Harbors
Duluth
Superior
Cloquet
Carlton
Bayfield
La Pointe
Madeline Island Museum
Red Cliff Ind. Res.
Big Bay S.P.
Cornucopia
Port Wing
Washburn
Ashland
Hurley
Ironwood
Bessemer
Montreal
Mellen
Copper Falls S.P.
CHEQUAMEGON NATL. FOR.
PORCUPINE MTS. WILDERNESS S.P.
Ontonagon
Houghton
Huron N.W.R.
HURON MTS.
OTTAWA NATL. FOR.
Marquette
Ishpeming
Escanaba
Gladstone
Iron Mountain
Menominee
Marinette
Crystal Falls
Iron River
Watersmeet
Land O' Lakes
Eagle River
Rhinelander
Minocqua
Woodruff
Tomahawk
Merrill
Wausau
Antigo
Shawano
Green Bay
Door
Sturgeon Bay
Algoma
Kewaunee
Two Rivers
Manitowoc
Sheboygan
Appleton
Kaukauna
Menasha
Neenah
Oshkosh
Fond du Lac
Ripon
Berlin
Waupaca
Stevens Point
Plover
Wisconsin Rapids
Marshfield
Abbotsford
Medford
Chippewa Falls
Eau Claire
Menomonie
Rice Lake
Hayward
Spooner
Ladysmith
Park Falls
Phillips
Hudson
St. Paul
Stillwater
Prescott
River Falls
Red Wing
Rochester
Winona
La Crosse
Onalaska
Holmen
Sparta
Tomah
Black River Falls
Mauston
Wisconsin Dells
Baraboo
Portage
Reedsburg
Richland Center
Prairie du Chien
Platteville
Dubuque
Dodgeville
Mount Horeb
Madison
Middleton
Monona
McFarland
Stoughton
Sun Prairie
Waunakee
Watertown
Beaver Dam
Hartford
West Bend
Port Washington
Menomonee Falls
Waukesha
Milwaukee
West Allis
Oak Creek
South Milwaukee
Racine
Kenosha
Pleasant Prairie
Waukegan
Burlington
Lake Geneva
Elkhorn
Delavan
Whitewater
Fort Atkinson
Jefferson
Janesville
Milton
Beloit
Monroe
Rockford
Freeport
Belvidere
McHenry
Elgin
Evanston
Chicago
Cicero
De Kalb
Sycamore
Rochelle
Dixon
Sterling
Clinton
Maquoketa
Cedar Rapids
Anamosa
Waterloo
Cedar Falls
Oelwein
Decorah
Cresco
Charles City
New Hampton
West Union
Manchester
Independence
minnesota 25
iowa 19
illinois 17
michigan 26
MINNESOTA
IOWA
ILLINOIS
MICH.
© GeoNova Publishing, Inc.

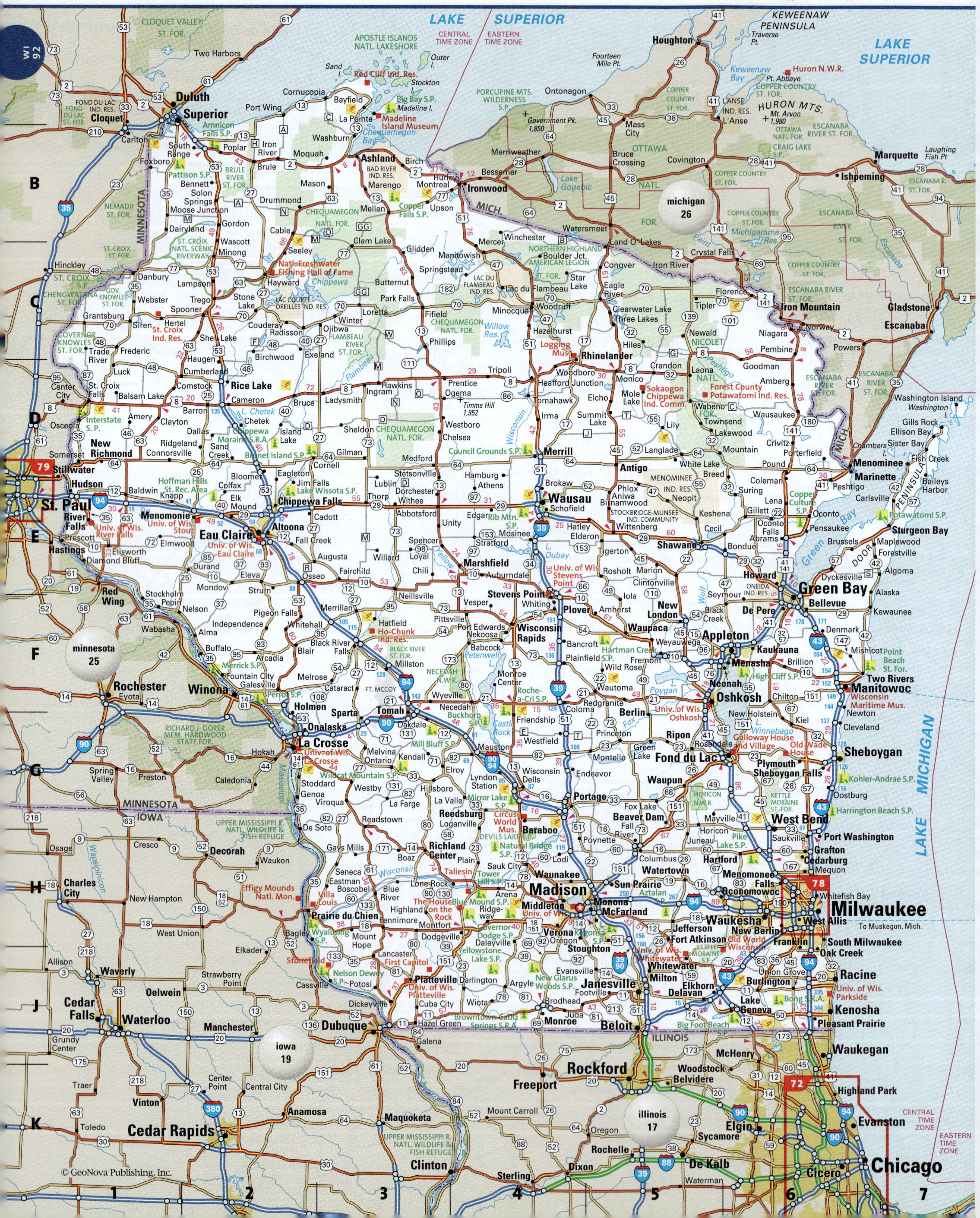

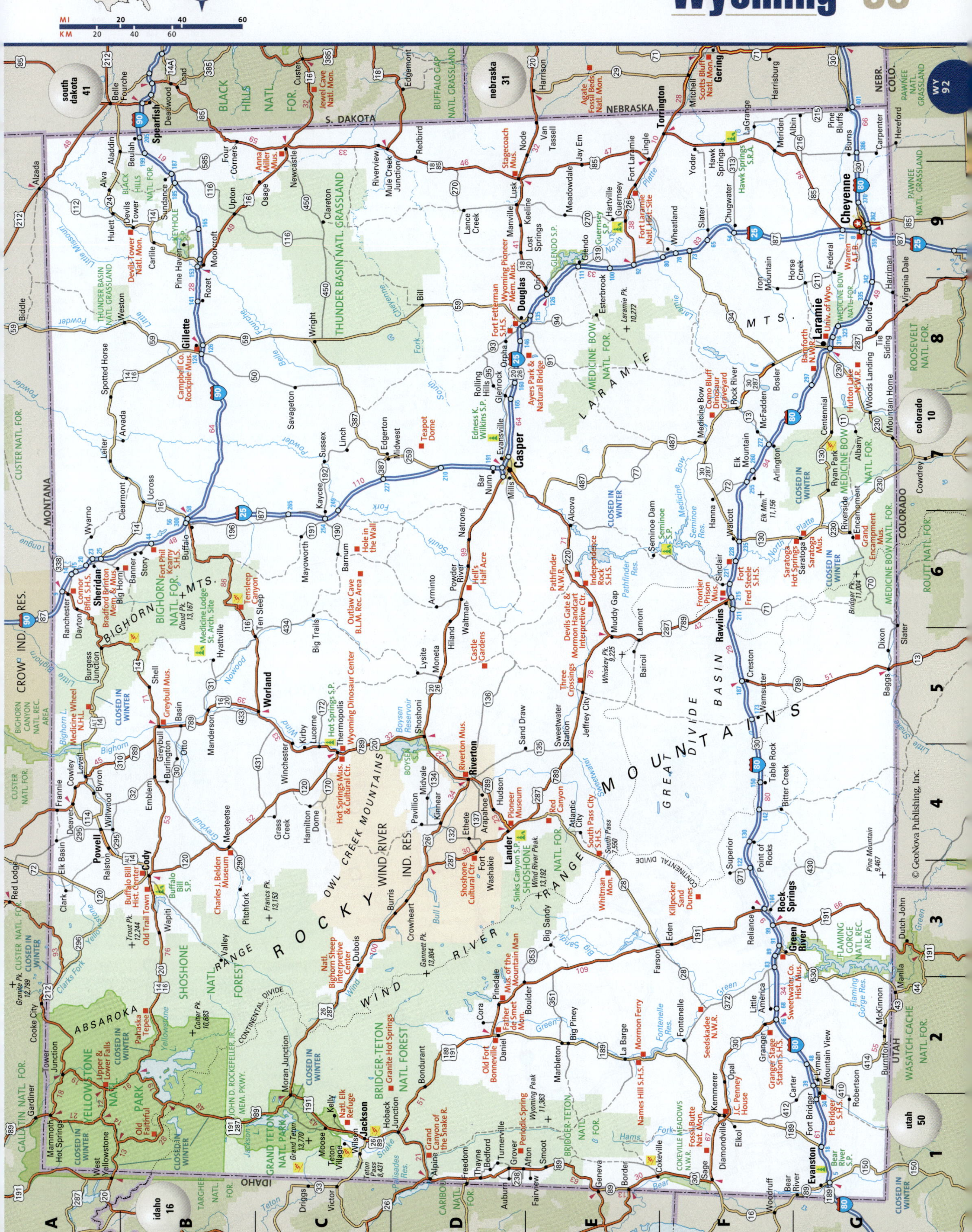

MI 20 40 60
KM 20 40 60
south dakota 41
nebraska 31
colorado 10
utah 50
idaho 16
WY 92
MONTANA
S. DAKOTA
NEBRASKA
COLORADO
UTAH
IDAHO
NEBR.
COLO.
Cheyenne
Casper
Laramie
Rawlins
Rock Springs
Green River
Evanston
Gillette
Sheridan
Buffalo
Worland
Cody
Powell
Riverton
Lander
Jackson
Douglas
Torrington
Kemmerer
Thermopolis
Newcastle
Sundance
Wheatland
BIGHORN NATL. FOR.
SHOSHONE NATL. FOREST
BRIDGER-TETON NATL. FOREST
MEDICINE BOW NATL. FOR.
THUNDER BASIN NATL. GRASSLAND
YELLOWSTONE NATL. PARK
GRAND TETON NATL. PARK
WIND RIVER IND. RES.
ROCKY MOUNTAINS
GREAT DIVIDE BASIN
WIND RIVER RANGE
OWL CREEK MOUNTAINS
LARAMIE MTS.
ABSAROKA
BIGHORN MTS.
BLACK HILLS NATL. FOR.
CROW IND. RES.
CLOSED IN WINTER
© GeoNova Publishing, Inc.

Canada

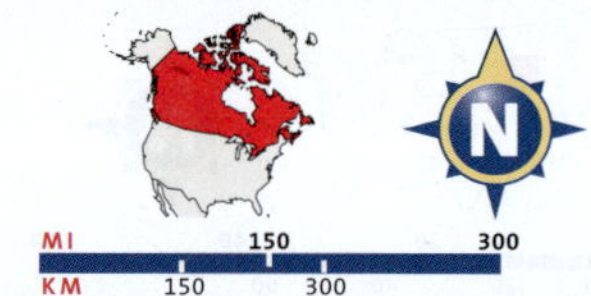

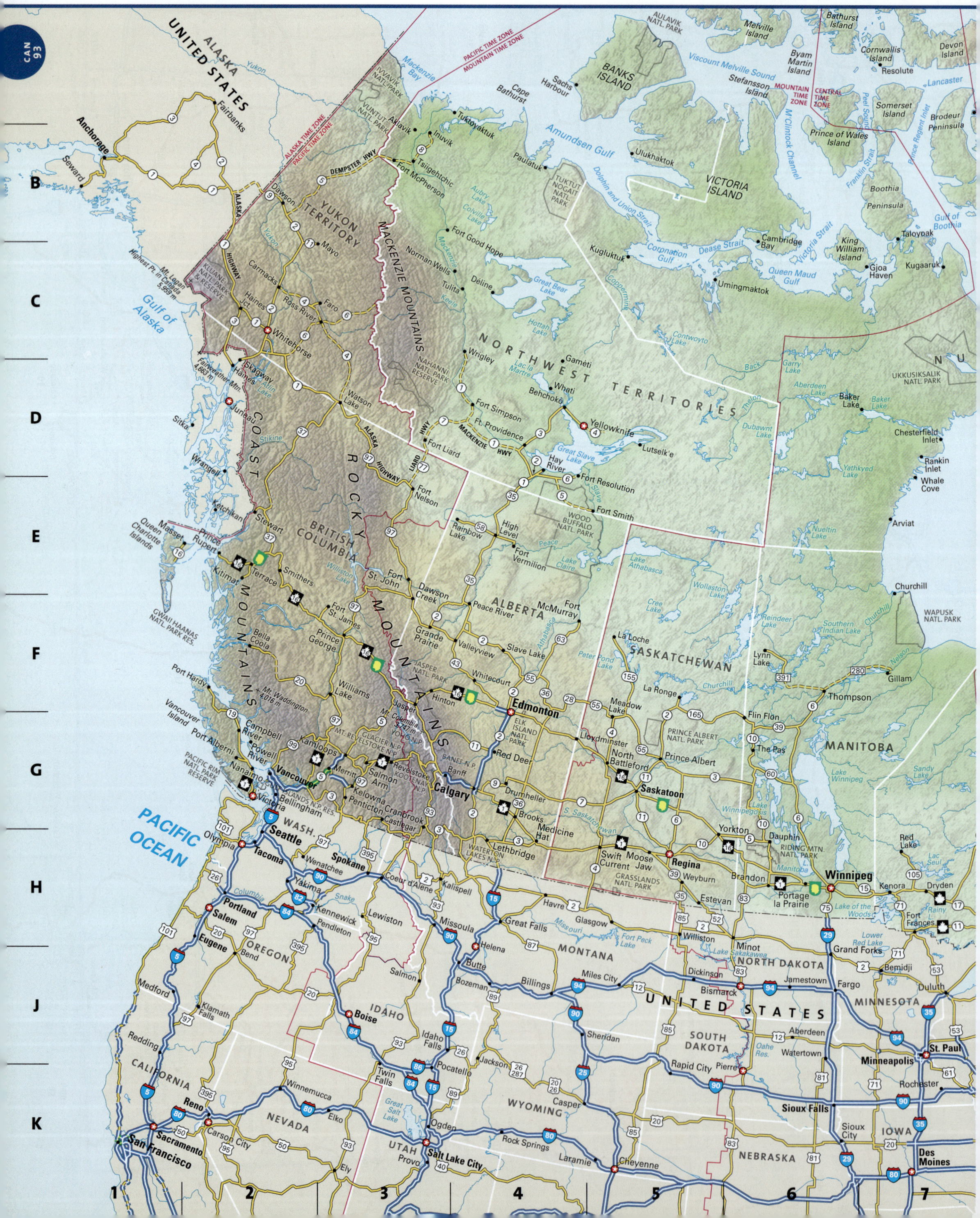

CAN 93

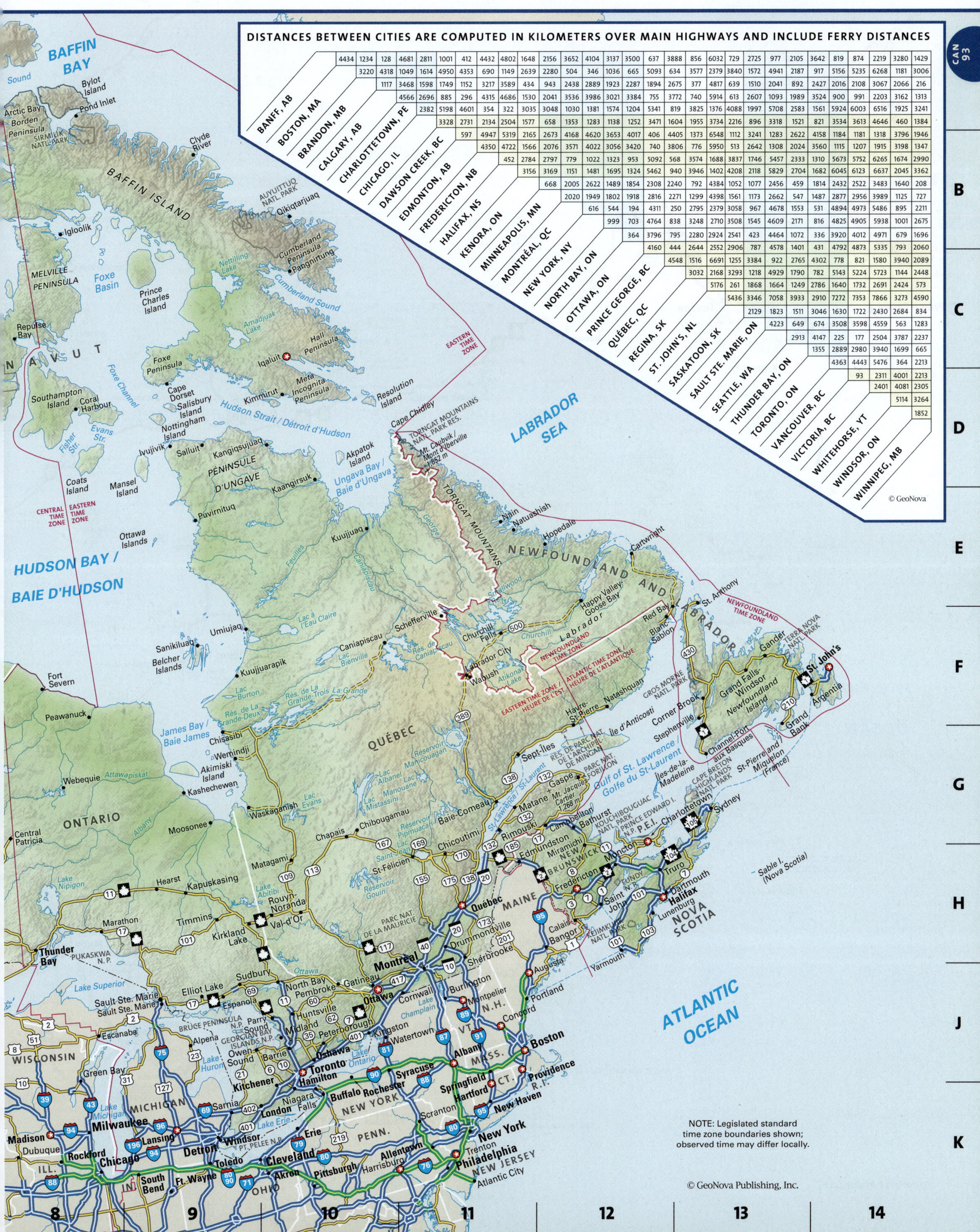

DISTANCES BETWEEN CITIES ARE COMPUTED IN KILOMETERS OVER MAIN HIGHWAYS AND INCLUDE FERRY DISTANCES

	BOSTON, MA	BRANDON, MB	CALGARY, AB	CHARLOTTETOWN, PE	CHICAGO, IL	DAWSON CREEK, BC	EDMONTON, AB	FREDERICTON, NB	HALIFAX, NS	KENORA, ON	MINNEAPOLIS, MN	MONTRÉAL, QC	NEW YORK, NY	NORTH BAY, ON	OTTAWA, ON	PRINCE GEORGE, BC	QUÉBEC, QC	REGINA, SK	ST. JOHN'S, NL	SASKATOON, SK	SAULT STE. MARIE, ON	SEATTLE, WA	THUNDER BAY, ON	TORONTO, ON	VANCOUVER, BC	VICTORIA, BC	WHITEHORSE, YT	WINDSOR, ON	WINNIPEG, MB
BANFF, AB	4434	1234	128	4681	2811	1001	412	4432	4802	1648	2156	3652	4104	3137	3500	637	3888	856	6032	729	2725	977	2105	3642	819	874	2219	3280	1429
BOSTON, MA		3220	4318	1049	1614	4950	4353	690	1149	2639	2280	504	346	1036	665	5093	634	3577	2379	3840	1572	4941	2187	917	5156	5235	6268	1181	3006
BRANDON, MB			1117	3468	1598	1749	1152	3217	3589	434	943	2438	2889	1923	2287	1894	2675	377	4817	639	1510	2041	892	2427	2016	2108	3067	2066	216
CALGARY, AB				4566	2696	885	296	4315	4686	1530	2041	3536	3986	3021	3384	755	3772	740	5914	613	2607	1093	1989	3524	900	991	2203	3162	1313
CHARLOTTETOWN, PE					2382	5198	4601	354	322	3035	3048	1030	1381	1574	1204	5341	819	3825	1376	4088	1997	5708	2583	1561	5924	6003	6516	1925	3241
CHICAGO, IL						3328	2731	2134	2504	1577	658	1353	1283	1138	1252	3471	1604	1955	3734	2216	896	3318	1521	821	3534	3613	4646	460	1384
DAWSON CREEK, BC							597	4947	5319	2165	2673	4168	4620	3653	4017	406	4405	1373	6548	1112	3241	1283	2622	4158	1184	1181	1318	3796	1946
EDMONTON, AB								4350	4722	1566	2076	3571	4022	3056	3420	740	3806	776	5950	513	2642	1308	2024	3560	1115	1207	1915	3198	1347
FREDERICTON, NB									452	2784	2797	779	1022	1323	953	5092	568	3574	1688	3837	1746	5457	2333	1310	5673	5752	6265	1674	2990
HALIFAX, NS										3156	3169	1151	1481	1695	1324	5462	940	3946	1402	4208	2118	5829	2704	1682	6045	6123	6637	2045	3362
KENORA, ON											668	2005	2622	1489	1854	2308	2240	792	4384	1052	1077	2456	459	1814	2432	2522	3483	1640	208
MINNEAPOLIS, MN												2020	1949	1802	1918	2816	2271	1299	4398	1561	1173	2662	547	1487	2877	2956	3989	1125	727
MONTRÉAL, QC													616	544	194	4311	250	2795	2379	3058	967	4678	1553	531	4894	4973	5486	895	2211
NEW YORK, NY														999	703	4764	838	3248	2710	3508	1545	4609	2171	816	4825	4905	5938	1001	2675
NORTH BAY, ON															364	3796	795	2280	2924	2541	423	4464	1072	336	3920	4012	4971	679	1696
OTTAWA, ON																4160	444	2644	2552	2906	787	4578	1401	431	4792	4873	5335	793	2060
PRINCE GEORGE, BC																	4548	1516	6691	1255	3384	922	2765	4302	778	821	1580	3940	2089
QUÉBEC, QC																		3032	2168	3293	1218	4929	1790	782	5143	5224	5723	1144	2448
REGINA, SK																			5176	261	1868	1664	1249	2786	1640	1732	2691	2424	573
ST. JOHN'S, NL																				5436	3346	7058	3933	2910	7272	7353	7866	3273	4590
SASKATOON, SK																					2129	1823	1511	3046	1630	1722	2430	2684	834
SAULT STE. MARIE, ON																						4223	649	674	3508	3598	4559	563	1283
SEATTLE, WA																							2913	4147	225	177	2504	3787	2237
THUNDER BAY, ON																								1355	2889	2980	3940	1699	665
TORONTO, ON																									4363	4443	5476	364	2213
VANCOUVER, BC																										93	2311	4001	2213
VICTORIA, BC																											2401	4081	2305
WHITEHORSE, YT																												5114	3264
WINDSOR, ON																													1852

© GeoNova

British Columbia

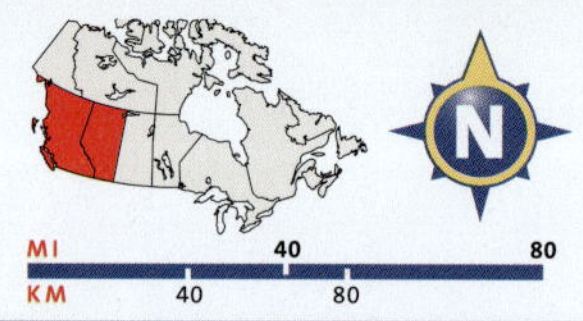

alaska 5

PACIFIC OCEAN

COAST MOUNTAINS

DISTANCES IN CANADA SHOWN IN KILOMETERS

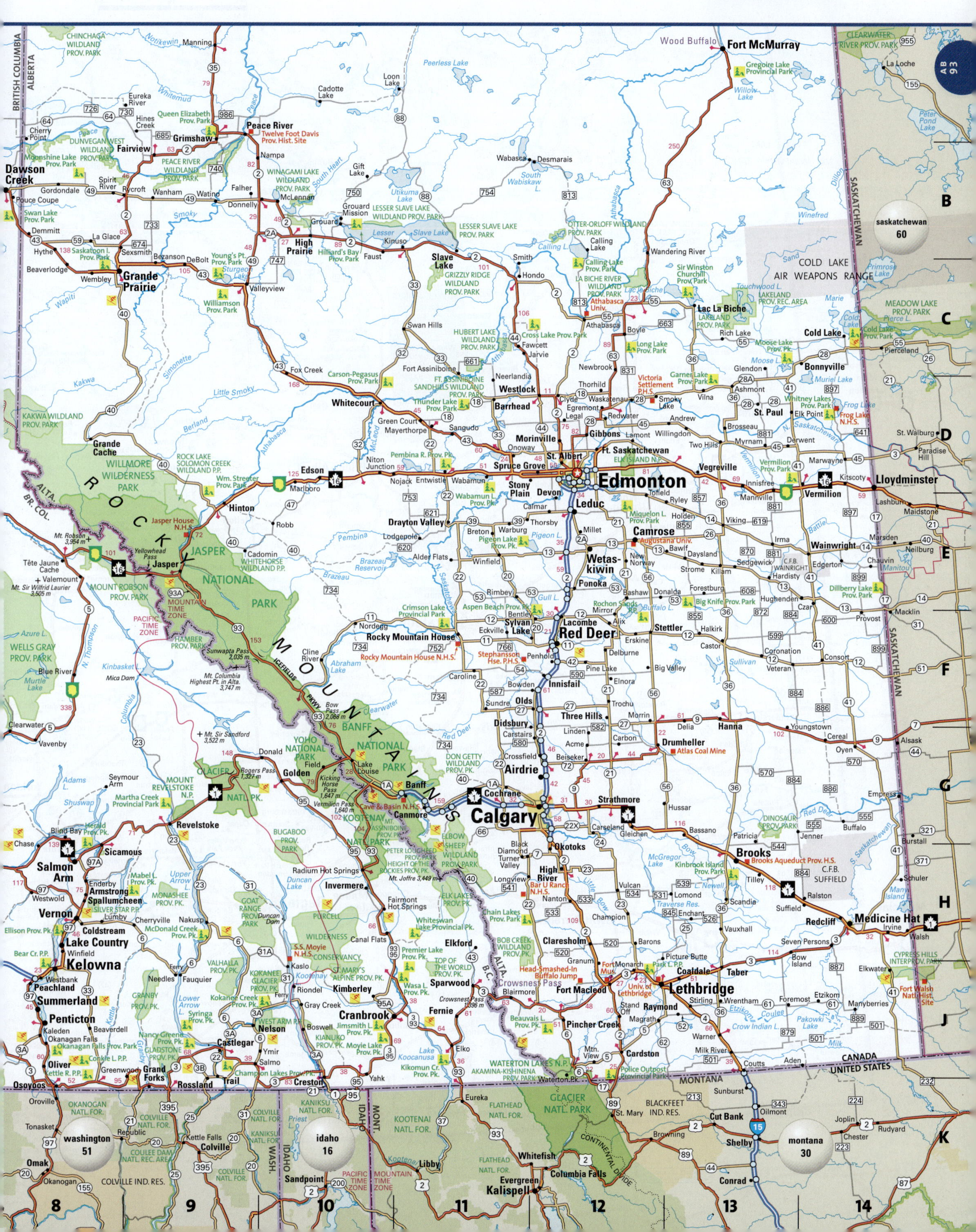
AB 93
BRITISH COLUMBIA
ALBERTA
SASKATCHEWAN
saskatchewan 60
washington 51
idaho 16
montana 30
COLD LAKE AIR WEAPONS RANGE
ROCKY MOUNTAINS
JASPER NATIONAL PARK
BANFF NATIONAL PARK
YOHO NATIONAL PARK
KOOTENAY NATL PARK
GLACIER NATL. PARK
WILLMORE WILDERNESS PARK
WATERTON LAKES N.P.
MOUNT REVELSTOKE N.P.
MOUNT ROBSON PROV. PARK
CANADA
UNITED STATES
Fort McMurray
Wood Buffalo
Peace River
Grimshaw
Fairview
Manning
Dawson Creek
Grande Prairie
High Prairie
Slave Lake
Athabasca
Lac La Biche
Cold Lake
Bonnyville
St. Paul
Whitecourt
Barrhead
Westlock
Edson
Hinton
Jasper
Grande Cache
Spruce Grove
St. Albert
Ft. Saskatchewan
Edmonton
Leduc
Camrose
Wetaskiwin
Vegreville
Vermilion
Lloydminster
Wainwright
Drayton Valley
Ponoka
Lacombe
Red Deer
Sylvan Lake
Rocky Mountain House
Stettler
Innisfail
Olds
Didsbury
Three Hills
Hanna
Drumheller
Airdrie
Cochrane
Calgary
Strathmore
Banff
Canmore
Okotoks
High River
Claresholm
Fort Macleod
Lethbridge
Coaldale
Taber
Pincher Creek
Cardston
Brooks
Medicine Hat
Golden
Revelstoke
Salmon Arm
Vernon
Kelowna
Penticton
Summerland
Lake Country
Cranbrook
Fernie
Sparwood
Kimberley
Invermere
Nelson
Castlegar
Trail
Rossland
Creston
Osoyoos
Oliver
Libby
Whitefish
Kalispell
Columbia Falls
Shelby
Cut Bank
Conrad
Colville
Sandpoint
8
9
10
11
12
13
14
B
C
D
E
F
G
H
J
K

Saskatchewan

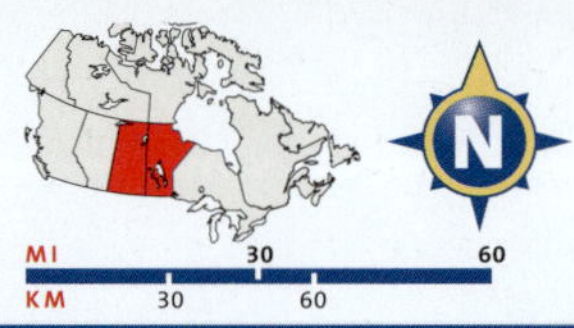

DISTANCES IN CANADA SHOWN IN KILOMETERS

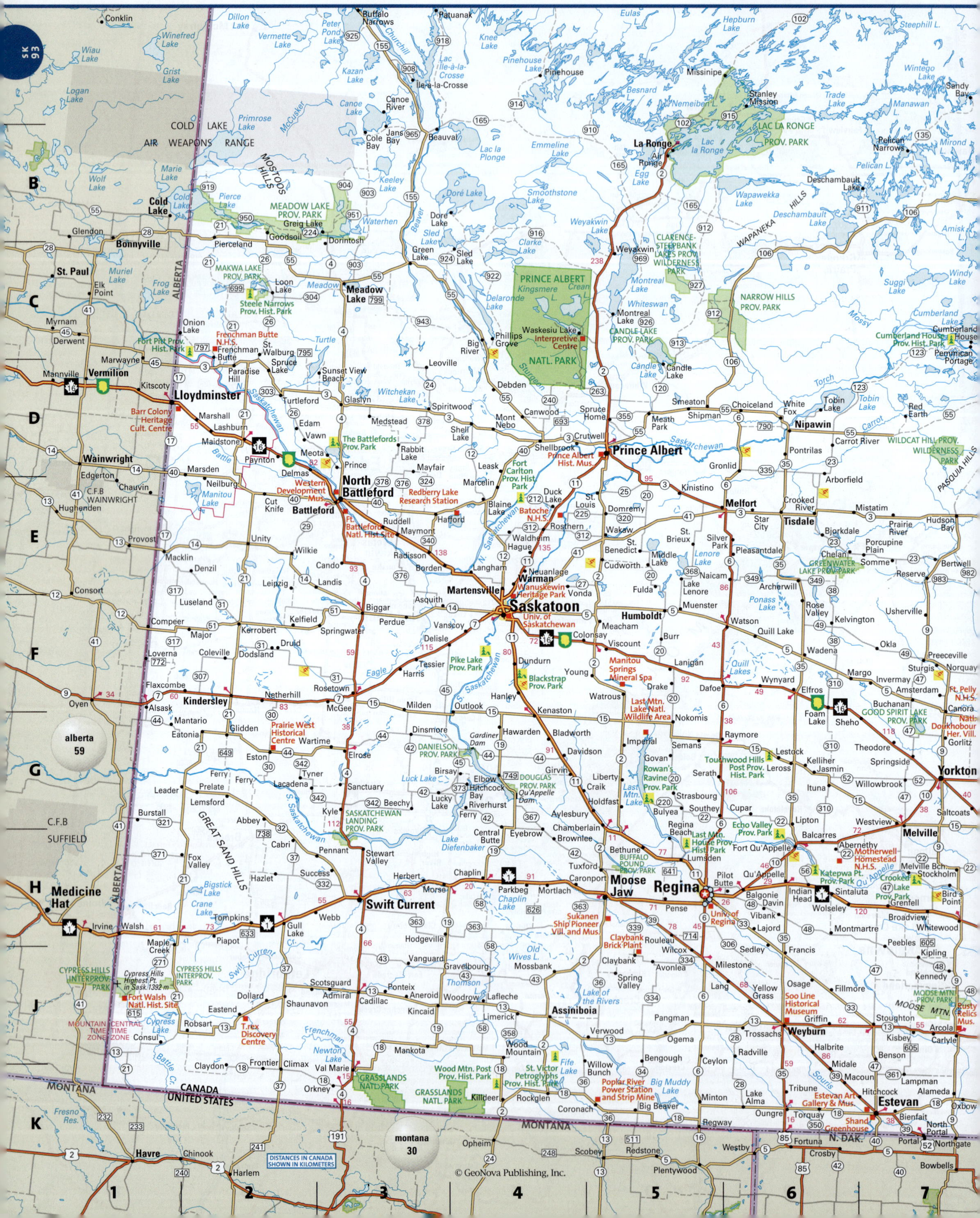

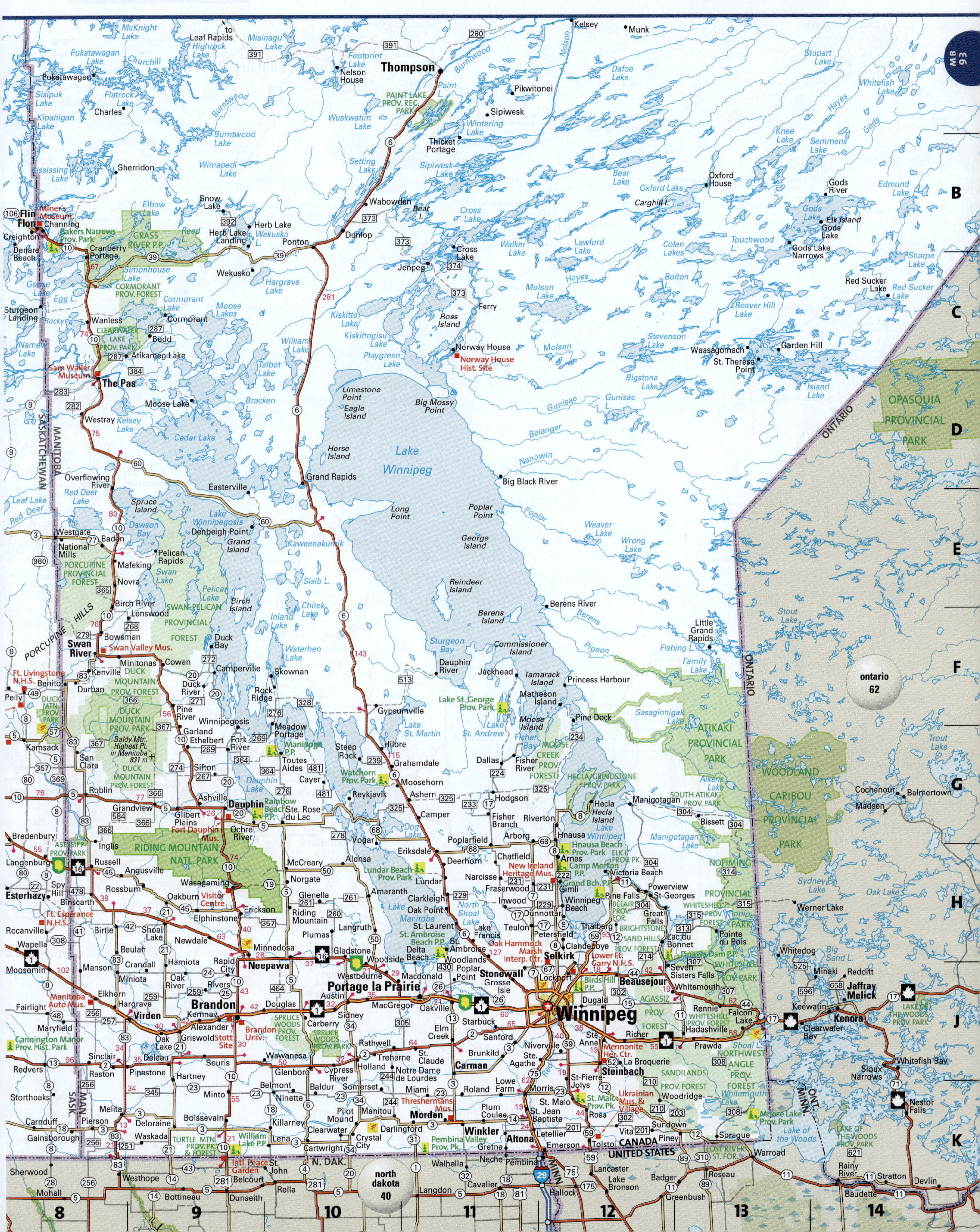

MB 93
Thompson
Flin Flon
The Pas
Swan River
Dauphin
Brandon
Portage la Prairie
Neepawa
Winnipeg
Selkirk
Steinbach
Morden
Winkler
Altona
Virden
Gimli
Beausejour
Norway House
Grand Rapids
Lake Winnipeg
Lake Winnipegosis
Lake Manitoba
Cedar Lake
RIDING MOUNTAIN NAT'L PARK
DUCK MOUNTAIN PROV. PARK
ATIKAKI PROVINCIAL PARK
WOODLAND CARIBOU PROVINCIAL PARK
OPASQUIA PROVINCIAL PARK
SASKATCHEWAN
MANITOBA
ONTARIO
ontario 62
north dakota 40
N. DAK.
MINN.
CANADA
UNITED STATES
Kenora
Jaffray Melick
Lake of the Woods
B
C
D
E
F
G
H
J
K
8
9
10
11
12
13
14

MI 25 50
KM 25 50

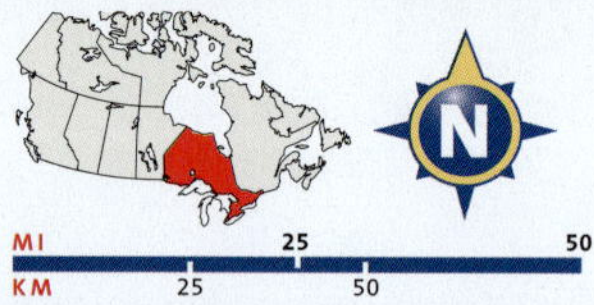

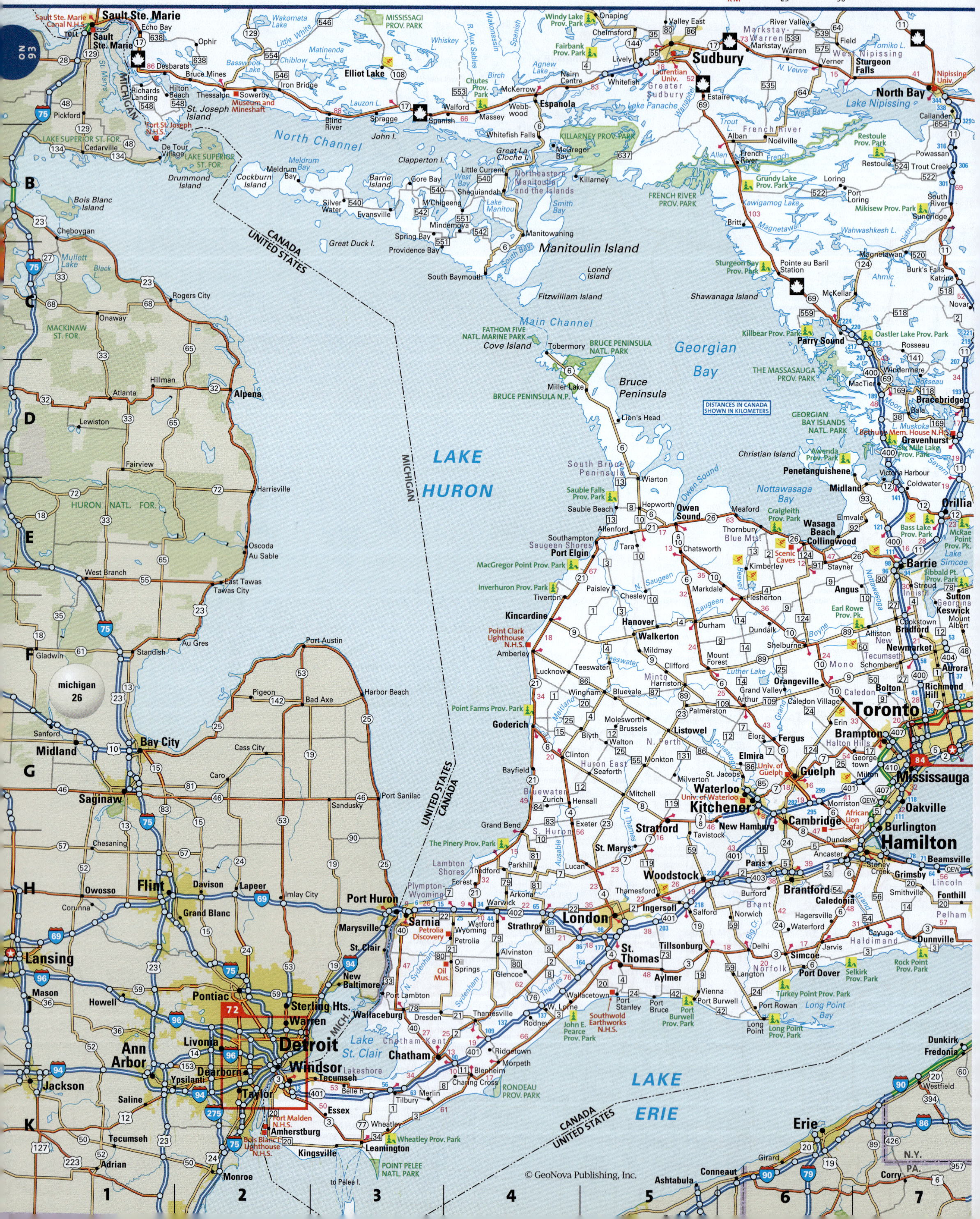

Sault Ste. Marie
Sudbury
North Bay
Espanola
Elliot Lake
North Channel
Manitoulin Island
Main Channel
Georgian Bay
Bruce Peninsula
LAKE HURON
MICHIGAN
CANADA
UNITED STATES
Owen Sound
Collingwood
Barrie
Orillia
Midland
Parry Sound
Gravenhurst
Bracebridge
Toronto
Mississauga
Brampton
Oakville
Burlington
Hamilton
Guelph
Waterloo
Kitchener
Cambridge
Stratford
Woodstock
Brantford
London
St. Thomas
Sarnia
Port Huron
Chatham
Windsor
Detroit
Lake St. Clair
LAKE ERIE
Erie
Alpena
Bay City
Saginaw
Flint
Lansing
Ann Arbor
Jackson
Midland
Pontiac
Kincardine
Goderich
Simcoe
Leamington
Tobermory
Wiarton
Alpena
Port Elgin
Newmarket
Aurora
michigan 26
© GeoNova Publishing, Inc.
1 2 3 4 5 6 7
B C D E F G H J K

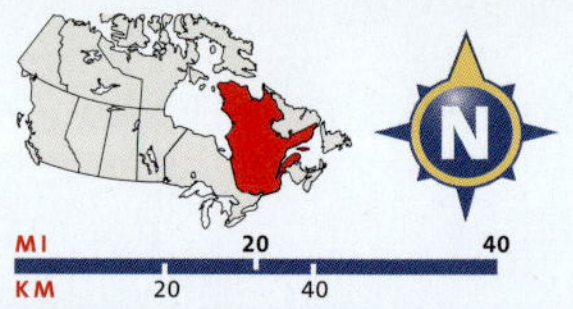

N
MI 20 40
KM 20 40

QC 93
DISTANCES IN CANADA SHOWN IN KILOMETERS
ONTARIO
EASTERN QUÉBEC
Normétal
Beaucanton
Lac Turgeon
La Reine
La Sarre
Lac Macamic
Macamic
Lake Abitibi
Palmarolle
Poularies
Taschereau
Trécesson
Amos
Pikogan
Lac Chicobi
Duparquet
Destor
PARC D'AIGUEBELLE
Lac Duparquet
Mont-Brun
Preissac
Lac Preissac
Rouyn-Noranda
Univ. du Québec en Abitibi-Témiscamingue
Lac Arnoux
Évain
Arntfield
Cadillac
Rivière-Héva
La Motte
La Corne
Lac Malartic
Lac-de Montigny
Malartic
Sullivan
Val-d'Or
Louvicourt
Landrienne
St-Marc-de-Figuery
Barraute
Senneterre
Lac Pascalis
Lac Tiblemont
Lac Obalski
Lac Castagnier
Rochebaucourt
vers/to Matagami
vers/to Chibougamau
Lebel-sur-Quévillon
Lac Quévillon
Lac Parent
Harricana
Cloutier
Rollet
Lac Caron
Lac Basserode
Lac Fournière
Lac Mourier
Lac Lemoine
Lac Sabourin
Lac Matchi-Manitou
Lac Villebon
Lac Rémigny
Lac Roger
Rapide-Sept
Outaouais
Nédélec
Lac des Quinze
Lac Simard
Winneway
Rés. Decelles
Notre-Dame-du-Nord
Angliers
Laforce
Lac Témiscamingue
Ville-Marie
Fugèreville
Lorrainville
Belleterre
Lieu Hist. Nat. du Fort-Témiscamingue
Lac Granet
Kitcisakik
Rés. Dozois
Lac Bouchette
ZEC CAPITACHOUANE
ZEC FESTUBERT
Lac Landron
Réservoir Cabonga
Lac-Rapide
Lac Poigan
Lac à la Truite
Lac Ostaboningue
Lac Saseginaga
ZEC KIPAWA
Lac des Baies
Lac Carrière
Lac aux Écorces
RÉSERVE FAUNIQUE LA VÉRENDRYE
Lac Giroux
Fabre
Laniel
Lac Kipawa
Lac Kikwissi
Kipawa
Lac Byrd
Lac Brûlé
Lac Dumoine
Lac Dix Milles
Lac Chavannes
Lac Delahey
Tomasine
Témiscaming
Lac Beauchêne
ZEC RESTIGO
Lac Bleu
Lac du Fils
Noire
Dumoine
Lac Nilgaut
Lac Doolittle
ZEC MAGANASIPI
ZEC DUMOINE
North Bay
Mattawa
Outaouais Ottawa
Lac Brodtkorb
Lac Désert
Lac Bryson
Lac de Abattis
Lac Lynch
Lac St-Patrice
Lac Duval
Coulonge
Lac Pythonga
Maniwaki
Lake Nipissing
Lake Nosbonsing
Powassan
Trout Creek
South River
Sundridge
Bernard Lake
Burks Falls
Kearney
ALGONQUIN PROVINCIAL PARK
Deep River
Chalk River
Petawawa
Pembroke
Sheenboro
Waltham
L'Isle-aux-Allumettes
Fort-Coulonge
Campbell's Bay
Shawville
Round L.
Golden L.
Killaloe
Cobden
Whitney
Barry's Bay
Renfrew
Arnprior
Madawaska
L. Clear
Huntsville
Lake of Bays
Bracebridge
Gravenhurst
Orillia
Black Donald Lake
White Lake
Almonte
Norcan Lake
Carleton Place
Centennial Lake
Bancroft
Weslemkoon Lake
SILENT LAKE PROV. PARK
BON ECHO PROV. PARK
Crotch L.
Big Gull L.
Sharbot Lake
Mississippi
Perth
Smiths Falls
Merrickville
Kemptville
Rideau
S. Nation
Morrisburg
Massena
ST. REGIS MOHAWK IND. RES.
Cornwall
Ingleside
Lancaster
Chesterville
Winchester
Alexandria
Casselman
St. Isidore
Vankleek Hill
Alfred
Hawkesbury
Calumet
Montebello
Manoir Papineau
Papineauville
Thurso
Parc de Plaisance
Buckingham
Masson-Angers
Rockland
Gatineau
Hull
Ottawa
Aylmer
Kanata
PARC DE LA GATINEAU
Lac Dumont
Lac Cayamant
Gracefield
Kazabazua
Lac Ste-Marie
Lac du Poisson Blanc
Poltimore
Val-des-Bois
Notre-Dame-de-la-Salette
Messines
Lac Blue Sea
Gatineau
Lac des Îles
Lac-des-Îles
Mont-Laurier
Grand-Remous
Désert
Lac-des-Écorces
Lac-Saguay
Réservoir Baskatong
Ferme-Neuve
Ste-Anne-du-Lac
Mont-St-Michel
Lac Piscatosine
Gens de Terre
ZEC PETAWAGA
ZEC LESUEUR
ZEC MITCHINAMECUS
ZEC NORMANDIE
ZEC MAZANA
Réservoir Mitchinamecus
Lièvre
Bazin
ZEC DE LA MAISON DE PIERRE
RÉS. FAUNIQUE ROUGE-MATAWIN
Réservoir Kiamika
L'Ascension
Ste-Véronique
Rivière-Rouge (L'Annonciation)
Grand Lac Nominingue
Nominingue
Labelle
Mont-Tremblant-Village
Mont Tremblant 968 m
La Conception
St-Jovite
St-Faustin-Lac-Carré
Notre-Dame-de-Pontmain
Lac Montjoie
Notre-Dame-du-Laus
Lac Gagnon
Duhamel
RÉS. FAUNIQUE DE PAPINEAU-LABELLE
Lac Écho
Lac Simon
Chénéville
St-Rémi-d'Amherst
Namur
Lac Papineau
Rouge
ontario 62
vers/to Labrador City
Rés. Manicouagan Trois
Rés. Outardes Quatre
ZEC VARIN
Outardes
Toulnustouc
Lac Ste-Anne
Godbout
Pentecôte
RÉS FAUNIQUE DE PORT-CARTIER SEPT-ÎLES
ZEC MATIMEK
Clarke City
Sept-Îles
Moisie
Port-Cartier
Rivière-Pentecôte
Pointe-aux-Anglais
ZEC TRINITÉ
Baie-Trinité
St-Laurent / St. Lawrence
Baie-Comeau
Chute-aux-Outardes
Pointe-Lebel
Les Buissons
Pointe-aux-Outardes
Betsiamites
Colombier
Forestville
vers/to Tadoussac
Pointe-au-Père
Rimouski
Pte-au-Père Lighthouse N.H.S.
Mont-Joli
Grand-Métis
Jardins de Métis
Sayabec
Matane
Petit-Matane
Ste-Félicité
St-René-de-Matane
RÉSERVE FAUNIQUE DE MATANE
ZEC CASAULT
RÉSERVE FAUNIQUE DE DUNIÈRE
Grosses-Roches
Les Méchins
Cap-Chat
Ste-Anne-des-Monts
La Martre
Marsoui
Mont-St-Pierre
Ste-Madeleine-de-la-Rivière-Madeleine
Gros-Morne
PARC DE LA GASPÉSIE
Mont Logan 1,135 m
Mont Jacques-Cartier 1,268 m
Murdochville
RÉSERVE FAUNIQUE DES CHIC-CHOCS
B
C
D
E
F
G
H
J
K
1
2
3
4
5
6
7

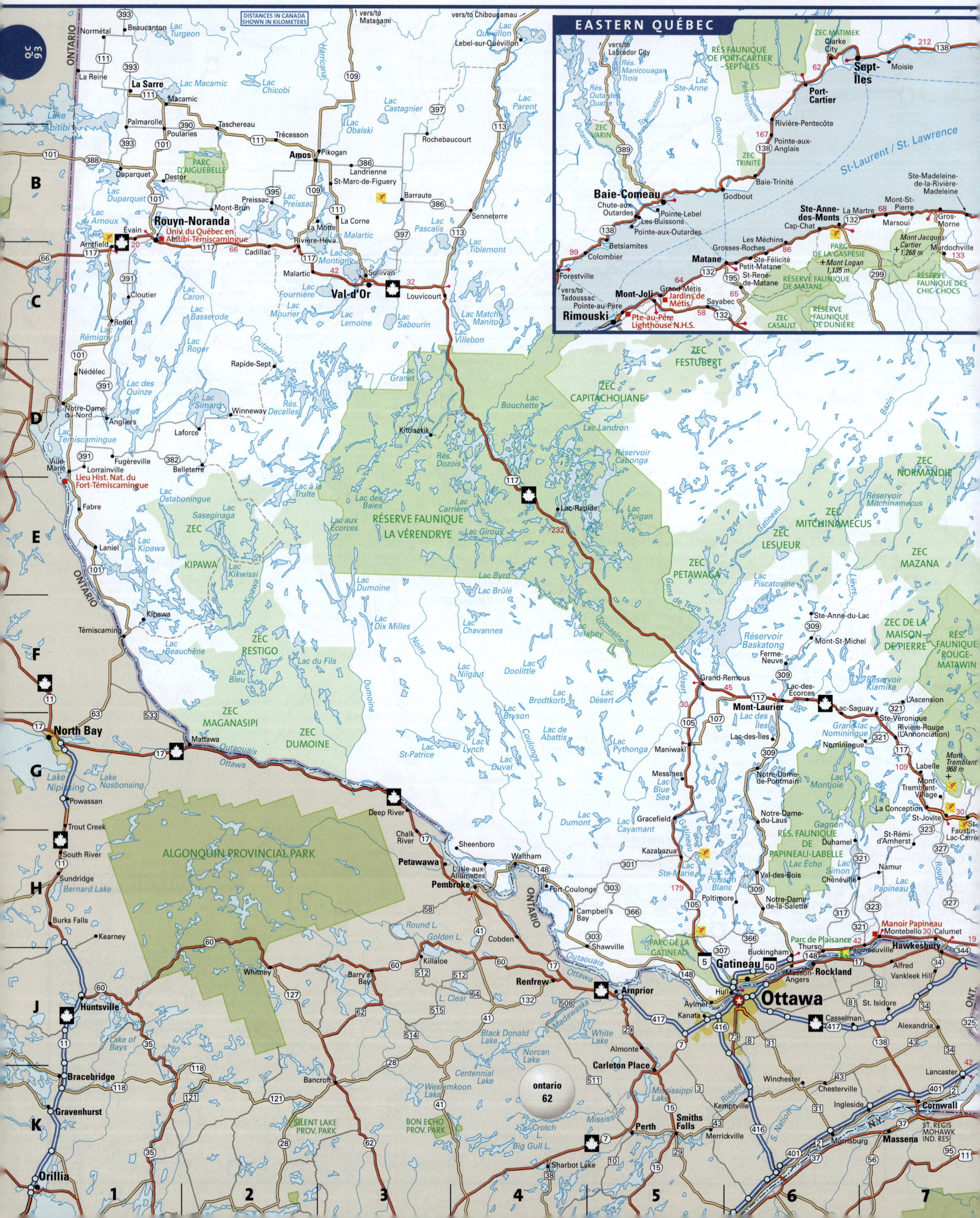

Québec
Montréal
Trois-Rivières
Sherbrooke
Chicoutimi
Jonquière
Alma
Roberval
Dolbeau-Mistassini
St-Félicien
La Tuque
Shawinigan
Drummondville
Victoriaville
Granby
St-Hyacinthe
St-Jean-sur-Richelieu
Longueuil
Laval
St-Jérôme
Joliette
Sorel-Tracy
Lévis
Montmagny
Rivière-du-Loup
Thetford Mines
St-Georges
Lac-Mégantic
Magog
Coaticook
Salaberry-de-Valleyfield
Châteauguay
Rimouski
Baie-Comeau
Forestville
Tadoussac
La Malbaie
Gaspé
Percé
Port-Menier
Île d'Anticosti
Détroit de Jacques-Cartier
Détroit d'Honguedo
PARC NAT. DE FORILLON
RÉSERVE DE PARC NATIONAL DE L'ARCHIPEL-DE-MINGAN
RÉS. FAUNIQUE DES LAURENTIDES
RÉS. FAUNIQUE MASTIGOUCHE
RÉS. FAUNIQUE DU ST-MAURICE
RÉS. FAUNIQUE DE PORTNEUF
PARC NATIONAL DE LA MAURICIE
PARC DE LA JACQUES-CARTIER
PARC DES GRANDS-JARDINS
PARC DES MONTS-VALIN
PARC DU SAGUENAY
LAURENTIDES
MONTS NOTRE DAME
Lac St-Jean
St-Laurent / St. Lawrence
CANADA
UNITED STATES
MAINE
N.H.
VERMONT
NEW YORK
maine 24
new hampshire 33
vermont 33
new york 36
ALLAGASH WILDERNESS WATERWAY
Skowhegan
Farmington
St. Albans
Malone
Newport
0 25 50 mi
0 25 50 km
© GeoNova
© GeoNova Publishing, Inc.
B C D E F G H J K
8 9 10 11 12 13 14

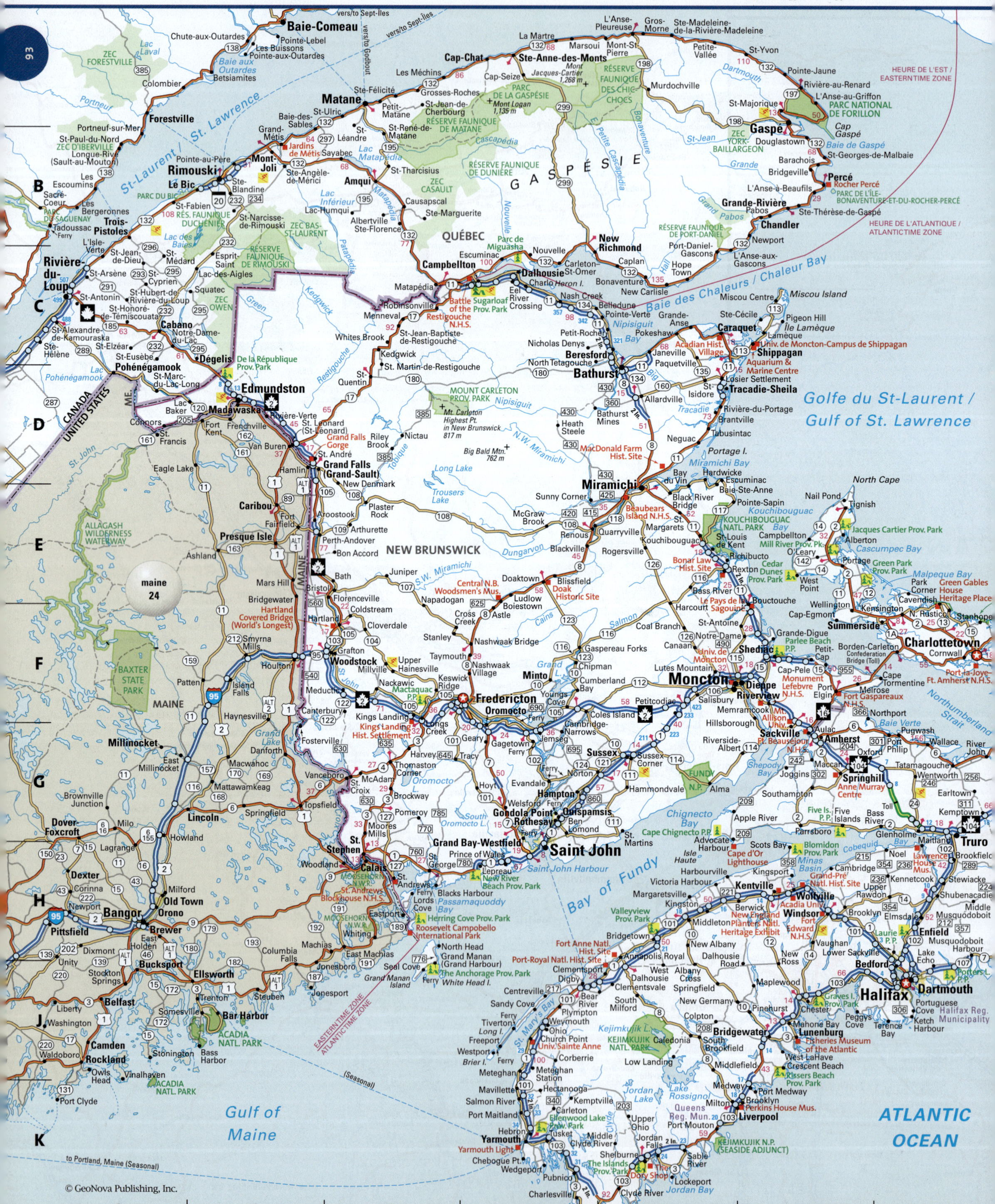

93

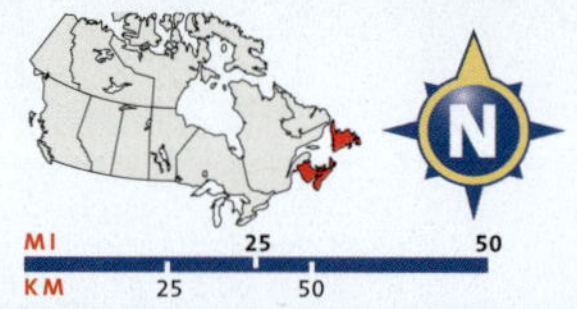

QUÉBEC

GASPÉSIE

NEW BRUNSWICK

MAINE

maine 24

CANADA
UNITED STATES

Golfe du St-Laurent / Gulf of St. Lawrence

Baie des Chaleurs / Chaleur Bay

Northumberland Strait

Bay of Fundy

Gulf of Maine

ATLANTIC OCEAN

St-Laurent / St. Lawrence

HEURE DE L'EST / EASTERN TIME ZONE

HEURE DE L'ATLANTIQUE / ATLANTIC TIME ZONE

EASTERN TIME ZONE / ATLANTIC TIME ZONE

Baie-Comeau

Matane

Rimouski

Gaspé

Percé

Campbellton

Dalhousie

Bathurst

Miramichi

Edmundston

Moncton

Fredericton

Saint John

Charlottetown

Summerside

Truro

Halifax

Dartmouth

Bangor

Yarmouth

1 2 3 4 5 6 7

B C D E F G H J K

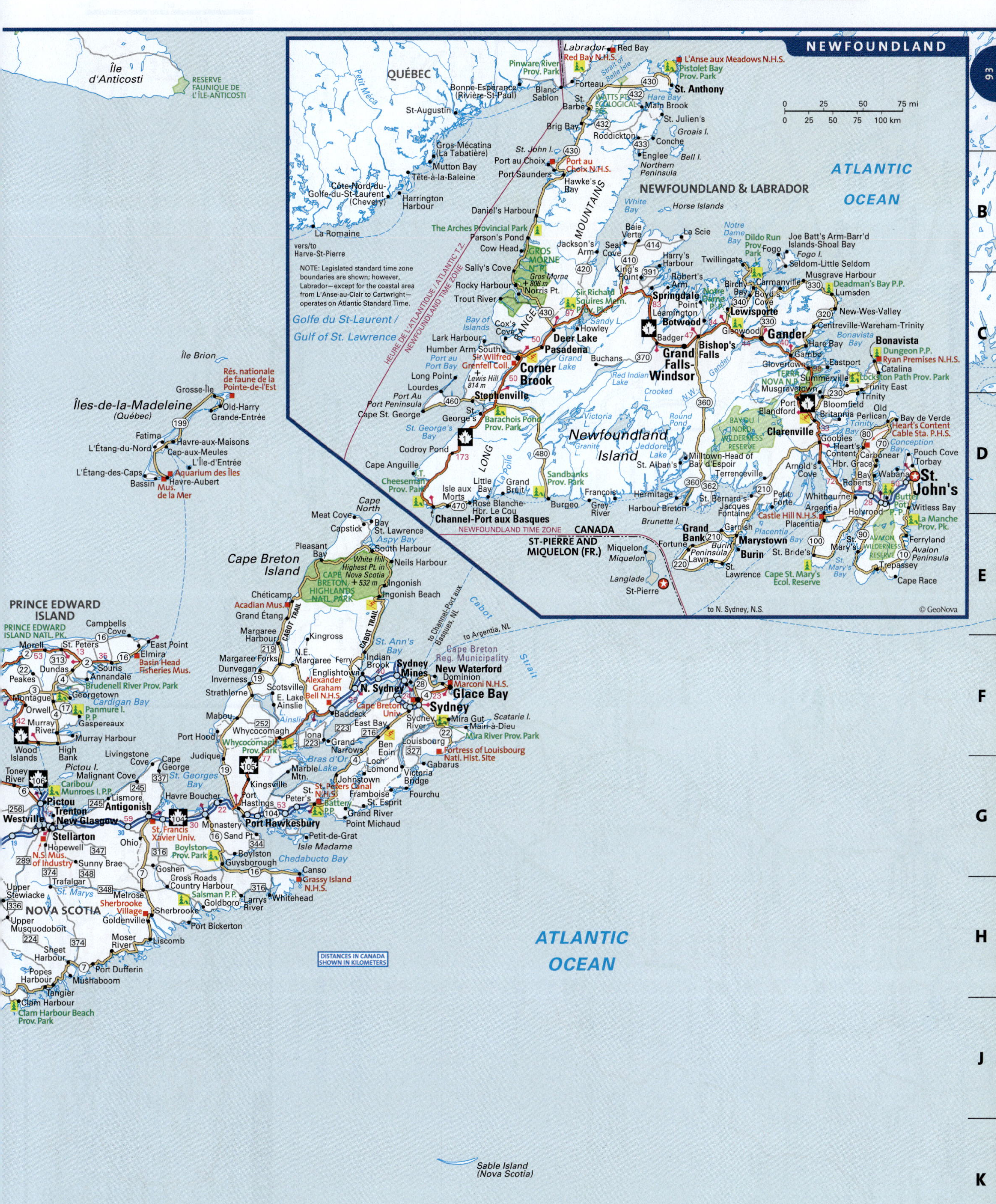
NEWFOUNDLAND
ATLANTIC OCEAN
NEWFOUNDLAND & LABRADOR
QUÉBEC
Golfe du St-Laurent / Gulf of St. Lawrence
NOTE: Legislated standard time zone boundaries are shown; however, Labrador—except for the coastal area from L'Anse-au-Clair to Cartwright—operates on Atlantic Standard Time.
NEWFOUNDLAND TIME ZONE
CANADA
ST-PIERRE AND MIQUELON (FR.)
Newfoundland Island
St. John's
Gander
Corner Brook
Grand Falls-Windsor
Channel-Port aux Basques
Cape Breton Island
PRINCE EDWARD ISLAND
NOVA SCOTIA
Îles-de-la-Madeleine (Québec)
Île d'Anticosti
Sydney
Glace Bay
Port Hawkesbury
Antigonish
New Glasgow
Cabot Strait
ATLANTIC OCEAN
DISTANCES IN CANADA SHOWN IN KILOMETERS
Sable Island (Nova Scotia)
© GeoNova

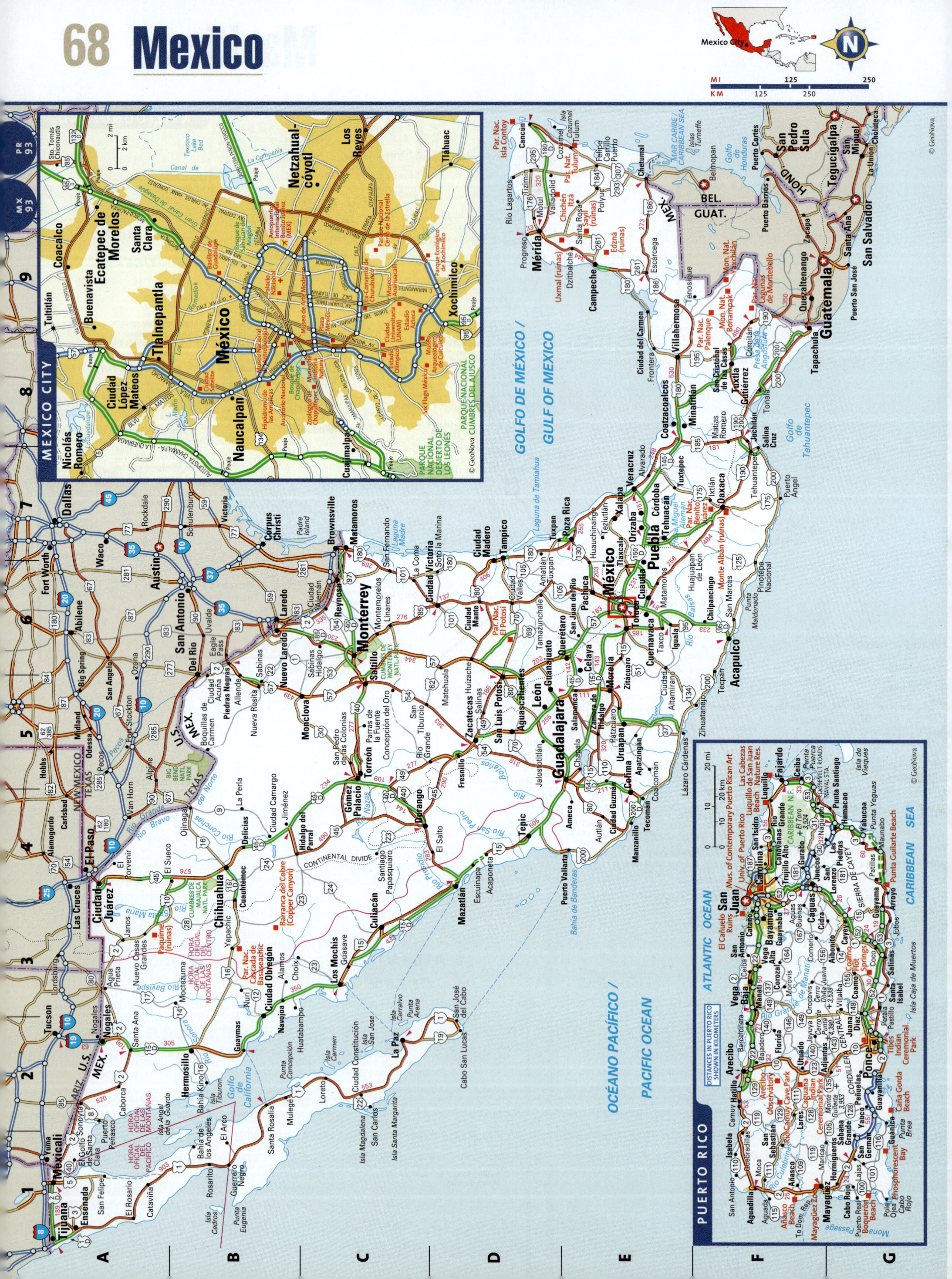

MEXICO CITY

PUERTO RICO

GOLFO DE MÉXICO / GULF OF MEXICO

OCÉANO PACÍFICO / PACIFIC OCEAN

ATLANTIC OCEAN

CARIBBEAN SEA

MAR CARIBE / CARIBBEAN SEA

DISTANCES IN PUERTO RICO SHOWN IN KILOMETERS

ALBUQUERQUE

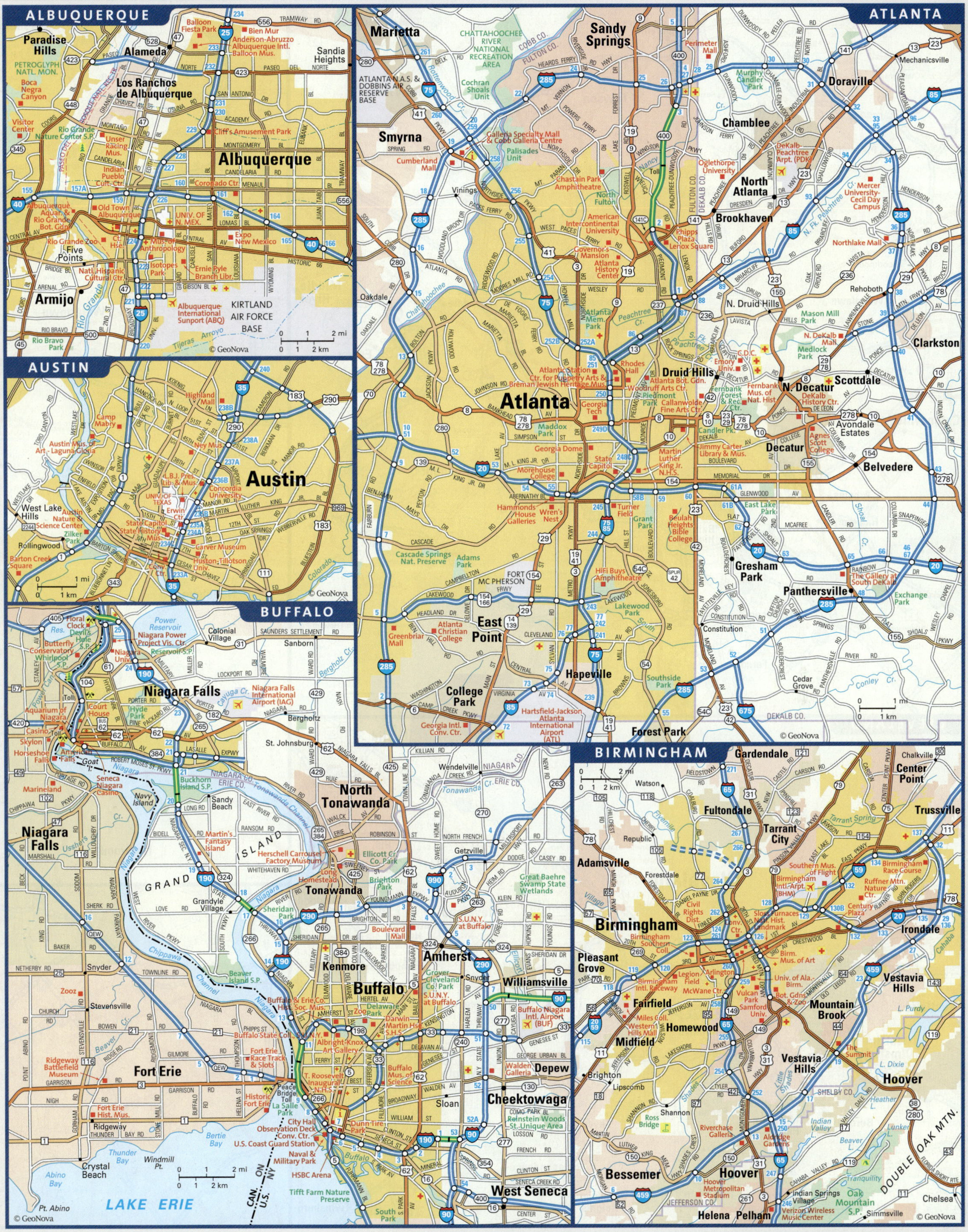

© GeoNova

ATLANTA

© GeoNova

AUSTIN

© GeoNova

BUFFALO

© GeoNova

BIRMINGHAM

© GeoNova

Cities

BALTIMORE

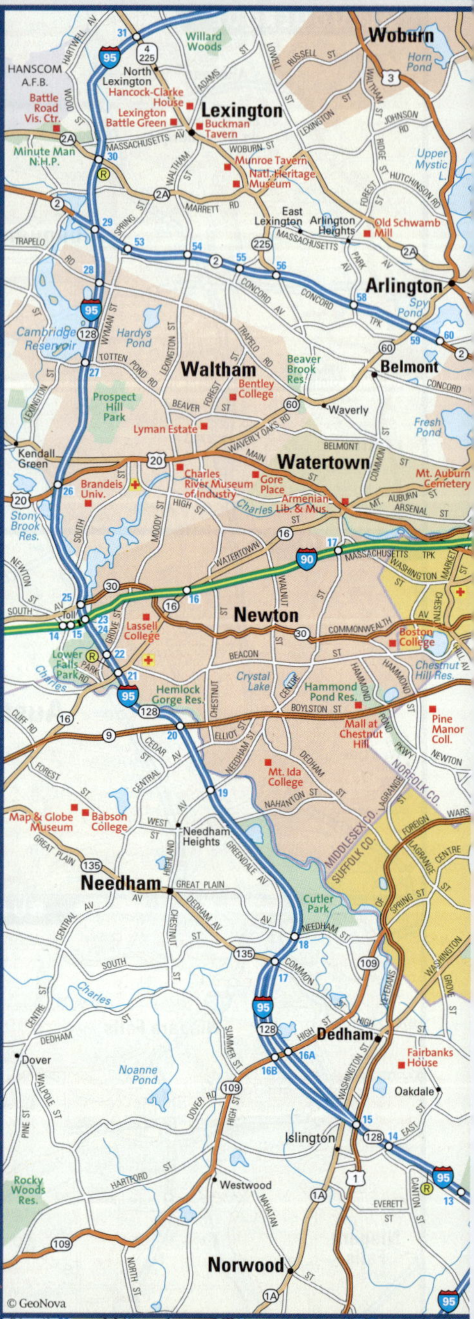

CLEVELAND

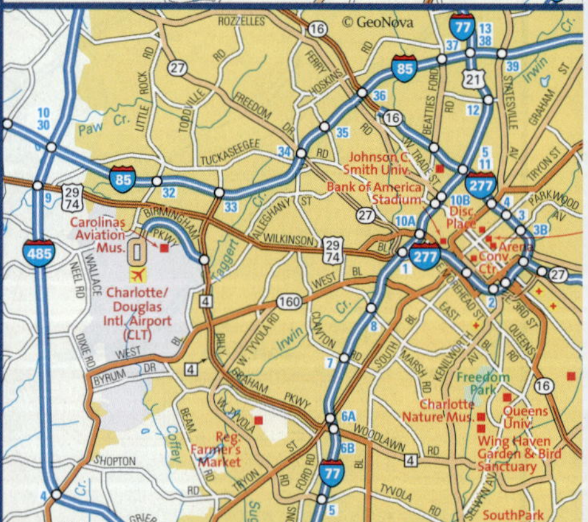

BOSTON
COLUMBUS, OH
CINCINNATI
CHARLOTTE
ATLANTIC OCEAN
Boston
Cambridge
Columbus
Cincinnati
Charlotte
© GeoNova

CHICAGO

LAKE MICHIGAN

© GeoNova

CHARLESTON, SC

© GeoNova

DETROIT

© GeoNova

DALLAS–FT. WORTH
Dallas
Fort Worth
Arlington
Grand Prairie
Irving
Garland
Mesquite
Plano
Carrollton
Richardson
Grapevine
DENVER
Denver
Aurora
Lakewood
Arvada
Westminster
Thornton
Golden
Littleton
Sterling Heights
Warren
Dearborn
Windsor
Troy
Roseville
LaSalle
© GeoNova

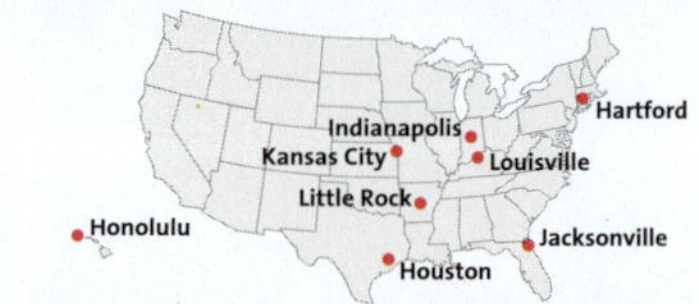

Hartford
Indianapolis
Kansas City
Louisville
Little Rock
Honolulu
Jacksonville
Houston

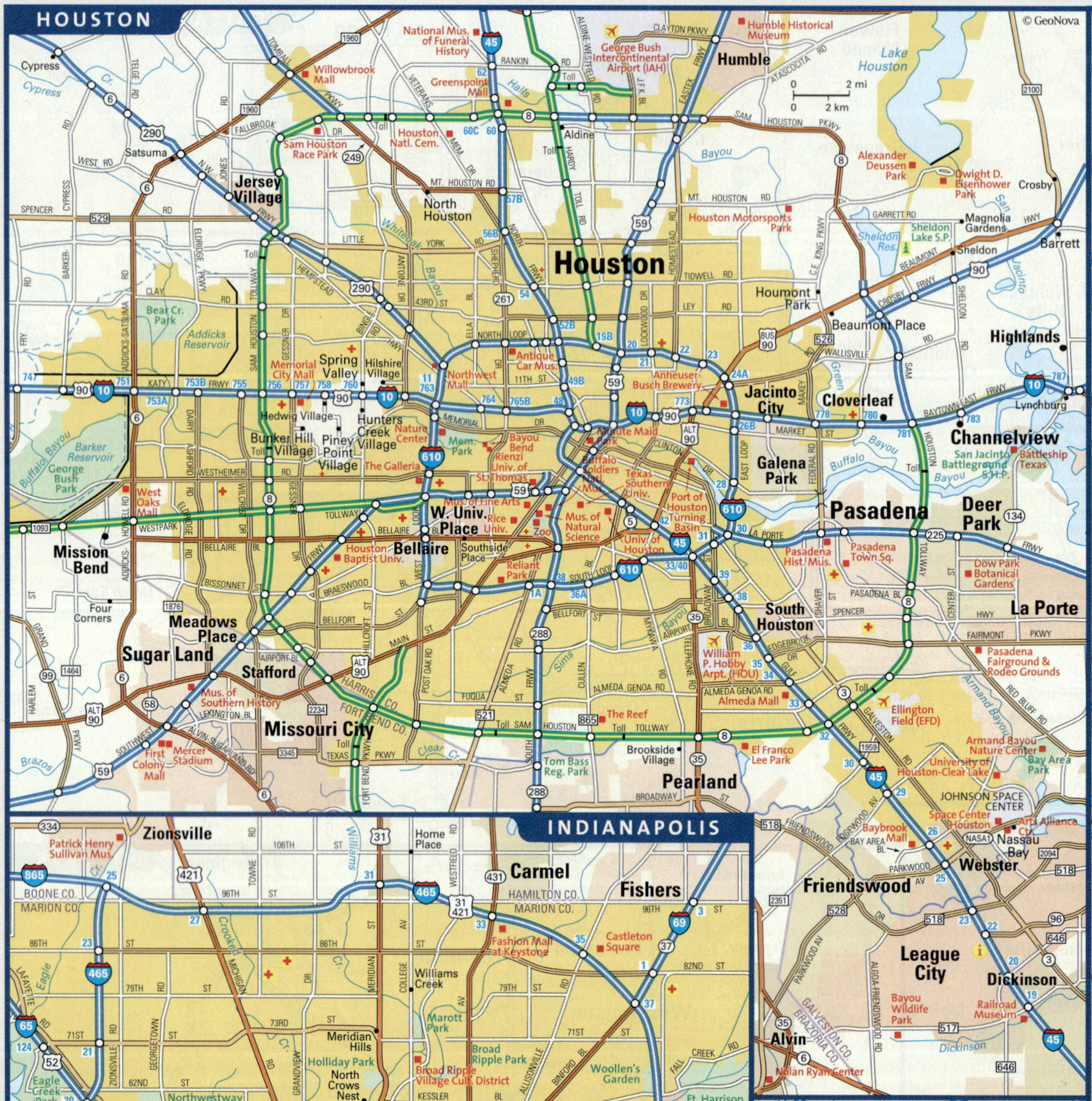
HOUSTON
© GeoNova
Houston
Humble
Aldine
North Houston
Jersey Village
Spring Valley
Hilshire Village
Hedwig Village
Hunters Creek Village
Bunker Hill Village
Piney Point Village
W. Univ. Place
Bellaire
Southside Place
Mission Bend
Four Corners
Meadows Place
Sugar Land
Stafford
Missouri City
Pasadena
Jacinto City
Galena Park
Cloverleaf
Channelview
Deer Park
La Porte
South Houston
Highlands
Crosby
Barrett
Sheldon
Pearland
Brookside Village
Friendswood
League City
Webster
Nassau Bay
Dickinson
Alvin
Lake Houston
Houston Natl. Cem.
George Bush Intercontinental Airport (IAH)
William P. Hobby Arpt. (HOU)
Ellington Field (EFD)
JOHNSON SPACE CENTER

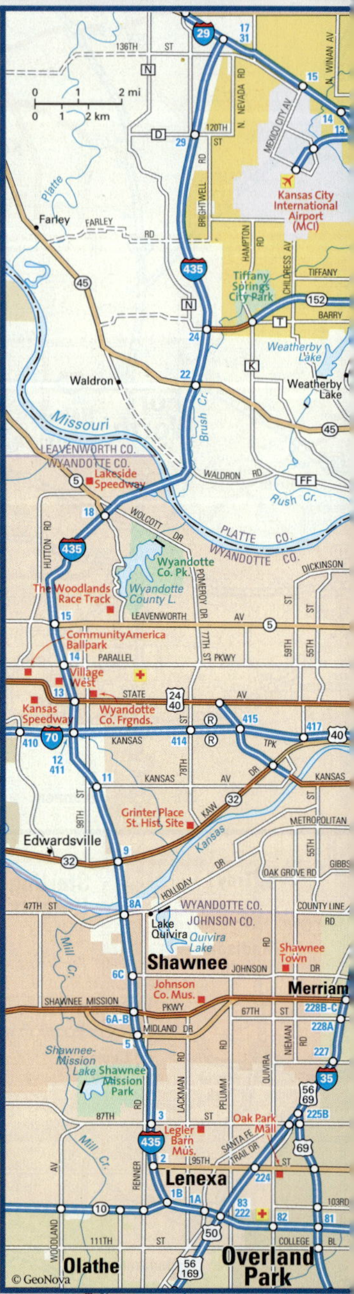
© GeoNova
Kansas City International Airport (MCI)
Farley
Waldron
Weatherby Lake
Edwardsville
Shawnee
Merriam
Lenexa
Olathe
Overland Park
Missouri
WYANDOTTE CO.
JOHNSON CO.

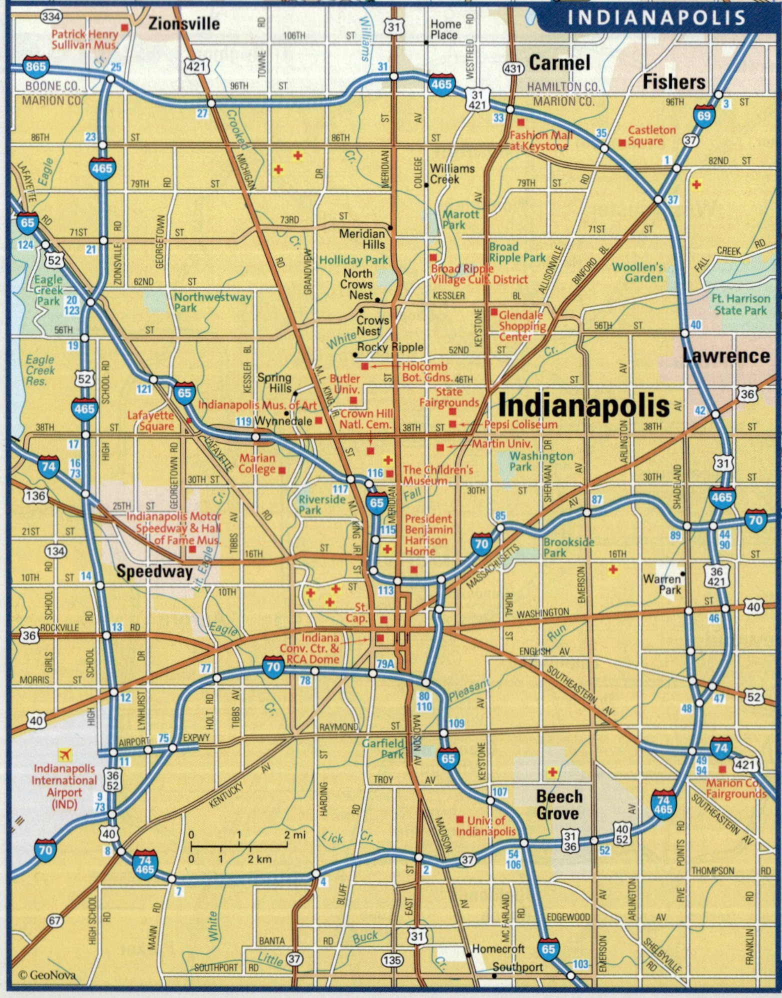
INDIANAPOLIS
© GeoNova
Indianapolis
Zionsville
Carmel
Fishers
Williams Creek
Meridian Hills
North Crows Nest
Crows Nest
Rocky Ripple
Spring Hills
Wynnedale
Lawrence
Speedway
Warren Park
Beech Grove
Homecroft
Southport
Indianapolis International Airport (IND)
Indianapolis Motor Speedway & Hall of Fame Mus.

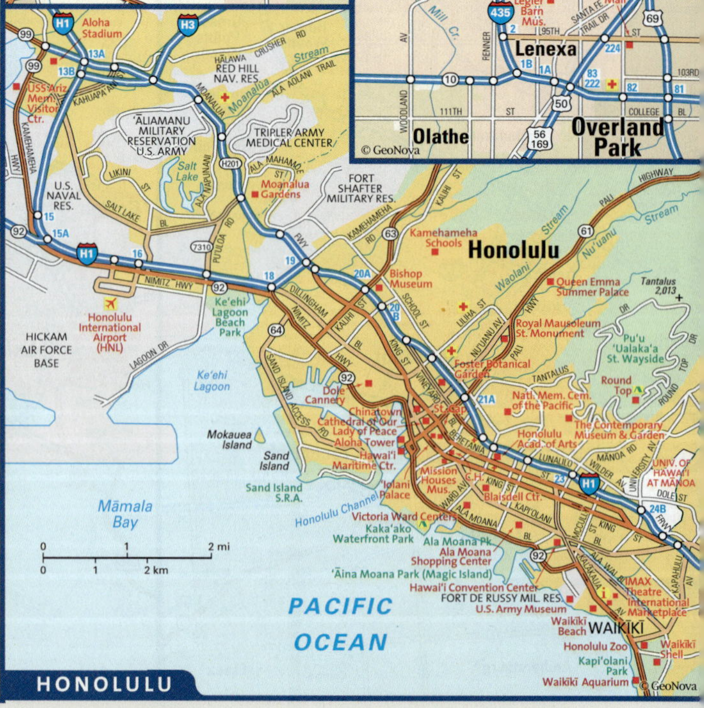
HONOLULU
© GeoNova
Honolulu
WAIKIKI
PACIFIC OCEAN
Māmala Bay
Ke'ehi Lagoon
Honolulu International Airport (HNL)
HICKAM AIR FORCE BASE
U.S. NAVAL RES.
ALIAMANU MILITARY RESERVATION U.S. ARMY
TRIPLER ARMY MEDICAL CENTER
FORT SHAFTER MILITARY RES.
Sand Island
Mokauea Island

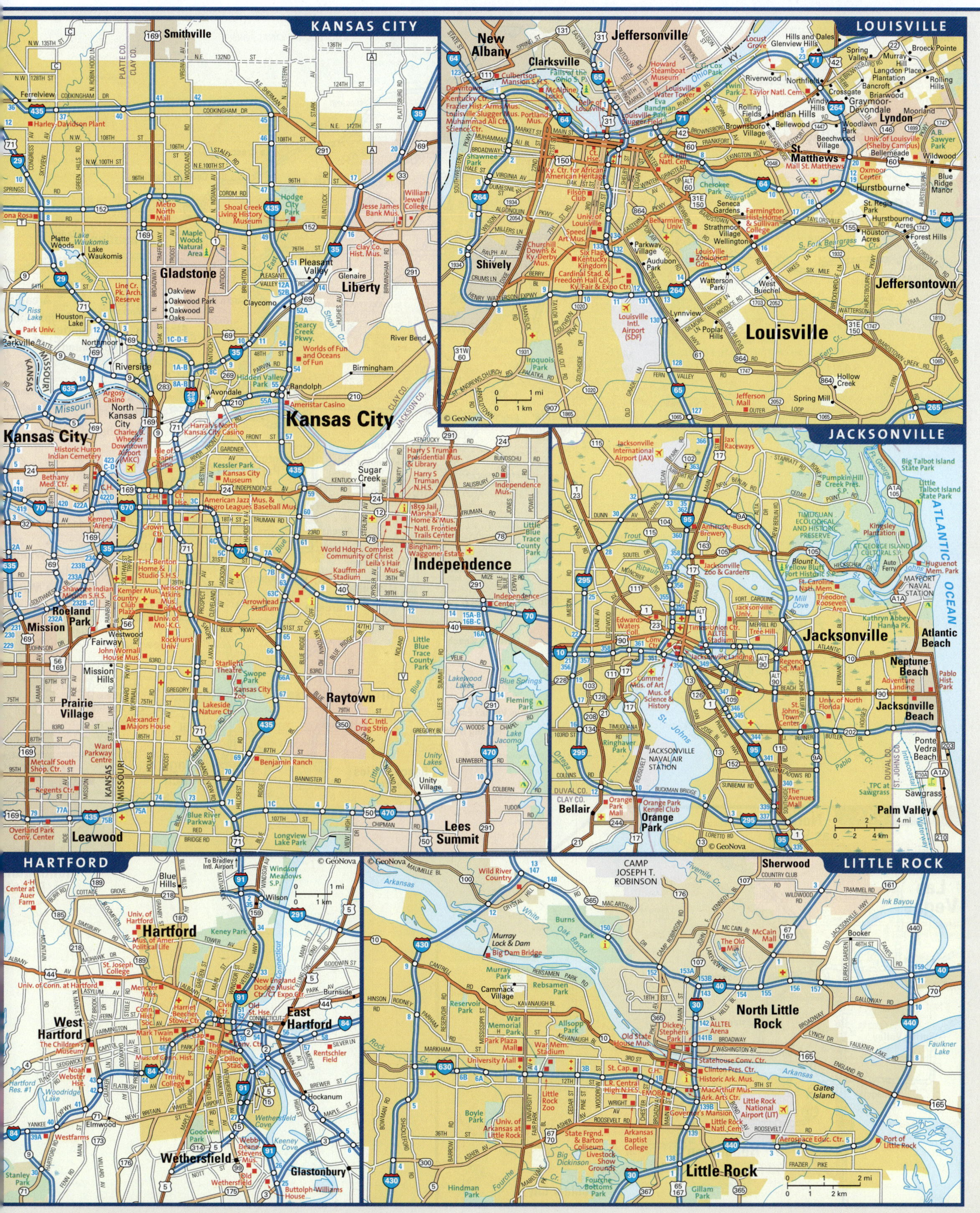
KANSAS CITY
Kansas City
Independence
Gladstone
Liberty
Raytown
Lees Summit
Leawood
Prairie Village
Mission
Roeland Park
Smithville
LOUISVILLE
Louisville
Jeffersonville
New Albany
Clarksville
Shively
St. Matthews
Jeffersontown
Lyndon
Hurstbourne
JACKSONVILLE
Jacksonville
Atlantic Beach
Neptune Beach
Jacksonville Beach
Ponte Vedra Beach
Orange Park
Bellair
Palm Valley
ATLANTIC OCEAN
HARTFORD
Hartford
West Hartford
East Hartford
Wethersfield
Glastonbury
LITTLE ROCK
Little Rock
North Little Rock
Sherwood
© GeoNova

ANGELES NATIONAL FOREST

Moorpark
Simi Valley
Thousand Oaks
Oak Park
Agoura Hills
Westlake Village
Calabasas
Hidden Hills
Chatsworth
Canoga Park
Northridge
Sylmar
San Fernando
Pacoima
Sunland
La Crescenta
Montrose
La Canada Flintridge
Altadena
Pasadena
Sierra Madre
Arcadia
Burbank
Glendale
North Hollywood
Studio City
Sherman Oaks
Encino
Woodland Hills
Topanga
Malibu
Point Dume
Los Angeles
West Hollywood
Beverly Hills
Santa Monica
Venice
Marina del Rey
Culver City
View Park
Windsor Hills
Ladera Hts.
Inglewood
Westchester
Lennox
El Segundo
Hawthorne
Lawndale
Manhattan Beach
Hermosa Beach
Redondo Beach
Torrance
Gardena
Palos Verdes Estates
Rolling Hills Estates
Rancho Palos Verdes
Lomita
Carson
Wilmington
San Pedro
Long Beach
Signal Hill
Seal Beach
Huntington Beach
South Pasadena
San Marino
Temple City
Alhambra
San Gabriel
Rosemead
El Monte
South El Monte
Monterey Park
S. San Gabriel
Montebello
E. Los Angeles
Commerce
Maywood
Bell
Bell Gdns.
Cudahy
Huntington Park
Vernon
Florence
Walnut Park
South Gate
Athens
Lynwood
Willowbrook
Compton
Paramount
Bellflower
Downey
Norwalk
Pico Rivera
Whittier
Santa Fe Springs
S. Whittier
La Mirada
Cerritos
Artesia
Lakewood
La Palma
Hawaiian Gardens
Los Alamitos
Cypress
Rossmoor
Westminster
Bassett

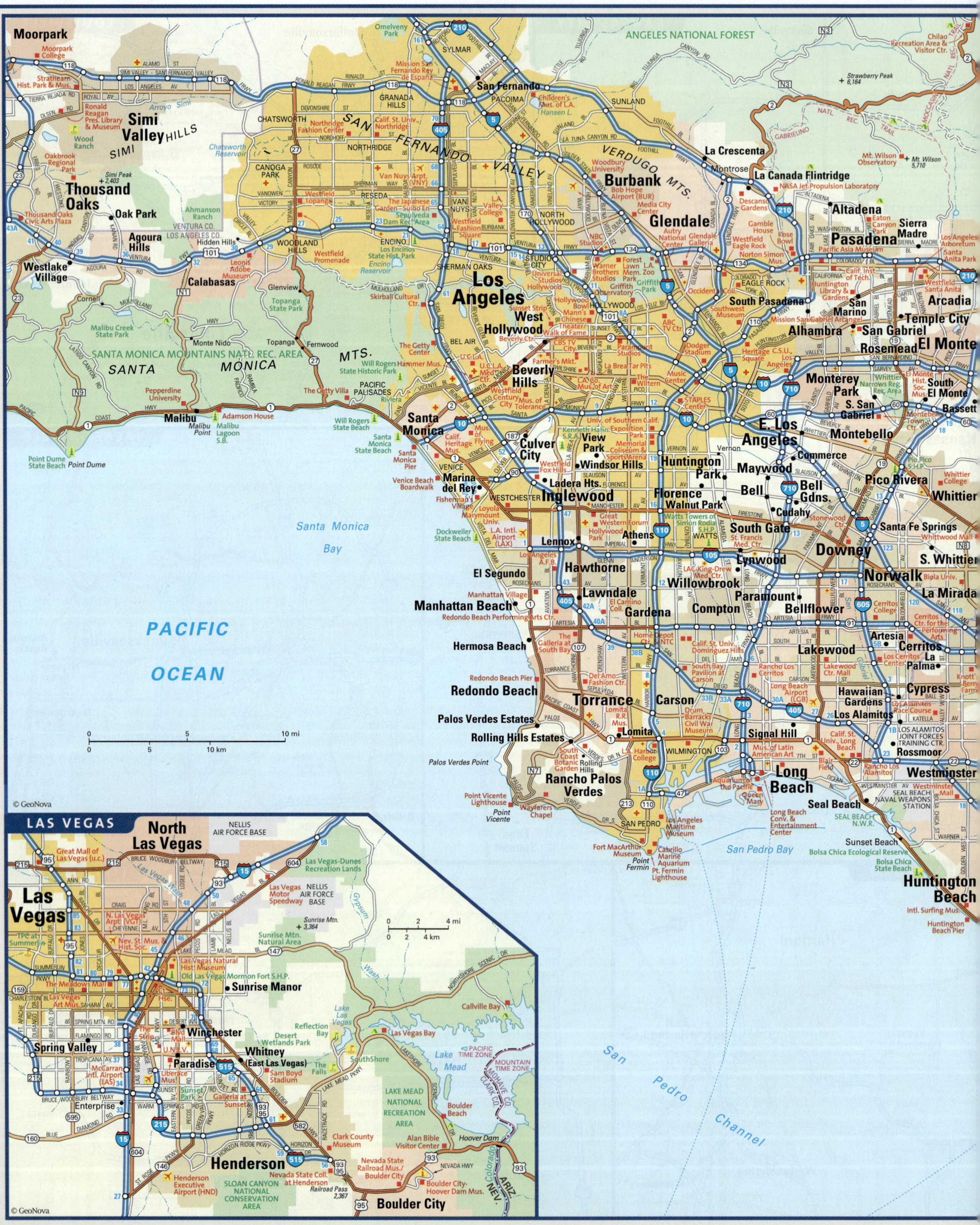

Santa Monica Bay
PACIFIC OCEAN
San Pedro Bay
San Pedro Channel

0 5 10 mi
0 5 10 km

© GeoNova

LAS VEGAS

North Las Vegas
Las Vegas
Sunrise Manor
Winchester
Spring Valley
Paradise
Whitney (East Las Vegas)
Enterprise
Henderson
Boulder City
Lake Mead
LAKE MEAD NATIONAL RECREATION AREA
NELLIS AIR FORCE BASE
SLOAN CANYON NATIONAL CONSERVATION AREA
Hoover Dam
PACIFIC TIME ZONE
MOUNTAIN TIME ZONE

0 2 4 mi
0 2 4 km

© GeoNova

LOS ANGELES
San Gabriel Wilderness
ANGELES NATIONAL FOREST
Sheep Mountain Wilderness
SAN BERNARDINO NATL. FOR.
Mt. Baldy
Cucamonga Wilderness
San Dimas Experimental Forest
Hesperia
Summit
Cajon Junction
Silverwood Lake
Lake Arrowhead
Crestline
Cedar Glen
Blue Jay
Twin Peaks
Rimforest
Crest Park
Skyforest
Lytle Creek
Devore
San Bernardino
Muscoy
Highland
Mentone
Redlands
Loma Linda
Grand Terrace
Colton
Bloomington
Rialto
Fontana
Rancho Cucamonga
Upland
San Antonio Heights
Claremont
La Verne
San Dimas
Glendora
Azusa
Monrovia
Duarte
Irwindale
Covina
Charter Oak
Baldwin Park
West Covina
Valinda
La Puente
Walnut
Pomona
Montclair
Ontario
Diamond Bar
Hacienda Hts.
Rowland Heights
La Habra Hts.
La Habra
Brea
Chino
Chino Hills
CHINO HILLS
Glen Avon
Mira Loma
Pedley
Rubidoux
Sunnyslope
Belltown
Crestmore
Highgrove
Riverside
Moreno Valley
Woodcrest
Norco
Home Gardens
Corona
El Cerrito
Perris
Nuevo
Romoland
Mead Valley
Yorba Linda
Fullerton
Buena Park
Placentia
Anaheim
Stanton
Garden Grove
Villa Park
Orange
Cowan Heights
Lemon Heights
E. Tustin
Tustin
Santa Ana
Midway City
Fountain Valley
Costa Mesa
Newport Beach
Irvine
Lake Forest
Laguna Woods
Laguna Hills
Mission Viejo
Rancho Santa Margarita
Trabuco Canyon
Coto de Caza
Aliso Viejo
Laguna Niguel
Laguna Beach
Emerald Bay
Dana Point
San Juan Capistrano
San Clemente
Silverado
Modjeska
CLEVELAND NATIONAL FOREST
MEMPHIS
Memphis
Bartlett
West Memphis
Presidents Island
Treasure Island
Mississippi
© GeoNova

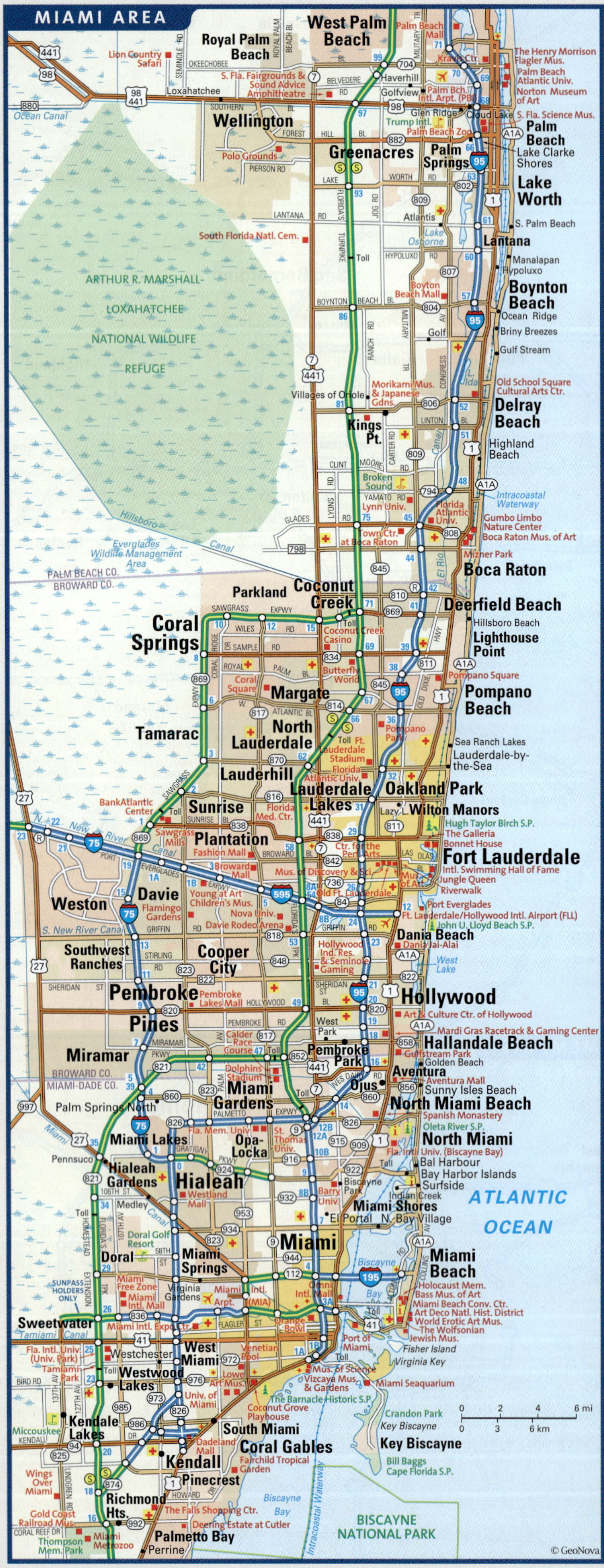

MIAMI AREA

West Palm Beach
Royal Palm Beach
Wellington
Greenacres
Palm Springs
Palm Beach
Lake Worth
Lantana
Boynton Beach
Delray Beach
Boca Raton
ARTHUR R. MARSHALL-LOXAHATCHEE NATIONAL WILDLIFE REFUGE
Parkland
Coconut Creek
Coral Springs
Deerfield Beach
Lighthouse Point
Margate
Pompano Beach
Tamarac
North Lauderdale
Lauderhill
Sunrise
Lauderdale Lakes
Oakland Park
Wilton Manors
Plantation
Fort Lauderdale
Weston
Davie
Dania Beach
Southwest Ranches
Cooper City
Hollywood
Pembroke Pines
Hallandale Beach
Miramar
Pembroke Park
Aventura
Miami Gardens
North Miami Beach
Miami Lakes
Opa-Locka
North Miami
Hialeah Gardens
Hialeah
Miami Shores
ATLANTIC OCEAN
Doral
Miami Springs
Miami
Miami Beach
Sweetwater
West Miami
Westwood Lakes
Kendale Lakes
South Miami
Coral Gables
Key Biscayne
Kendall
Pinecrest
Richmond Hts.
Palmetto Bay
BISCAYNE NATIONAL PARK

© GeoNova

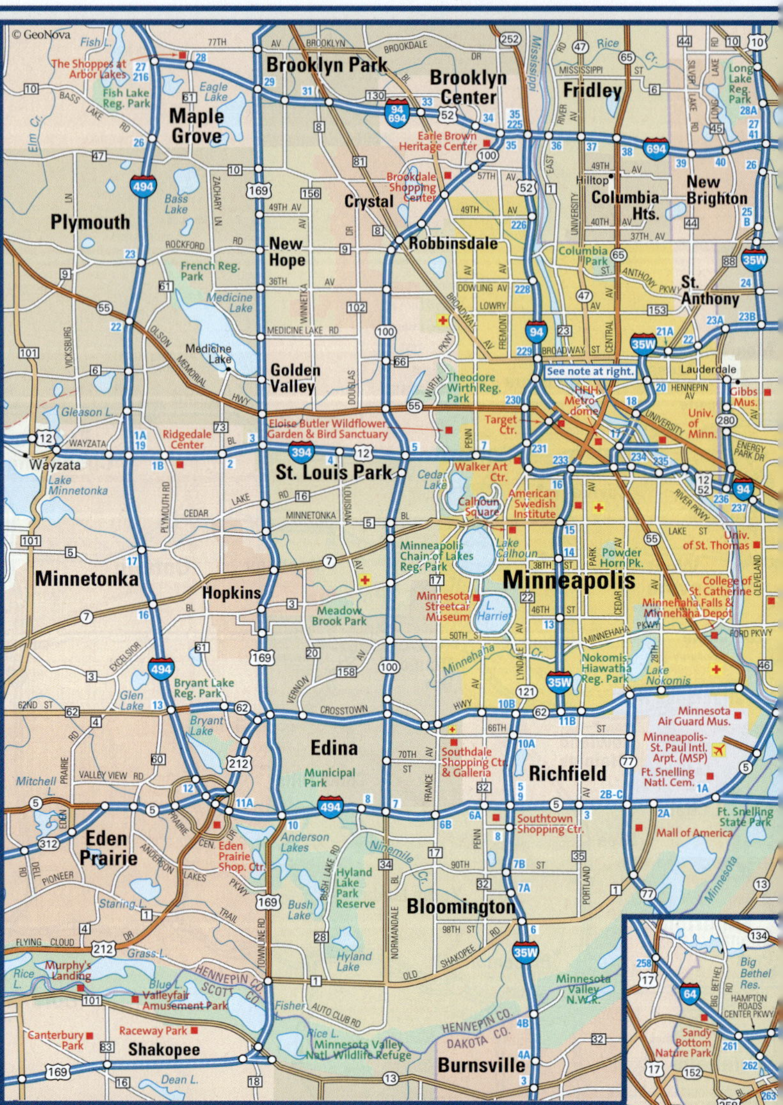

MINNEAPOLIS–ST. PAUL

Brooklyn Park
Brooklyn Center
Fridley
Maple Grove
Plymouth
Crystal
New Hope
Robbinsdale
Columbia Hts.
New Brighton
St. Anthony
Golden Valley
Wayzata
St. Louis Park
Minnetonka
Hopkins
Minneapolis
Edina
Richfield
Eden Prairie
Bloomington
Shakopee
Burnsville

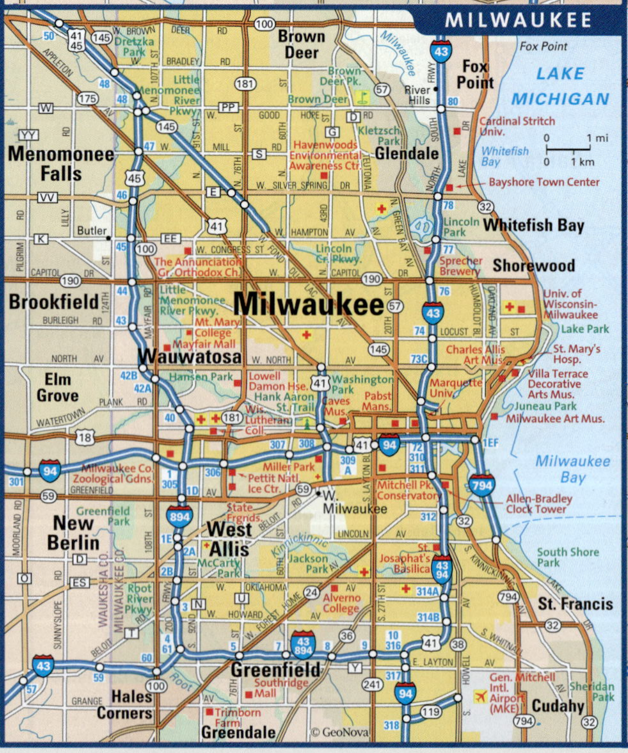

© GeoNova

MILWAUKEE

Brown Deer
Fox Point
LAKE MICHIGAN
Menomonee Falls
Glendale
Whitefish Bay
Shorewood
Brookfield
Milwaukee
Wauwatosa
Elm Grove
West Milwaukee
New Berlin
West Allis
St. Francis
Greenfield
Hales Corners
Cudahy
Greendale

© GeoNova

NORFOLK–VA. BEACH–NEWPORT NEWS

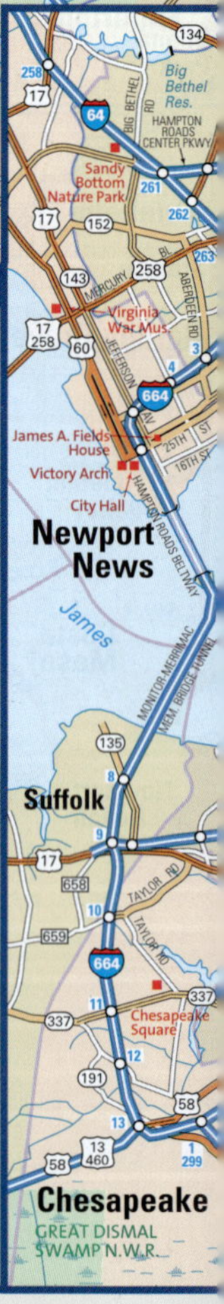

Newport News
Suffolk
Chesapeake
GREAT DISMAL SWAMP N.W.R.

MINNEAPOLIS–ST. PAUL
TRAVEL NOTE: Interstate 35W bridge closed by collapse 8/1/07. Designated detour route is I-94 and Minnesota highway 280. Highway 280 will be converted to temporary limited access for the duration of detour. Thru travelers should use I-35E or I-494 and I-694. Minnesota DOT hopes to have bridge rebuilt by the end of 2008.
Arden Hills
Vadnais Heights
White Bear Lake
Mahtomedi
Roseville
Little Canada
Maplewood
North St. Paul
Falcon Heights
Oakdale
Lake Elmo
St. Paul
Woodbury
Mendota Heights
West St. Paul
South St. Paul
Eagan
Inver Grove Heights
St. Paul Park
MONTRÉAL
Laval
Montréal
Longueuil
Boucherville
Saint-Lambert
Hampstead
Côte-St-Luc
Westmount
Montréal-Ouest
Dorval
Brossard
NEW ORLEANS
Lake Pontchartrain
Kenner
Metairie
New Orleans
Arabi
Chalmette
Meraux
Violet
St. Rose
River Ridge
Jefferson
Harahan
Destrehan
Avondale
Marrero
Harvey
Gretna
Terrytown
Westwego
Estelle
Belle Chasse
Lake Borgne
Chesapeake Bay
Hampton
Norfolk
Portsmouth
Virginia Beach
NASHVILLE
Nashville
Belle Meade
Oak Hill
NORFOLK–VIRGINIA BEACH–NEWPORT NEWS
© GeoNova

NEW YORK CITY

OKLAHOMA CITY
Edmond
The Village
Nichols Hills
Warr Acres
Bethany
Spencer
Choctaw
Midwest City
Del City
Smith Village
Valley Brook
Tinker Air Force Base
Mustang
Moore
Oklahoma City
Lake Hefner
Lake Overholser
Lake Stanley Draper
Arcadia Lake
Will Rogers World Arpt. (OKC)
© GeoNova
PITTSBURGH
West View
Ben Avon Heights
Avalon
Bellevue
Evergreen
Millvale
Etna
Sharpsburg
Aspinwall
Fox Chapel
Oakmont
Verona
Blawnox
McKees Rocks
West Park
Pittsburgh
Ingram
Thornburg
Crafton
Green Tree
Carnegie
Mount Lebanon
Dormont
Mount Oliver
Castle Shannon
Brentwood
Baldwin
West Mifflin
Munhall
Homestead
West Homestead
Swissvale
Edgewood
Wilkinsburg
Forest Hills
Churchill
Braddock
North Braddock
Rankin
Whitaker
Duquesne
Chalfant
East Pittsburgh
Sandy Creek
Monongahela
Allegheny
Ohio
PHILADELPHIA
Hatboro
Holland
Feasterville
Trevose
Oakford
Blue Bell
Ambler
Fort Washington
Willow Grove
Bryn Athyn
Trooper
Jeffersonville
Norristown
Bridgeport
Plymouth Meeting
Whitemarsh
Oreland
Roslyn
Abington
Huntingdon Valley
Glenside
Jenkintown
Wyncote
Rockledge
King of Prussia
Swedeland
Lafayette Hill
Conshohocken
West Conshohocken
Elkins Pk.
Ogontz
Melrose Park
Cheltenham
Andalusia
Radnor
Wayne
St. Davids
Villanova
Rosemont
Bryn Mawr
Gladwyne
Haverford
Ardmore
Narberth
Bala-Cynwyd
Wynnewood
Philadelphia
Riverside
Delanco
Riverton
Palmyra
Cinnaminson
Delran
Havertown
Penn Wynne
Broomall
Manoa
Upper Darby
Drexel Hill
East Lansdowne
Lansdowne
Clifton Hts.
Yeadon
Springfield
Aldan
Collingdale
Darby
Sharon Hill
Colwyn
Glenolden
Media
Marple
Rose Tree
Swarthmore
Rutledge
Morton
Prospect Park
Folsom
Ridley Park
Norwood
Folcroft
Woodlyn
Brookhaven
Upland
Chester
Eddystone
Essington
Paulsboro
Gibbstown
Thorofare
Woodbury
Woodbury Heights
National Park
Westville
Brooklawn
Gloucester City
Mt. Ephraim
Audubon
Audubon Park
Oaklyn
Collingswood
Woodlynne
Camden
Pennsauken
Merchantville
Maple Shade
Lenola
Cherry Hill
Westmont
Haddonfield
Haddon Heights
Bellmawr
Barrington
Lawnside
Magnolia
Runnemede
Somerdale
Stratford
Hi-Nella
Laurel Springs
Lindenwold
Kirkwood
Gibbsboro
Ashland
Springdale
Almonesson
Deptford
Fellowship
Philadelphia International Airport (PHL)
PENNSYLVANIA
NEW JERSEY
Delaware
Schuylkill
© GeoNova
Great Neck
Kings Point
Great Neck Gardens
Plandome Heights
Manhasset
Kensington
Saddle Rock
Great Neck Plaza
Thomaston
Lake Success
Manhasset Hills
Mineola
North New Hyde Park
New Hyde Park
Garden City
Floral Park
Bellerose
Elmont
Franklin Square
North Valley Stream
Lakeview
Valley Stream
Malverne
Lynbrook
South Valley Stream
Hewlett
East Rockaway
Woodmere
Cedarhurst
Inwood
Lawrence
Island Park
Long Beach
Atlantic Beach
East Atlantic Beach
Far Rockaway
Hollis
St. Albans
Bayside
Little Neck Bay
ATLANTIC OCEAN
© GeoNova

Cities

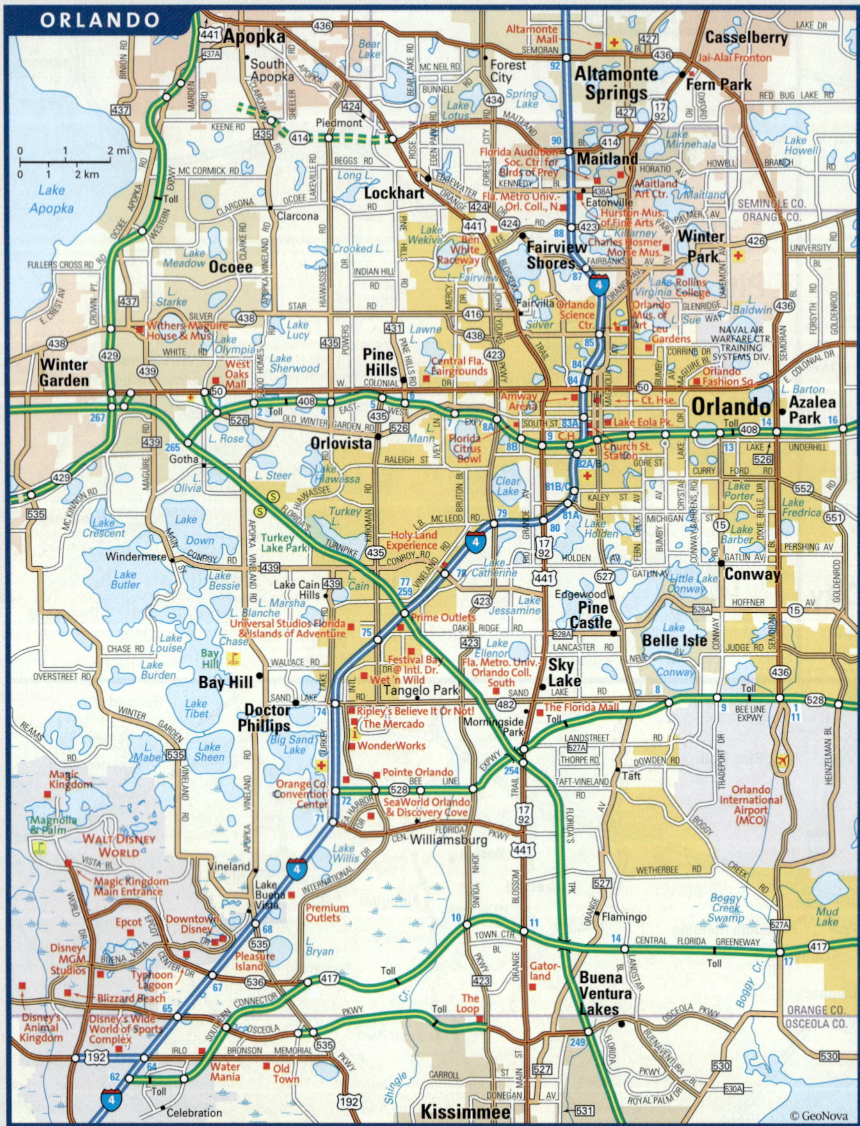

ORLANDO

PORTLAND, OR

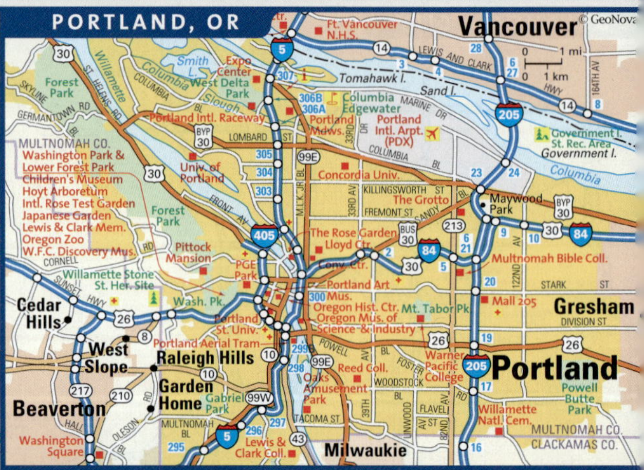

PROVIDENCE

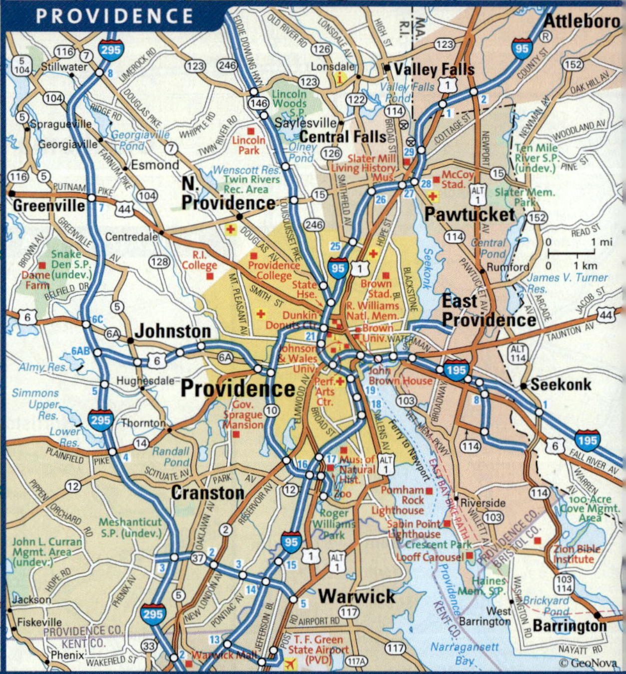

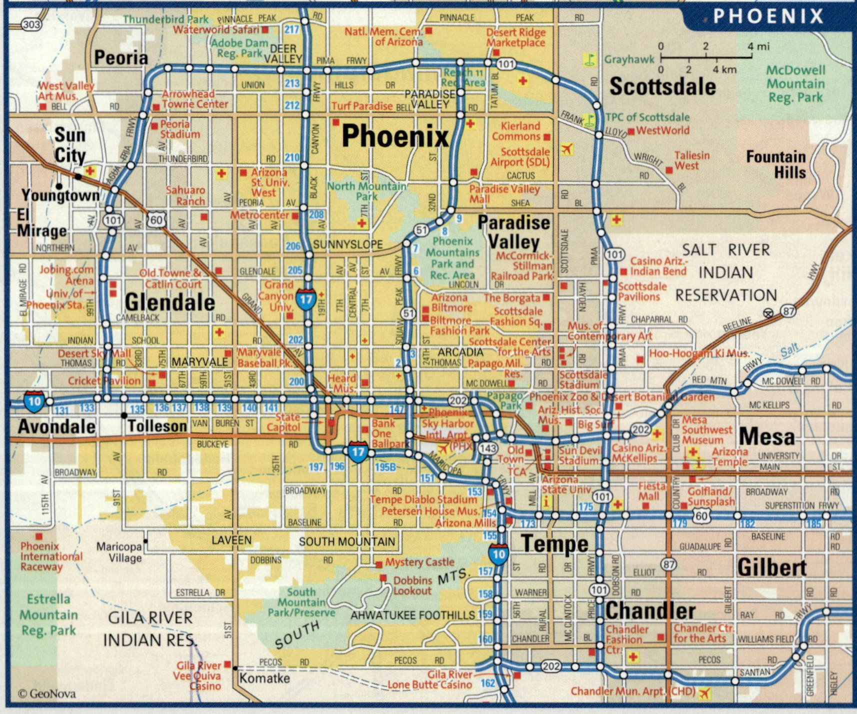

PHOENIX

RICHMOND

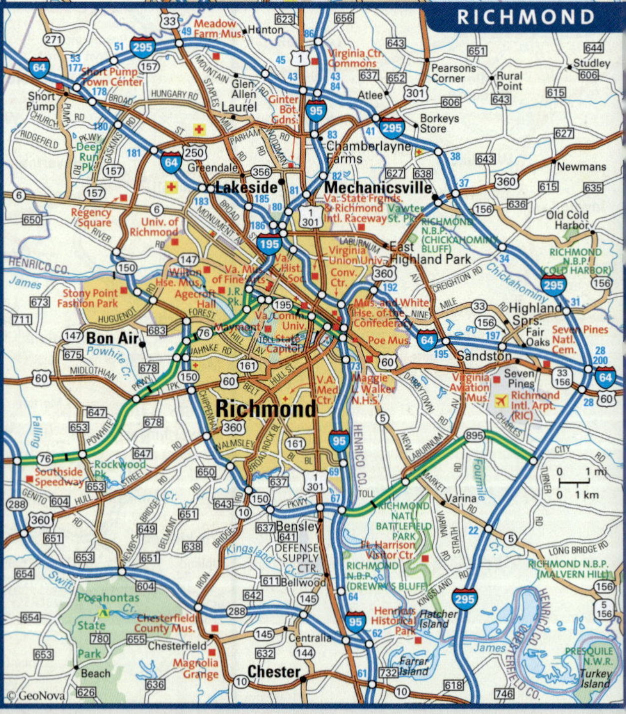

SAN FRANCISCO BAY
SAN DIEGO
SACRAMENTO
PACIFIC OCEAN
San Pablo Bay
San Francisco Bay
SANTA CRUZ MOUNTAINS
San Francisco
Oakland
Berkeley
Richmond
San Rafael
San Anselmo
Fairfax
Kentfield
Larkspur
Corte Madera
Mill Valley
Tiburon
Sausalito
Tamalpais Valley
San Pablo
El Cerrito
Albany
Emeryville
Piedmont
Alameda
Pinole
Hercules
Rodeo
Crockett
El Sobrante
Orinda
Daly City
Broadmoor
Colma
Brisbane
South San Francisco
San Bruno
Millbrae
Burlingame
San Mateo
Hillsborough
Foster City
Belmont
San Carlos
Redwood City
North Fair Oaks
Menlo Park
Atherton
East Palo Alto
Palo Alto
Mountain View
Los Altos
Los Altos Hills
Sunnyvale
Santa Clara
Cupertino
Campbell
San Jose
Saratoga
Los Gatos
Monte Sereno
Milpitas
Fremont
Newark
Union City
Hayward
San Lorenzo
San Leandro
Ashland
Castro Valley
Pleasanton
Sunol
Pacifica
Montara
Moss Beach
El Granada
Half Moon Bay
Woodside
Portola Valley
Ladera
La Honda
San Diego
La Jolla
Santee
Spring Valley
Lemon Grove
National City
Bonita
Chula Vista
Imperial Beach
Coronado
Tijuana
Sacramento
West Sacramento
Rio Linda
Arcade
Arden
Rosemont
© GeoNova

SEATTLE–TACOMA

ST. LOUIS

TORONTO

SAN ANTONIO

WASHINGTON, DC AREA
VANCOUVER
TAMPA–ST. PETERSBURG AREA
SALT LAKE CITY
© GeoNova

Ortsregister

Note: Population figures are from the latest census or the most recent available estimates

ALABAMA
PG. 4

CAPITAL
Montgomery

NICKNAME
Heart of Dixie

POPULATION
4,447,100, rank 23

AREA
51,705 sq mi, rank 29

ALASKA
PG. 5

CAPITAL
Juneau

NICKNAME
Great Land

POPULATION
626,932, rank 48

AREA
591,004 sq mi, rank 1

ARIZONA
PG. 6

CAPITAL
Phoenix

NICKNAME
Grand Canyon State

POPULATION
5,130,632, rank 20

AREA
114,000 sq mi, rank 6

ARKANSAS
PG. 7

CAPITAL
Little Rock

NICKNAME
Natural State

POPULATION
2,673,400, rank 33

AREA
53,187 sq mi, rank 27

CALIFORNIA
PG. 8–9

CAPITAL
Sacramento

NICKNAME
Golden State

POPULATION
33,871,648, rank 1

AREA
158,706 sq mi, rank 3

COLORADO
PG. 10

CAPITAL
Denver

NICKNAME
Centennial State

POPULATION
4,301,261, rank 24

AREA
104,091 sq mi, rank 8

CONNECTICUT
PG. 12–13

CAPITAL
Hartford

NICKNAME
Constitution State

POPULATION
3,405,565, rank 29

AREA
5,018 sq mi, rank 48

DELAWARE
PG. 11

CAPITAL
Dover

NICKNAME
First State

POPULATION
783,600, rank 45

AREA
2,044 sq mi, rank 49

DISTRICT OF COLUMBIA
PG. 85

POPULATION
572,059

AREA
69 sq mi

FLORIDA

PG. 14

CAPITAL
Tallahassee

NICKNAME
Sunshine State

POPULATION
15,982,378, rank 4

AREA
58,664 sq mi, rank 22

GEORGIA

PG. 15

CAPITAL
Atlanta

NICKNAME
Empire State of the South

POPULATION
8,186,453, rank 10

AREA
58,910 sq mi, rank 21

HAWAI'I

PG. 5

CAPITAL
Honolulu

NICKNAME
Aloha State

POPULATION
1,211,537, rank 42

AREA
6,471 sq mi, rank 47

IDAHO

PG. 16

CAPITAL
Boise

NICKNAME
Gem State

POPULATION
1,293,953, rank 39

AREA
83,564 sq mi, rank 13

ILLINOIS

PG. 17

CAPITAL
Springfield

NICKNAME
Land of Lincoln

POPULATION
12,419,293, rank 5

AREA
56,345 sq mi, rank 24

INDIANA

PG. 18

CAPITAL
Indianapolis

NICKNAME
Hoosier State

POPULATION
6,080,485, rank 14

AREA
36,185 sq mi, rank 38

IOWA

PG. 19

CAPITAL
Des Moines

NICKNAME
Hawkeye State

POPULATION
2,926,324, rank 30

AREA
56,275 sq mi, rank 25

KANSAS

PG. 22

CAPITAL
Topeka

NICKNAME
Sunflower State

POPULATION
2,688,418, rank 32

AREA
82,277 sq mi, rank 14

KENTUCKY

PG. 20-21

CAPITAL
Frankfort

NICKNAME
Bluegrass State

POPULATION
4,041,769, rank 25

AREA
40,409 sq mi, rank 37

LOUISIANA

PG. 23

CAPITAL
Baton Rouge

NICKNAME
Pelican State

POPULATION
4,468,976, rank 22

AREA
47,751 sq mi, rank 31

MAINE

PG. 24

CAPITAL
Augusta

NICKNAME
Pine Tree State

POPULATION
1,274,923, rank 40

AREA
33,265 sq mi, rank 39

MARYLAND

PG. 11

CAPITAL
Annapolis

NICKNAME
Old Line State

POPULATION
5,296,486, rank 19

AREA
10,460 sq mi, rank 42

MASSACHUSETTS

PG. 12–13

CAPITAL
Boston

NICKNAME
Bay State

POPULATION
6,349,097, rank 13

AREA
8,284 sq mi, rank 45

MICHIGAN

PG. 26–27

CAPITAL
Lansing

NICKNAME
Great Lakes State

POPULATION
9,938,444, rank 8

AREA
58,527 sq mi, rank 23

- Pinckney, 2141 ... N8
- Plainwell, 3933 ... N5
- Pontiac, 66337 ... M9
- Portage, 44897 ... N5
- Port Huron, 32338 ... M10
- Portland, 3789 ... M6
- Potterville, 2168 ... M6
- Prudenville, 1737 ... J6
- Quincy, 1701 ... P6
- Reed City, 2430 ... K5
- Richmond, 4897 ... M10
- Rockford, 4626 ... L5
- Rockwood, 3442 ... N9
- Rogers City, 3322 ... G8
- Romeo, 3721 ... M9
- Romulus, 22979 ... N8
- Saginaw, 61799 ... L7
- St. Charles, 2215 ... L7
- St. Clair, 5802 ... M10
- St. Helen, 2993 ... J7
- St. Ignace, 2678 ... F6
- St. Johns, 7485 ... M6
- St. Joseph, 8789 ... N3
- St. Louis, 4494 ... L6
- Saline, 8034 ... N8
- Sandusky, 2745 ... L9
- Sault Ste. Marie, 16542 D7
- Sebewaing, 1974 ... K8
- Shelby, 1914 ... K3
- Shields, 6590 ... L7
- Skidway Lake, 3147 ... J7
- S. Haven, 5021 ... N4
- S. Lyon, 10036 ... N8
- Sparta, 4159 ... L5
- Springfield, 5189 ... N5
- Sterling Hts., 124471 ... M9
- Sturgis, 11285 ... P5
- Swartz Creek, 5102 ... M8
- Tawas City, 2005 ... J8
- Taylor, 65868 ... N9
- Tecumseh, 8574 ... P8
- Temperance, 7757 ... P8
- Three Rivers, 7328 ... P5
- Traverse City, 14532 ... H4
- Troy, 80959 ... M9
- Union City, 1804 ... N5
- Vassar, 2823 ... L8
- Vicksburg, 2320 ... N5
- Wakefield, 2085 ... C7
- Walker, 21842 ... M4
- Warren, 138247 ... N9
- Watervliet, 1843 ... N4
- Wayland, 3939 ... M5
- W. Branch, 1926 ... J7
- Whitehall, 2884 ... L3
- Whitmore Lake, 6574 ... N8
- Williamston, 3441 ... M7
- Wixom, 13263 ... M8
- Wolf Lake, 4455 ... L4
- Wyoming, 69368 ... M5
- Yale, 2063 ... L9
- Ypsilanti, 22362 ... N8
- Zeeland, 5805 ... M4
- Zilwaukee, 1799 ... L7

MINNESOTA

PG. 25

CAPITAL
St. Paul

NICKNAME
Gopher State

POPULATION
4,919,479, rank 21

AREA
84,402 sq mi, rank 12

- Ada, 1657 ... D1
- Aitkin, 1984 ... E4
- Albany, 1796 ... F3
- Albert Lea, 18356 ... J4
- Alexandria, 8820 ... F2
- Annandale, 2684 ... G3
- Anoka, 18076 ... G4
- Appleton, 2871 ... G2
- Arlington, 2048 ... H3
- Aurora, 1850 ... C5
- Austin, 23314 ... J5
- Babbitt, 1670 ... C5
- Bagley, 1235 ... C2
- Barnesville, 2173 ... E1
- Baxter, 5555 ... E3
- Belle Plaine, 3789 ... H4
- Bemidji, 11917 ... C3
- Benson, 3376 ... G2
- Big Lake, 6063 ... G4
- Blooming Prairie, 1933 ... J4
- Bloomington, 85172 ... H4
- Blue Earth, 3621 ... J3
- Braham, 1276 ... F4
- Brainerd, 13178 ... E3
- Breckenridge, 3559 ... E1
- Buffalo, 10097 ... G4
- Caledonia, 2965 ... J6
- Cambridge, 5520 ... F4
- Canby, 1903 ... H1
- Cannon Falls, 3795 ... H5
- Chanhassen, 20321 ... G4
- Chaska, 17449 ... H4
- Chatfield, 2394 ... J5
- Chisholm, 4960 ... C5
- Clara City, 1393 ... G2
- Cloquet, 11201 ... E5
- Cohasset, 2481 ... D4
- Cokato, 2727 ... G3
- Cold Spr., 2975 ... G3
- Coon Rapids, 61607 ... G4
- Corcoran, 5630 ... G4
- Crookston, 8192 ... C1
- Crosby, 2299 ... E4
- Crosslake, 1893 ... E3
- Dawson, 1539 ... G2
- Detroit Lakes, 7348 ... D2
- Dilworth, 3001 ... D1
- Dodge Ctr., 2226 ... J5
- Duluth, 86918 ... E5
- E. Bethel, 10941 ... G4
- E. Grand Forks, 7501 ... C1
- Elbow Lake, 1275 ... F2
- Elk River, 16447 ... G4
- Ely, 3724 ... C5
- Eveleth, 3865 ... D5
- Eyota, 1644 ... J5
- Fairfax, 1295 ... H3
- Fairmont, 10889 ... J3
- Faribault, 20818 ... H4
- Farmington, 12365 ... H4
- Fergus Falls, 13471 ... E2
- Foley, 2154 ... F4
- Forest Lake, 15098 ... G5
- Fosston, 1575 ... C2
- Frazee, 1377 ... E2
- Fulda, 1283 ... J2
- Gaylord, 2279 ... H3
- Glencoe, 5453 ... H3
- Glenwood, 2594 ... F2
- Goodview, 3373 ... J6
- Grand Marais, 1353 ... C7
- Grand Rapids, 7764 ... D4
- Granite Falls, 3070 ... H2
- Hastings, 18204 ... H5
- Hawley, 1882 ... D1
- Hayfield, 1325 ... J5
- Hermantown, 7448 ... E5
- Hibbing, 17071 ... D5
- Hinckley, 1291 ... F5
- Howard Lake, 1853 ... G3
- Hoyt Lakes, 2082 ... C5
- Hutchinson, 13080 ... G3
- International Falls, 6703 B4
- Jackson, 3501 ... J3
- Janesville, 2109 ... J4
- Jordan, 3833 ... H4
- Kasson, 4398 ... J5
- Kenyon, 1661 ... H4
- La Crescent, 4923 ... J6
- Lake City, 4950 ... H5
- Lake Crystal, 2420 ... J3
- Lakefield, 1721 ... J2
- Lakeville, 43128 ... H4
- Le Center, 2240 ... H4
- Le Sueur, 3922 ... H4
- Litchfield, 6562 ... G3
- Little Falls, 7719 ... F3
- Long Prairie, 3040 ... F3
- Luverne, 4617 ... J1
- Madelia, 2340 ... J3
- Madison, 1768 ... G1
- Mankato, 32427 ... J4
- Mapleton, 1678 ... J4
- Marshall, 12735 ... H2
- Melrose, 3091 ... F3
- Milaca, 2580 ... F4
- Minneapolis, 382618 ... G4
- Minneota, 1449 ... H2
- Montevideo, 5346 ... G2
- Montgomery, 2794 ... H4
- Monticello, 7868 ... G4
- Moorhead, 32177 ... D1
- Moose Lake, 2239 ... E5
- Mora, 3193 ... F4
- Morris, 5068 ... F2
- Mtn. Iron, 2999 ... C5
- Mtn. Lake, 2082 ... J3
- New Prague, 4559 ... H4
- New Ulm, 13594 ... H3
- Nisswa, 1953 ... E3
- N. Branch, 8023 ... F5
- Northfield, 17147 ... H4
- Norwood Young America, 3108 ... H4
- Olivia, 2570 ... H3
- Ortonville, 2158 ... G1
- Osakis, 1567 ... F2
- Otsego, 6389 ... G4
- Owatonna, 22434 ... J4
- Park Rapids, 3276 ... D3
- Paynesville, 2267 ... G3
- Pelican Rapids, 2374 ... E2
- Perham, 2559 ... E2
- Pierz, 1277 ... F3
- Pine City, 3043 ... F5
- Pine Island, 2337 ... J5
- Pipestone, 4280 ... J1
- Plainview, 3190 ... J5
- Preston, 1426 ... J5
- Princeton, 3933 ... F4
- Prior Lake, 15917 ... H4
- Ramsey, 18510 ... G4
- Red Lake, 1430 ... C3
- Red Lake Falls, 1590 ... C1
- Red Wing, 16116 ... H5
- Redwood Falls, 5459 ... H2
- Renville, 1323 ... H2
- Rochester, 85806 ... J5
- Roseau, 2756 ... A2
- Rush City, 2102 ... F5
- Rushford, 1696 ... J6
- St. Charles, 3295 ... J5
- St. Cloud, 59107 ... F3
- St. Francis, 4910 ... G4
- St. James, 4695 ... J3
- St. Joseph, 4681 ... F3
- St. Michael, 9099 ... G4
- St. Paul, 287151 ... G4
- St. Peter, 9747 ... H4
- Sandstone, 1549 ... F5
- Sartell, 9641 ... F3
- Sauk Centre, 3930 ... F3
- Sauk Rapids, 10213 ... F3
- Shakopee, 20568 ... H4
- Silver Bay, 2068 ... D6
- Slayton, 2072 ... J2
- Sleepy Eye, 3515 ... H3
- Springfield, 2215 ... H3
- Spring Grove, 1304 ... J6
- Spring Valley, 2518 ... J5
- Staples, 3104 ... E3
- Starbuck, 1314 ... F2
- Stewartville, 5411 ... J5
- Stillwater, 15143 ... G5
- Thief River Falls, 8410 ... B2
- Tracy, 2268 ... H2
- Truman, 1259 ... J3
- Two Harbors, 3613 ... D6
- Virginia, 9157 ... C5
- Wabasha, 2599 ... H5
- Wadena, 4294 ... E2
- Warren, 1678 ... B1
- Warroad, 1722 ... A2
- Waseca, 8493 ... J4
- Waterville, 1833 ... H4
- Wells, 2494 ... J4
- Wheaton, 1619 ... F1
- White Bear Lake, 24325 ... G4
- Willmar, 18351 ... G3
- Windom, 4490 ... J2
- Winnebago, 1487 ... J3
- Winona, 27069 ... J6
- Winthrop, 1367 ... H3
- Worthington, 11283 ... J2
- Zumbrota, 2789 ... H5

MISSISSIPPI

PG. 28

CAPITAL
Jackson

NICKNAME
Magnolia State

POPULATION
2,844,658, rank 31

AREA
47,689 sq mi, rank 32

- Aberdeen, 6415 ... C6
- Ackerman, 1696 ... D5
- Alcorn, 1200 ... G2
- Amory, 6956 ... C6
- Baldwyn, 3321 ... B6
- Batesville, 7113 ... B4
- Bay St. Louis, 8209 ... K5
- Bay Sprs., 2097 ... G5
- Belmont, 1961 ... B6
- Belzoni, 2663 ... D3
- Biloxi, 50644 ... K6
- Booneville, 8625 ... B6
- Brandon, 16436 ... F4
- Brookhaven, 9861 ... H3
- Bruce, 2097 ... C5
- Byram, 7386 ... F3
- Calhoun City, 1872 ... C5
- Canton, 12911 ... F4
- Carthage, 4637 ... E5
- Centreville, 1680 ... J2
- Charleston, 2198 ... C4
- Clarksdale, 20645 ... B3
- Cleveland, 13841 ... C3
- Clinton, 23347 ... F3
- Coldwater, 1674 ... A4
- Collins, 2683 ... H4
- Collinsville, 1823 ... F5
- Columbia, 6603 ... H4
- Columbus, 25944 ... D6
- Como, 1310 ... B4
- Corinth, 14054 ... A6
- Crystal Sprs., 5873 ... G3
- Decatur, 1426 ... F5
- Diamondhead, 5912 ... K5
- Drew, 2434 ... C3
- Durant, 2932 ... E4
- Ellisville, 3465 ... H5
- Eupora, 2326 ... D5
- Fayette, 2242 ... G2
- Flora, 1546 ... F3
- Florence, 2396 ... G4
- Forest, 5987 ... F5
- Fulton, 3882 ... B6
- Gautier, 11681 ... K6
- Goodman, 1252 ... E4
- Greenville, 41633 ... D2
- Greenwood, 18425 ... D4
- Grenada, 14879 ... C4
- Gulfport, 71127 ... K5
- Hattiesburg, 44779 ... H5
- Hazlehurst, 4400 ... G3
- Hernando, 6812 ... A4
- Hollandale, 3437 ... D3
- Holly Sprs., 7957 ... A5
- Horn Lake, 14099 ... A4
- Houston, 4079 ... C5
- Indianola, 12066 ... D3
- Itta Bena, 2208 ... D3
- Iuka, 3059 ... A6
- Jackson, 184256 ... F4
- Jonestown, 1701 ... B3
- Kiln, 2040 ... K5
- Kosciusko, 7372 ... E4
- Lambert, 1967 ... B3
- Laurel, 18393 ... G5
- Leland, 5502 ... D2
- Lexington, 2025 ... E4
- Long Beach, 17320 ... K5
- Louisville, 7006 ... E5
- Lucedale, 2458 ... J6
- Lumberton, 2228 ... J5
- Macon, 2461 ... E6
- Madison, 14692 ... F4
- Magee, 4200 ... G4
- Magnolia, 2071 ... J3
- Marion, 1305 ... F6
- Marks, 1551 ... B3
- McComb, 13337 ... H3
- Mendenhall, 2555 ... G4
- Meridian, 39968 ... F6
- Monticello, 1726 ... H4
- Moorhead, 2573 ... D3
- Morton, 3482 ... F4
- Moss Pt., 15851 ... K6
- Mound Bayou, 2102 ... C3
- Natchez, 18464 ... H2
- New Albany, 7607 ... B5
- Newton, 3699 ... F5
- Nicholson, 1400 ... K4
- Ocean Sprs., 17225 ... K5
- Okolona, 3056 ... C6
- Olive Branch, 21054 ... A4
- Oxford, 11756 ... B4
- Pascagoula, 26200 ... K6
- Pass Christian, 6579 ... K5
- Pearl, 21961 ... F4
- Pelahatchie, 1461 ... F4
- Petal, 7579 ... H5
- Philadelphia, 7303 ... E5
- Picayune, 10535 ... K4
- Pickens, 1325 ... E4
- Pontotoc, 5253 ... B5
- Poplarville, 2601 ... J4
- Port Gibson, 1840 ... G2
- Purvis, 2164 ... J5
- Quitman, 2463 ... G6
- Raleigh, 1255 ... G5
- Raymond, 1664 ... F3
- Ridgeland, 20173 ... F4
- Ripley, 5478 ... A5
- Rolling Fork, 2486 ... E3
- Rosedale, 2414 ... C2
- Ruleville, 3234 ... C3
- Saltillo, 3393 ... B6
- Sardis, 2038 ... B4
- Saucier, 1303 ... K5
- Senatobia, 6682 ... B4
- Shannon, 1657 ... C6
- Shaw, 2312 ... D3
- Shelby, 2926 ... C3
- Southaven, 28977 ... A4
- Starkville, 21869 ... D6
- Summit, 1428 ... H3
- Taylorsville, 1341 ... G5
- Tchula, 2332 ... D3
- Tupelo, 34211 ... B6
- Tutwiler, 1364 ... C3
- Tylertown, 1910 ... J4
- Union, 2021 ... F5
- Vancleave, 4910 ... K6
- Verona, 3334 ... B6
- Vicksburg, 26407 ... F3
- Water Valley, 3677 ... C4
- Waynesboro, 5197 ... G6
- Wesson, 1693 ... H3
- W. Point, 12145 ... D6
- Wiggins, 3849 ... J5
- Winona, 5482 ... D4
- Yazoo City, 14550 ... E3

MISSOURI

PG. 29

CAPITAL
Jefferson City

NICKNAME
Show Me State

POPULATION
5,595,211, rank 17

AREA
69,697 sq mi, rank 19

- Adrian, 1780 ... D3
- Albany, 1937 ... A3
- Anderson, 1856 ... G3
- Arnold, 19965 ... D8
- Ash Grove, 1430 ... F4
- Ashland, 1869 ... C6
- Aurora, 7014 ... F4
- Ava, 3021 ... F5
- Belton, 21730 ... C3
- Bernie, 1777 ... G9
- Bethany, 3087 ... A3
- Bismarck, 1470 ... E8
- Bloomfield, 1952 ... F9
- Blue Sprs., 48080 ... C3
- Bolivar, 9143 ... E4
- Bonne Terre, 4039 ... E8
- Boonville, 8202 ... C5
- Bowling Green, 3260 ... C7
- Branson, 6050 ... G4
- Brookfield, 4769 ... B5
- Buffalo, 2781 ... E5
- Butler, 4209 ... D3
- Cabool, 2168 ... F6
- California, 4005 ... D5
- Camdenton, 2779 ... E5
- Cameron, 8312 ... B3
- Campbell, 1883 ... G9
- Canton, 2557 ... A7
- Cape Girardeau, 35349 ... F9
- Carrollton, 4122 ... C4
- Carthage, 12668 ... F3
- Caruthersville, 6760 ... G9
- Cassville, 2890 ... G3
- Cedar Hill, 1703 ... D8
- Centralia, 3774 ... C6
- Chaffee, 3044 ... F9
- Charleston, 4732 ... F10
- Chesterfield, 46802 ... D8
- Chillicothe, 8968 ... B4
- Clinton, 9311 ... D4
- Columbia, 84531 ... C6
- Concordia, 2360 ... C4
- Cuba, 3230 ... E7
- De Soto, 6375 ... D8
- Dexter, 7356 ... F9
- Dixon, 1570 ... E6
- Doniphan, 1932 ... G8
- E. Prairie, 3227 ... F10
- Eldon, 4895 ... D5
- El Dorado Sprs., 3775 ... E3
- Elsberry, 2047 ... C8
- Eureka, 7676 ... D8
- Excelsior Sprs., 10847 ... C3
- Farmington, 13924 ... E8
- Fayette, 2793 ... C5
- Festus, 9660 ... D8
- Forsyth, 1686 ... G4
- Fredericktown, 3928 ... E8
- Fulton, 12128 ... C6
- Gallatin, 1789 ... B3
- Garden City, 1500 ... D3
- Granby, 2121 ... F3
- Grandview, 24881 ... C3
- Hamilton, 1813 ... B3
- Hannibal, 17757 ... B7
- Harrisonville, 8946 ... D3
- Hayti, 3207 ... G9
- Hermann, 2674 ... D7
- Higginsville, 4682 ... C4
- Hillsboro, 1675 ... D8
- Holden, 2510 ... D3
- Hollister, 3867 ... G4
- Holts Summit, 2935 ... D6
- Houston, 1992 ... F6
- Huntsville, 1553 ... B5
- Independence, 113288 ... C3
- Ironton, 1471 ... E8
- Jackson, 11947 ... F9
- Jefferson City, 39636 ... D6
- Joplin, 45504 ... F3
- Kahoka, 2241 ... A6
- Kansas City, 441545 ... C3
- Kennett, 11260 ... G9
- Kirksville, 16988 ... A5
- Knob Noster, 2462 ... D4
- Lake Ozark, 1489 ... D5
- Lamar, 4425 ... E3
- La Plata, 1486 ... B5
- Lathrop, 2092 ... B3
- Lawson, 2336 ... B3
- Lebanon, 12155 ... E5
- Lees Summit, 70700 ... C3
- Lexington, 4453 ... C3
- Licking, 1471 ... E6
- Louisiana, 3863 ... B7
- Macon, 5538 ... B5
- Malden, 4782 ... G9
- Marble Hill, 1502 ... F9
- Marceline, 2558 ... B5
- Marshall, 12433 ... C4
- Marshfield, 5720 ... F5
- Maryville, 10581 ... A2
- Memphis, 2061 ... A6
- Mexico, 11320 ... C6
- Milan, 1958 ... A4
- Moberly, 11945 ... C5
- Monett, 7396 ... F3
- Monroe City, 2588 ... B6
- Montgomery City, 2442 ... C7
- Mtn. Grove, 4574 ... F6
- Mtn. View, 2430 ... F6
- Mt. Vernon, 4017 ... F4
- Neosho, 10505 ... F3
- Nevada, 8607 ... E3
- New Haven, 1867 ... D7
- New Madrid, 3334 ... G9
- Nixa, 12124 ... F4
- Noel, 1480 ... G3
- Odessa, 4818 ... C3
- O'Fallon, 46169 ... C7
- Osage Beach, 3662 ... D5
- Owensville, 2500 ... D7
- Ozark, 9665 ... F4
- Pacific, 5482 ... D8
- Palmyra, 3467 ... B7
- Paris, 1529 ... B6
- Park Hills, 7861 ... E8
- Peculiar, 2604 ... D3
- Perryville, 7667 ... E9
- Pevely, 3768 ... D8
- Piedmont, 1992 ... F8
- Plattsburg, 2354 ... B3
- Pleasant Hill, 5582 ... C3
- Poplar Bluff, 16651 ... F8
- Portageville, 3295 ... G9
- Potosi, 2662 ... E8
- Republic, 8438 ... F4
- Rich Hill, 1461 ... D3
- Richland, 1805 ... E5
- Richmond, 6116 ... C3
- Rogersville, 1508 ... F5
- Rolla, 16367 ... E6
- St. Charles, 60321 ... C8
- St. Clair, 4390 ... D7
- Ste. Genevieve, 4476 ... E9
- St. James, 3704 ... E6
- St. Joseph, 73990 ... B2
- St. Louis, 348189 ... D8
- St. Peters, 51381 ... C8
- Salem, 4854 ... E7
- Salisbury, 1726 ... C5
- Savannah, 4762 ... B2
- Scott City, 4591 ... F9
- Sedalia, 20339 ... D4
- Senath, 1650 ... G8
- Seneca, 2135 ... F2
- Seymour, 1834 ... F5
- Shelbina, 1943 ... B6
- Sikeston, 16992 ... F9
- Slater, 2083 ... C5
- Smithville, 5514 ... C3
- Springfield, 151580 ... F4
- Steele, 2263 ... G9
- Steelville, 1429 ... E7
- Stockton, 1960 ... E4
- Sullivan, 6351 ... D7
- Sweet Sprs., 1628 ... C4
- Tarkio, 1935 ... A2
- Thayer, 2201 ... G7
- Tipton, 3261 ... D5
- Trenton, 6216 ... B4
- Troy, 6737 ... C7
- Union, 7757 ... D7
- Unionville, 2041 ... A5
- Vandalia, 2529 ... C7
- Versailles, 2565 ... D5
- Warrensburg, 16340 ... C4
- Warrenton, 5281 ... C7
- Warsaw, 2070 ... D4
- Washington, 13243 ... D7
- Waynesville, 3507 ... E6
- Webb City, 9812 ... F3
- Wellsville, 1423 ... C7
- Wentzville, 6896 ... C7
- W. Plains, 10866 ... G6
- Willard, 3193 ... F4
- Willow Sprs., 2147 ... F6
- Windsor, 3087 ... D4

MONTANA

PG. 30

CAPITAL
Helena

NICKNAME
Treasure State

POPULATION
902,195, rank 44

AREA
147,046 sq mi, rank 4

- Absarokee, 1234 ... E6
- Anaconda, 9417 ... E3
- Arlee, 602 ... D2
- Ashland, 464 ... E8
- Baker, 1695 ... D10
- Belgrade, 5728 ... E4
- Belt, 633 ... C5
- Bigfork, 1421 ... C2
- Big Sandy, 703 ... C5
- Big Sky, 1221 ... E4
- Big Timber, 1650 ... E5
- Billings, 89847 ... E7
- Boulder, 1300 ... E4
- Box Elder, 794 ... B5
- Bozeman, 27509 ... E4
- Bridger, 745 ... E6
- Broadus, 451 ... E9
- Browning, 1065 ... B3
- Busby, 695 ... E8
- Butte, 34606 ... E3
- Cascade, 819 ... C4
- Chester, 871 ... B5
- Chinook, 1386 ... B6
- Choteau, 1781 ... C4
- Circle, 644 ... C9
- Clancy, 1406 ... D4
- Colstrip, 2346 ... E8
- Columbia Falls, 3645 ... B2
- Columbus, 1748 ... E6
- Conrad, 2753 ... C4
- Crow Agency, 1552 ... E7
- Culbertson, 716 ... B10
- Cut Bank, 3105 ... B4
- Darby, 710 ... E2
- Deer Lodge, 3421 ... D3
- Dillon, 3752 ... F3
- E. Helena, 1642 ... D4
- Ennis, 840 ... E4
- Eureka, 1017 ... B1
- Evergreen, 6215 ... B2
- Fairfield, 659 ... C4
- Fairview, 709 ... C10
- Florence, 901 ... D2
- Forsyth, 1944 ... D8
- Ft. Belknap Agency, 1262 ... B6
- Ft. Benton, 1594 ... C5
- Frazer, 452 ... C8
- Fromberg, 486 ... E6
- Gardiner, 851 ... F5
- Glasgow, 3253 ... B8
- Glendive, 4729 ... D10
- Grantsdale, 750 ... D2
- Great Falls, 56690 ... C4
- Hamilton, 3705 ... D2
- Hardin, 3384 ... E7
- Harlem, 848 ... B6
- Harlowton, 1062 ... D5
- Havre, 9621 ... B6
- Hays, 702 ... C6
- Heart Butte, 698 ... B3
- Helena, 25780 ... D4
- Hot Sprs., 531 ... C2
- Joliet, 575 ... E6
- Kalispell, 14223 ... B2
- Lame Deer, 2018 ... E8
- Laurel, 6255 ... E6
- Lewistown, 5813 ... D6
- Libby, 2626 ... B1
- Lincoln, 1100 ... D3
- Livingston, 6851 ... E5
- Lodge Grass, 510 ... E7
- Lolo, 3388 ... D2
- Malta, 2120 ... B7
- Manhattan, 1396 ... E4
- Miles City, 8487 ... D9
- Missoula, 57053 ... D2
- Pablo, 1814 ... C2
- Philipsburg, 914 ... D3
- Plains, 1126 ... C2
- Plentywood, 2061 ... B10
- Polson, 4041 ... C2
- Poplar, 911 ... C9
- Pryor, 628 ... E7
- Red Lodge, 2177 ... F6
- Ronan, 1812 ... C2
- Roundup, 1931 ... D7
- St. Ignatius, 788 ... C2
- Scobey, 1082 ... B9
- Seeley Lake, 1436 ... D3
- Shelby, 3216 ... B4
- Sheridan, 659 ... E4
- Sidney, 4774 ... C10
- Somers, 556 ... C2
- Stanford, 454 ... D5
- Stevensville, 1553 ... D2
- Superior, 893 ... C2
- Terry, 611 ... D9
- Thompson Falls, 1321 ... C1
- Three Forks, 1728 ... E4
- Townsend, 1867 ... D4
- Troy, 957 ... B1
- Ulm, 750 ... C4
- Valier, 498 ... B4
- Vaughn, 701 ... C4
- W. Yellowstone, 1177 ... F4
- Whitefish, 5032 ... B2
- Whitehall, 1044 ... E4
- White Sulphur Sprs., 984 ... D5
- Wibaux, 567 ... D10
- Wolf Pt., 2663 ... C9

NEBRASKA

PG. 31

CAPITAL
Lincoln

NICKNAME
Cornhusker State

POPULATION
1,711,263, rank 38

AREA
77,355 sq mi, rank 15

- Ainsworth, 1862 ... C5
- Albion, 1797 ... D7
- Alliance, 8959 ... C2
- Alma, 1214 ... F6
- Arapahoe, 1028 ... F5
- Arlington, 1197 ... D9
- Ashland, 2262 ... E9
- Atkinson, 1244 ... C6
- Auburn, 3350 ... E10
- Aurora, 4225 ... E7
- Battle Creek, 1158 ... C8
- Bayard, 1247 ... D1
- Beatrice, 12496 ... F9
- Bellevue, 44382 ... D10
- Benkelman, 1006 ... F3
- Blair, 7512 ... D9
- Bloomfield, 1126 ... C8
- Blue Hill, 867 ... F7
- Bridgeport, 1594 ... D2
- Broken Bow, 3491 ... D5
- Burwell, 1130 ... D6
- Cambridge, 1041 ... F5
- Central City, 2998 ... E7
- Ceresco, 920 ... E9
- Chadron, 5634 ... B2
- Chappell, 983 ... E2
- Clay Ctr., 861 ... E7
- Columbus, 20971 ... D8
- Cozad, 4163 ... E5
- Crawford, 1107 ... B1
- Creighton, 1270 ... C7
- Crete, 6028 ... E8
- Dakota City, 1821 ... C9
- David City, 2597 ... D8
- Deshler, 879 ... F8
- Eagle, 1105 ... E9
- Elkhorn, 6062 ... D9
- Elm Creek, 894 ... E6
- Fairbury, 4262 ... F8
- Falls City, 4671 ... F10
- Franklin, 1026 ... F6
- Fremont, 25174 ... D9
- Friend, 1174 ... E8
- Fullerton, 1378 ... D7
- Geneva, 2226 ... E8
- Genoa, 981 ... D8
- Gering, 7751 ... D1
- Gibbon, 1759 ... E6
- Gordon, 1756 ... B3
- Gothenburg, 3619 ... E5
- Grand Island, 42940 ... E7
- Grant, 1225 ... E3
- Hartington, 1640 ... C8
- Hastings, 24064 ... E7
- Hebron, 1565 ... F8
- Hemingford, 993 ... C2
- Henderson, 986 ... E8
- Hickman, 1084 ... E9
- Holdrege, 5636 ... F6
- Humboldt, 941 ... F10
- Imperial, 1982 ... E3
- Kearney, 27431 ... E6
- Kimball, 2559 ... D1
- Laurel, 986 ... C8
- Lexington, 10011 ... E5
- Lincoln, 225581 ... E9
- Loup City, 996 ... D6
- Lyons, 963 ... C9
- Macy, 956 ... C9
- Madison, 2367 ... D8
- McCook, 7994 ... F4
- Milford, 2070 ... E8
- Minden, 2964 ... E6
- Mitchell, 1831 ... C1
- Morrill, 957 ... C1
- Nebraska City, 7228 ... E10
- Neligh, 1651 ... C7
- Norfolk, 23516 ... C8
- N. Bend, 1213 ... D9
- N. Platte, 23878 ... E4
- Oakland, 1367 ... D9
- Ogallala, 4930 ... E3
- Omaha, 390007 ... D10
- O'Neill, 3733 ... C7
- Ord, 2269 ... D6
- Osceola, 921 ... D8
- Oshkosh, 887 ... D2
- Oxford, 876 ... F5
- Papillion, 16363 ... D9
- Pawnee City, 1033 ... F9
- Pender, 1148 ... C9
- Pierce, 1774 ... C8
- Plainview, 1353 ... C7
- Plattsmouth, 6887 ... E10
- Ponca, 1062 ... C9
- Randolph, 955 ... C8
- Ravenna, 1341 ... E6
- Red Cloud, 1131 ... F7
- Rushville, 999 ... B2
- St. Paul, 2218 ... D7
- Schuyler, 5371 ... D8
- Scottsbluff, 14732 ... D1
- Seward, 6319 ... E8
- Sidney, 6282 ... D2
- S. Sioux City, 11925 ... C9
- Springfield, 1450 ... E9
- Stanton, 1627 ... C8
- Stromsburg, 1232 ... E8
- Superior, 2055 ... F7
- Sutherland, 1129 ... D4
- Sutton, 1447 ... E7
- Syracuse, 1762 ... E9
- Tecumseh, 1716 ... E9
- Tekamah, 1892 ... D9
- Tilden, 1078 ... C7
- Valentine, 2820 ... B4
- Valley, 1788 ... D9
- Wahoo, 3942 ... D9
- Wakefield, 1411 ... C8
- Waverly, 2448 ... E9
- Wayne, 5583 ... C8
- Weeping Water, 1103 ... E9
- W. Point, 3660 ... D9
- Wilber, 1761 ... E8
- Wisner, 1270 ... C8
- Wood River, 1204 ... E7
- Wymore, 1656 ... F9
- York, 8081 ... E8

NEVADA

PG. 32

CAPITAL
Carson City

NICKNAME
Silver State

POPULATION
1,998,257, rank 35

AREA
110,561 sq mi, rank 7

- Austin, 600 ... D4
- Battle Mtn., 2871 ... C4
- Beatty, 1154 ... H4
- Blue Diamond, 282 ... J6
- Boulder City, 14966 ... J6
- Caliente, 1123 ... G6
- Cal Nev Ari, 278 ... K6
- Carlin, 2161 ... C5
- Carson City, 52457 ... E1
- Dayton, 5907 ... E2
- Elko, 16708 ... B5
- Ely, 4041 ... E6
- Empire, 499 ... C2
- Eureka, 550 ... D5
- Fallon, 7536 ... D2
- Fernley, 8959 ... D2
- Gabbs, 318 ... E3
- Gardnerville, 3357 ... E1
- Gerlach, 499 ... C2
- Hawthorne, 3311 ... F2
- Henderson, 175381 ... J6
- Imlay, 300 ... C3
- Incline Vil., 9952 ... E1
- Indian Sprs., 1302 ... H5
- Jackpot, 1100 ... A6
- Las Vegas, 478434 ... J6
- Laughlin, 7076 ... K6
- Lovelock, 2003 ... C3
- McGill, 1054 ... D6
- Mesquite, 9389 ... H7
- Mill City, 300 ... C3
- Mina, 275 ... F3
- Minden, 2836 ... E1
- Nixon, 418 ... D2
- N. Las Vegas, 115488 ... J6
- Overton, 1700 ... H6
- Owyhee, 1017 ... A5
- Pahrump, 24631 ... J5
- Panaca, 550 ... G6
- Pioche, 475 ... F6
- Reno, 180480 ... D1
- Round Mtn., 550 ... E4
- Ruth, 500 ... E6
- Schurz, 721 ... E2
- Searchlight, 576 ... K6
- Silver Sprs., 4708 ... D2
- Sparks, 66346 ... D1
- Spring Creek, 10548 ... C5
- Steamboat, 1100 ... D1
- Sun Valley, 19461 ... D1
- Sutcliffe, 281 ... D2
- Tonopah, 2627 ... F4
- Verdi, 2949 ... D1
- Virginia City, 800 ... D2
- Wadsworth, 881 ... D2
- Wells, 1346 ... B6
- W. Wendover, 4721 ... C7
- Winnemucca, 7174 ... B3
- Yerington, 2883 ... E2
- Zephyr Cove, 1649 ... E1

NEW HAMPSHIRE

PG. 33

CAPITAL
Concord

NICKNAME
Granite State

POPULATION
1,235,786, rank 41

AREA
9,279 sq mi, rank 44

- Alton, 650 ... G6
- Amherst, 1600 ... J5
- Antrim, 1389 ... J4
- Ashland, 1100 ... F5
- Belmont, 950 ... G5
- Berlin, 10331 ... D6
- Bethlehem, 700 ... D5
- Bristol, 1670 ... G5
- Brookline, 650 ... K5
- Canaan, 800 ... G4
- Center Ossipee, 650 ... F6
- Charlestown, 1145 ... H3
- Claremont, 13151 ... H3
- Colebrook, 1400 ... B5
- Concord, 40687 ... H5
- Contoocook, 1444 ... H5
- Conway, 1692 ... E6
- Derry, 22661 ... J6
- Dover, 26884 ... H7
- Durham, 9024 ... H6
- Enfield, 1698 ... G4
- Epping, 1673 ... J6
- Exeter, 9759 ... J6
- Farmington, 3468 ... G6
- Franklin, 8405 ... G5
- Goffstown, 2400 ... J5
- Gorham, 1773 ... D6
- Greenville, 1131 ... K4
- Groveton, 1197 ... C5
- Hampton, 9126 ... J7
- Hanover, 8162 ... F3
- Henniker, 1627 ... H4
- Hillsborough, 1842 ... H4
- Hinsdale, 1713 ... K3
- Hooksett, 3609 ... J5
- Hopkinton, 700 ... H5
- Hudson, 7814 ... K5
- Jaffrey, 2802 ... K4
- Keene, 22563 ... J3
- Kingston, 1700 ... J6
- Laconia, 16411 ... G5
- Lancaster, 1695 ... D5
- Lebanon, 12568 ... G4
- Lincoln, 750 ... E5
- Lisbon, 1070 ... E4
- Littleton, 4431 ... D5
- Londonderry, 11417 ... J6
- Manchester, 107006 ... J5
- Marlborough, 1089 ... J4
- Meredith, 1739 ... F5
- Merrimack, 1600 ... J5
- Milford, 8293 ... K5
- Milton, 950 ... G6
- Nashua, 86605 ... K5
- New London, 1000 ... G4
- Newmarket, 5124 ... J6
- Newport, 4008 ... H4
- N. Conway, 2069 ... E6
- Northfield, 2200 ... G5
- N. Woodstock, 750 ... E5
- Peterborough, 2944 ... J4
- Pinardville, 5779 ... J5
- Pittsfield, 1669 ... H6
- Plaistow, 2800 ... J6
- Plymouth, 3528 ... F5
- Portsmouth, 20784 ... J7
- Raymond, 2839 ... J6
- Rindge, 750 ... K4
- Rochester, 28461 ... H6
- Rollinsford, 1500 ... H7
- Rye, 1100 ... J7
- Rye Beach, 750 ... J7
- Salem, 28112 ... K6
- Sanbornville, 950 ... G6
- Seabrook, 2300 ... J7
- Somersworth, 11477 ... H7
- S. Hooksett, 5282 ... J5
- Sunapee, 750 ... G4
- Suncook, 5362 ... H5
- Tilton, 3231 ... G5
- Troy, 1300 ... J4
- Walpole, 700 ... J3
- Warner, 650 ... H4
- W. Swanzey, 1118 ... J3
- Whitefield, 1089 ... D5
- Wilton, 1236 ... J5
- Winchester, 1832 ... K3
- Wolfeboro, 2979 ... G6
- Woodsville, 1081 ... E4

NEW JERSEY

PG. 34

CAPITAL
Trenton

NICKNAME
Garden State

POPULATION
8,414,350, rank 9

AREA
7,787 sq mi, rank 46

- Absecon, 7638 ... H5
- Allentown, 1882 ... E4
- Alpha, 2482 ... C3
- Asbury Park, 16930 ... E6
- Atlantic City, 40517 ... J5
- Atlantic Highlands, 4705 ... D6
- Avalon, 2143 ... K4
- Bayonne, 61842 ... C6
- Beachwood, 10375 ... F5
- Belmar, 6045 ... E6
- Belvidere, 2771 ... C3
- Berlin, 6149 ... G3
- Bernardsville, 7345 ... C4
- Blackwood, 4692 ... G3
- Boonton, 8496 ... B5
- Bordentown, 3969 ... E4
- Bridgeton, 22771 ... H3
- Bridgewater, 3200 ... D4
- Brigantine, 12594 ... H5
- Browns Mills, 11257 ... F4
- Budd Lake, 8100 ... C4
- Buena, 3873 ... H3
- Burlington, 9736 ... F4
- Butler, 7420 ... B5
- Camden, 79904 ... F3
- Cape May, 4034 ... K3
- Cape May C.H., 4704 ... K4
- Chatham, 8460 ... C5
- Cherry Hill, 69300 ... F3
- Clayton, 7139 ... G3
- Clifton, 78672 ... C5
- Clinton, 2632 ... C3
- Cranford, 22578 ... C5
- Dayton, 6235 ... E5
- Dover, 18188 ... C4
- E. Brunswick, 46756 ... D5
- Eatontown, 14008 ... E6
- Edison, 97687 ... D5
- Egg Harbor City, 4545 ... H4
- Elizabeth, 120568 ... C5
- Englewood, 26203 ... B6
- Fairfield, 7063 ... C5
- Fairton, 2253 ... J3
- Flemington, 4200 ... D4
- Folsom, 1972 ... H4
- Forked River, 4914 ... G5
- Franklin, 5160 ... B4
- Freehold, 10976 ... E5
- Glassboro, 19068 ... G3
- Gloucester City, 11484 ... G3
- Hackensack, 42677 ... C6
- Hackettstown, 10403 ... C4
- Hamburg, 3105 ... A4
- Hammonton, 12604 ... H4
- High Bridge, 3776 ... C4
- Highlands, 5097 ... D6
- Hightstown, 5216 ... E5
- Hopatcong, 15888 ... B4
- Hopewell, 2035 ... D4
- Jamesburg, 6025 ... E5
- Jersey City, 240055 ... C6
- Keansburg, 10732 ... D6
- Lakehurst, 2522 ... F5
- Lakewood, 36065 ... F5
- Lambertville, 3868 ... E3
- Linden, 39394 ... D5
- Lindenwold, 17414 ... G3
- Little Silver, 6170 ... E6
- Livingston, 27391 ... C5
- Long Branch, 31340 ... E6
- Madison, 16530 ... C5
- Mahwah, 5200 ... B6
- Manahawkin, 2004 ... G5
- Manasquan, 6310 ... F6
- Manville, 10343 ... D4
- Margate City, 8193 ... J5
- Marlboro, 3300 ... E5
- Marlton, 10260 ... G3
- Matawan, 8910 ... E5
- Mays Landing, 2321 ... H4
- Medford, 3500 ... G4
- Medford Lakes, 4173 ... G4
- Metuchen, 12840 ... D5
- Middlesex, 13717 ... D5
- Millville, 26847 ... J3
- Moorestown, 13860 ... F3
- Morris Plains, 5236 ... C5
- Morristown, 18544 ... C5
- Mt. Holly, 10600 ... F4
- Neptune City, 5218 ... E6
- Netcong, 2580 ... B4
- Newark, 273546 ... C5
- New Brunswick, 48573 D5
- New Egypt, 2519 ... F5
- New Providence, 11907 C5
- Newton, 8244 ... B4
- N. Cape May, 3618 ... K3
- Northfield, 7725 ... J4
- N. Wildwood, 4935 ... K4
- Oakland, 12466 ... B5
- Ocean City, 15378 ... J4
- Ogdensburg, 2638 ... B4
- Old Bridge, 22833 ... D5
- Paramus, 25737 ... B6
- Passaic, 67861 ... C6
- Paterson, 149222 ... B5
- Paulsboro, 6160 ... G3
- Pennington, 2696 ... E4
- Penns Grove, 4886 ... G2
- Pennsville, 11657 ... G2
- Perth Amboy, 47303 ... D5
- Phillipsburg, 15166 ... C3
- Pitman, 9331 ... G3
- Plainfield, 47829 ... D5
- Pleasantville, 19012 ... J5
- Pt. Pleasant, 19306 ... F6
- Port Monmouth, 3742 ... D6
- Princeton, 14203 ... E4
- Rahway, 26500 ... D5
- Ramsey, 14351 ... B5
- Red Bank, 11844 ... E6
- Ridgewood, 24936 ... B6
- Ringwood, 12396 ... A5
- Rio Grande, 2444 ... K4
- Rockaway, 6473 ... B5
- Rumson, 7137 ... E6
- Salem, 5857 ... H2
- Sayreville, 40377 ... D5
- Sea Girt, 2148 ... F6
- Sea Isle City, 2835 ... J4
- Seaside Hts., 3155 ... F6
- Seaside Park, 2263 ... F6
- Silverton, 9200 ... F6
- Smithville, 3100 ... H5
- Somerdale, 5192 ... G3
- Somers Pt., 11614 ... J4
- Somerville, 12423 ... D4
- S. River, 15322 ... D5
- Sparta, 9755 ... B4
- Spring Lake, 3567 ... E6
- Sussex, 2145 ... A4
- Swedesboro, 2055 ... G2
- Toms River, 86327 ... F5
- Trenton, 85403 ... E4
- Tuckerton, 3517 ... H5
- Union, 54405 ... C5
- Union City, 67088 ... C6
- Ventnor City, 12910 ... J5
- Villas, 9064 ... K3
- Vineland, 56271 ... H3
- Washington, 6712 ... C3
- Wayne, 54069 ... B5

Ortsregister

New Jersey – Oklahoma

OREGON
PG.45

CAPITAL
Salem

NICKNAME
Beaver State

POPULATION
3,421,399, rank 28

AREA
97,073 sq mi, rank 10

PENNSYLVANIA
PG. 46–47

CAPITAL
Harrisburg

NICKNAME
Keystone State

POPULATION
12,281,054, rank 6

AREA
45,308 sq mi, rank 33

RHODE ISLAND
PG. 12–13

CAPITAL
Providence

NICKNAME
Ocean State

POPULATION
1,048,319, rank 43

AREA
1,212 sq mi, rank 50

SOUTH CAROLINA
PG. 38–39

CAPITAL
Columbia

NICKNAME
Palmetto State

POPULATION
4,012,012, rank 26

AREA
31,113 sq mi, rank 40

SOUTH DAKOTA
PG. 41

CAPITAL
Pierre

NICKNAME
Mount Rushmore State

POPULATION
754,844, rank 46

AREA
77,116 sq mi, rank 16

TENNESSEE
PG. 20–21

CAPITAL
Nashville

NICKNAME
Volunteer State

POPULATION
5,689,283, rank 16

AREA
42,144 sq mi, rank 34

TEXAS
PG. 48–49

CAPITAL
Austin

NICKNAME
Lone Star State

POPULATION
20,851,820, rank 2

AREA
266,807 sq mi, rank 2

Ortsregister

Texas – Wyoming

UTAH
PG. 50
CAPITAL
Salt Lake City
NICKNAME
Beehive State
POPULATION
2,233,169, rank 34
AREA
84,899 sq mi, rank 11

VERMONT
PG. 33
CAPITAL
Montpelier
NICKNAME
Green Mountain State
POPULATION
608,827, rank 49
AREA
9,614 sq mi, rank 43

VIRGINIA
PG. 52–53
CAPITAL
Richmond
NICKNAME
Old Dominion
POPULATION
7,078,515, rank 12
AREA
40,767, rank 36

WASHINGTON
PG. 51
CAPITAL
Olympia
NICKNAME
Evergreen State
POPULATION
5,894,121, rank 15
AREA
68,138 sq mi, rank 20

WEST VIRGINIA
PG. 52–53
CAPITAL
Charleston
NICKNAME
Mountain State
POPULATION
1,808,344, rank 37
AREA
24,231 sq mi, rank 41

WISCONSIN
PG. 54
CAPITAL
Madison
NICKNAME
Badger State
POPULATION
5,363,675, rank 18
AREA
56,153 sq mi, rank 26

WYOMING
PG. 55
CAPITAL
Cheyenne
NICKNAME
Equality State
POPULATION
493,782, rank 50
AREA
97,809 sq mi, rank 9

Canada

ALBERTA
PG. 59
CAPITAL
Edmonton
POPULATION
2,974,807, rank 4
AREA
255,541 sq mi, rank 6

BRITISH COLUMBIA
PG. 58–59
CAPITAL
Victoria
POPULATION
3,907,738, rank 3
AREA
364,764 sq mi, rank 5

MANITOBA
PG. 61
CAPITAL
Winnipeg
POPULATION
1,119,583, rank 5
AREA
250,116 sq mi, rank 8

NEW BRUNSWICK
PG. 66
CAPITAL
Fredericton
POPULATION
729,498, rank 8
AREA
28,150 sq mi, rank 11

NEWFOUNDLAND & LAB.
PG. 67
CAPITAL
St. John's
POPULATION
512,930, rank 9
AREA
156,453 sq mi, rank 10

NORTHWEST TERRITORIES
PG. 56
CAPITAL
Yellowknife
POPULATION
37,360, rank 11
AREA
519,734 sq mi. rank 3

NOVA SCOTIA
PG. 66–67
CAPITAL
Halifax
POPULATION
908,007, rank 7
AREA
21,345 sq mi, rank 12

NUNAVUT
PG. 56–57
CAPITAL
Iqaluit
POPULATION
26,745, rank 13
AREA
808,185 sq mi, rank 1

ONTARIO
PG. 62–63
CAPITAL
Toronto
POPULATION
11,410,046, rank 1
AREA
415,598 sq mi, rank 4

PRINCE EDWARD ISLAND
PG. 66–67
CAPITAL
Charlottetown
POPULATION
135,294, rank 10
AREA
2,185 sq mi, rank 13

QUÉBEC
PG. 64–65
CAPITAL
Québec
POPULATION
7,237,479, rank 2
AREA
595,391 sq mi, rank 2

* City indexed to pg. 66

SASKATCHEWAN
PG. 60–61
CAPITAL
Regina
POPULATION
978,933, rank 6
AREA
251,366 sq mi, rank 7

YUKON TERRITORY
PG. 56
CAPITAL
Whitehorse
POPULATION
28,674, rank 12
AREA
186,272 sq mi, rank 9

Mexico

MEXICO
PG. 68
CAPITAL
Mexico City
POPULATION
95,772,462
AREA
756,066 sq mi

Puerto Rico

PUERTO RICO
PG. 68
CAPITAL
San Juan
POPULATION
3,808,610
AREA
3,435 sq mi

Quellen/Tourismus-Informationen

TOURISM INFORMATION

Alabama
Alabama Bureau of Tourism & Travel
401 Adams Ave., P.O. Box 4927
Montgomery, AL 36103
800.252.2262, 334.242.4169
www.800alabama.com

Alaska
Alaska Travel Industry Association
2600 Cordova St., Suite 201
Anchorage, AK 99503-2745
800.862.5275
www.travelalaska.com

Arizona
Arizona Office of Tourism
1110 W. Washington, Suite 155
Phoenix, AZ 85007
866.275.5816, 602.374.3700
www.arizonaguide.com

Arkansas
Arkansas Dept. of Parks & Tourism
One Capitol Mall, Department 7701
Little Rock, AR 72201
800.628.8725, 501.682.7777
www.arkansasstateparks.com

California
California Division of Tourism
980 9th St., Suite 480
Sacramento, CA 95814
800.862.2543, 916.444.4429
www.visitcalifornia.com

Colorado
Colorado Tourism Office
1625 Broadway, Suite 2700
Denver, CO 80202
800.265.6723, 303.892.3885
www.colorado.com

Connecticut
Connecticut Office of Tourism
1 Financial Plaza
755 Main St
Hartford, CT 06103
888.288.4748, 860.256.2800
www.ctvisit.com

Delaware
Delaware Tourism Office
99 Kings Hwy
Dover, DE 19901
866.284.7483, 302.739.4271
www.visitdelaware.com

Florida
Visit Florida
661 E. Jefferson St., Suite 300
Tallahassee, FL 32301
850.488.5607, 888.735.2872
www.visitflorida.com

Georgia
Georgia Department of Industry, Trade &Tourism
75 Fifth St. NW, Suite 1200
Atlanta, GA 30308
800.847.4842
www.georgia.org/travel

Hawaii
Hawaii Visitors & Conv. Bureau
2270 Kalakaua Ave., 8th Floor
Honolulu, HI 96815
800.464.2924, 808.923.1811
www.gohawaii.com

Idaho
Idaho Department of Commerce
700 W. State St.
P.O. Box 83720
Boise, ID 83720-0093
800.635.7820, 208.334.2470
www.visitid.org

Illinois
Illinois Bureau of Tourism
100 W. Randolph St., Suite 3-400
Chicago, IL 60601
800.406.6418
www.enjoyillinois.com

Indiana
Indiana Tourism
1 N. Capitol Ave., Suite 700
Indianapolis, IN 46204
800.759.9191, 317.232.8860
www.enjoyindiana.com

Iowa
Iowa Division of Tourism
200 E. Grand Ave.
Des Moines, IA 50309
888.472.6035, 515.242.4705
www.traveliowa.com

Kansas
Kansas Travel & Tourism
1000 S.W. Jackson St., Suite 100
Topeka, KS 66612-1354
800.252.6727, 785.296.2009
www.travelks.com

Kentucky
Department of Tourism
Capital Plaza Tower
500 Mero St., Suite 2200
Frankfort, KY 40601
800.225.8747, 502.564.4930
www.kentuckytourism.com

Louisiana
Louisiana Office of Tourism
1051 N. 3rd St.
Baton Rouge, LA 70802
225.342.8119
www.louisianatravel.com

Maine
Maine Office of Tourism & Film
59 State House Station
Augusta, ME 04333-0059
888.624.6345, 207.624.7843
www.visitmaine.com

Maryland
Maryland Office of Tourism Develop.
217 E. Redwood St., 9th Floor
Baltimore, MD 21202
877.333.4455
www.visitmaryland.org

Massachusetts
Massachusetts Office of Travel & Tourism
10 Park Plaza, Suite 4510
Boston, MA 02116
800.227.6277, 617.973.8500
www.massvacation.com

Michigan
Travel Michigan
300 N. Washington Square, 2nd Floor
Lansing, MI 48913
888.784.7328, 517.373.0670
www.michigan.org

Minnesota
Minnesota Tourism
100 Metro Square
121 Seventh Place East
St. Paul, MN 55101
888.868.7476, 651.296.5029
www.exploreminnesota.com

Mississippi
Mississippi Development Authority/Tourism
PO Box 849
Jackson, MS 39205
866.733.6477, 601.359.3297
www.visitmississippi.org

Missouri
Missouri Division of Tourism
PO Box 1055
Jefferson City, MO 65102
800.519.2100, 573.751.4133
www.visitmo.com

Montana
Travel Montana
301 South Park
PO Box 200533
Helena, MT 59620
800.847.4868, 406.841.2870
www.visitmt.com

Nebraska
Nebraska Travel & Tourism
PO Box 98907
Lincoln, NE 68509-8907
877.632.7275, 402.471.3796
www.visitnebraska.org

Nevada
Nevada Commission on Tourism
401 N. Carson St.
Carson City, NV 89701
800.638.2328, 775.687.4322
www.travelnevada.com

New Hampshire
New Hampshire Division of Travel & Tourism Development
172 Pembroke Rd., PO Box 1856
Concord, NH 03302
800.386.4664, 603.271.2665
www.visitnh.gov

New Jersey
New Jersey Office of Travel & Tourism
PO Box 820
Trenton, NJ 08625-0820
800.847.4865, 609.777.0885
www.visitnj.org

New Mexico
New Mexico Department of Tourism
491 Old Santa Fe Trail
Santa Fe, NM 87503
800.545.2070, 505.827.7400
www.newmexico.org

New York
New York State Division of Tourism
PO Box 2603
Albany, NY 12220-0603
800.225.5697, 518.474.4116
www.iloveny.com

North Carolina
North Carolina Division of Tourism, Film & Sports Development
301 N. Wilmington St.
Raleigh, NC 27601
800.847.4862, 919.733.4171
www.visitnc.com

North Dakota
North Dakota Tourism
1600 E. Century Ave., Suite 2
P.O. Box 2057
Bismarck, ND 58503
800.435.5663, 701.328.2525
www.ndtourism.com

Ohio
Ohio Division of Travel & Tourism
77 S. High St., 29th Floor
Columbus, OH 43215
800.282.5393, 614-466-8844
www.discoverohio.com

Oklahoma
Oklahoma Department of Tourism & Recreation
120 N. Robinson Ave., Suite 600
P.O. Box 52002
Oklahoma City, OK 73152-2002
800.652.6552, 405.230.8420
www.travelok.com

Oregon
Oregon Tourism Commission, d.b.a. Travel Oregon
670 Hawthorne Ave. SE, Suite 240
Salem, OR 97301
800.547.7842, 503.378.8850
www.traveloregon.com

Pennsylvania
Pennsylvania Tourism Office
Commonwealth Keystone Building
400 North St., 4th Floor
Harrisburg, PA 17120
800.847.4872
www.visitpa.com

Puerto Rico
Puerto Rico Tourism Company
P.O. Box 902-3960
#2 Paseo La Princesa
San Juan, PR 00902-3960
800.866.7827, 787.721.2400
www.gotopuertorico.com

Rhode Island
Rhode Island Tourism Division
1 W. Exchange St.
Providence, RI 02903
800.556.2484, 401.222.2601
www.visitrhodeisland.com

South Carolina
South Carolina Department of Parks, Recreation & Tourism
1205 Pendleton St., Room 505
Columbia, SC 29201
888.727.6453, 803.734.1700
www.discoversouthcarolina.com

South Dakota
South Dakota Department of Tourism
711 E. Wells Ave.
Pierre, SD 57501-3369
800.732.5682, 605.773.3301
www.travelsd.com

Tennessee
Tennessee Department of Tourist Development
312 8th Ave. N, 25th Floor
Nashville, TN 37243
800.462.8366, 615.741.2159
www.tnvacation.com

Texas
Texas Department of Economic Development, Tourism Division
PO Box 12728
Austin, TX 78711-2728
800.888.8839
www.traveltex.com

Utah
Utah Office of Tourism
300 N. State St.
Salt Lake City, UT 84114
800.200.1160, 801.538.1030
www.utah.com

Vermont
Vermont Department of Tourism & Marketing
National Life Building, Drawer 20
Montpelier, VT 05620-1501
800.837.6668, 802.828.3237
www.vermontvacation.com

Virginia
Virginia Tourism Corporation
901 E. Byrd St.
Richmond, VA 23219
800.847.4882, 804.786.4485
www.virginia.org

Virgin Islands
United States Virgin Islands Department of Tourism
PO Box 6400
St. Thomas, VI 00804
800.372.8784, 340.774.8784
www.usvitourism.vi

Washington
Dept. of Community Trade & Economic Development
Washington State Tourism Div.
PO Box 42525
Olympia, WA 98504-2525
800.544.1800
www.experiencewashington.com

Washington, DC
DC Convention and Tourism Corp.
901 7th St. NW, 4th Floor
Washington, DC 20001-3719
800.422.8644, 202.789.7000 or 7030
www.washington.org

West Virginia
West Virginia Division of Tourism
90 MacCorkle Ave. SW
South Charleston, WV 25303
800.225.5982, 304.558.2200
www.wvtourism.com

Wisconsin
Wisconsin Department of Tourism
201 W. Washington Ave.
Madison, WI 53703
800.432.8747, 608.266.2161
www.travelwisconsin.com

Wyoming
Wyoming Division of Tourism
I-25 at College Dr.
Cheyenne, WY 82002
800.225.5996, 307.777.7777
www.wyomingtourism.org

Alberta
Travel Alberta Canada
PO Box 2500
Edmonton, AB, Canada T5J 2Z4
800.252.3782, 780.427.4321
www.travelalberta.com

British Columbia
Tourism British Columbia
Box 9830
Stn. Prov. Govt.
Victoria, BC, Canada V8W 9W5
800.663.6000, 250.356.6363
www.hellobc.com

Manitoba
Travel Manitoba
155 Carlton St., Seventh Floor
Winnipeg, MB, Canada R3C 3H8
800.665.0040
www.travelmanitoba.com

New Brunswick
Tourism Communication Center
26 Roseberry St.
Campbellton, NB, Canada E3N 2G4
800.561.0123, 506.444.5205
www.tourismnewbrunswick.ca

Newfoundland & Labrador
Newfoundland & Labrador Tourism
PO Box 8730
St. John's, NL, Canada A1B 4K2
800.563.6353, 709.729.2830
www.gov.nl.ca/tourism

Nova Scotia
Tourism Nova Scotia
PO Box 456
Halifax, NS, Canada B3J 2R5
800.565.0000, 902.425.5781
www.novascotia.com

Ontario
Ontario Tourism
10th Floor, Hearst Block
900 Bay St.
Toronto, ON, Canada M7A 2E1
800.668.2746, 905.282.1721
www.ontariotravel.net

Prince Edward Island
PEI Tourism
53 Watts Ave., P.O. Box 940
Charlottetown, PE, Canada C1A 7M5
800.734.7529, 902.368.4444
www.gentleisland.com

Québec
Tourisme Québec
1255 Peel Street, 4th Floor, Room 400
PO Box 979
Montréal, QC, Canada H3B 4V4
877.266.5687, 514.873.2015
www.bonjourquebec.com

Saskatchewan
Tourism Saskatchewan
1922 Park St.
Regina, SK, Canada S4N 7M4
877.237.2273, 306.787.9600
www.sasktourism.com

Mexico
Mexico Ministry of Tourism
Ave. Presidente Masaryk 172
Col. Chapultepec Morales
11587 México, D.F. Mexico
800.446.3942
www.visitmexico.com

INTERNET LINKS

American Association of Botanical Gardens & Arboreta
www.aabga.org
Information and links to member gardens.

American Zoo & Aquarium Association
www.aza.org
Information and links to member zoos and aquariums.

Amtrak
www.amtrak.com
Information on fares and schedules.

AOL Box Office
www.aolboxoffice.com
Find event information and buy tickets to concerts, sports events, the arts and theater, family attractions, and other local entertainment choices.

Art Museum Network
www.amn.org
Links to museums and exhibition calendars.

Association of Science-Technology Centers
www.astc.org
Information and links to science centers in the United States and Canada.

CNN
www.cnn.com
The latest top news stories from the U.S. and around the world; including political, financial, sports, health, technology and entertainment news.

Digital City
www.digitalcity.com
Your local city resource, with information on dining, entertainment and other helpful subjects.

Federal Aviation Administration
www.faa.gov
Airport security information, trip preparation tips and links to airports and airlines worldwide.

Golf
www.golfcourse.com
From the publishers of *Golf Magazine*, this site provides useful information about golf courses throughout the United States and Canada; including tee times, course ratings, dress codes, locations, and fees.

Google.com
www.google.com/maps
Get free driving directions, interactive maps, and satellite/aerial imagery.Find local businesses. Click and drag maps to view adjacent sections immediately. View satellite image with or without map data.

Government of Canada
www.canada.gc.ca
The official website of the Canadian government; it includes information on travelling to Canada.

Major League Baseball
www.mlb.com
Team and schedule information.

Major League Soccer
www.mlsnet.com
Team and schedule information.

Meteorological Service of Canada
www.weatheroffice.ec.gc.ca
Find weather forecasts for cities and communities throughout Canada.

NASCAR
www.nascar.com
Information on drivers, tracks, and races for each NASCAR series.

National Basketball Association
www.nba.com
Team and schedule information.

National Football League
www.nfl.com
Team and schedule information.

National Hockey League
www.nhl.com
Team and schedule information.

National Register of Historic Places
www.nationalregisterofhistoric places.com
Official list of cultural resources worthy of preservation.

National Ski Areas Association
www.nsaa.org
Links to ski areas in the United States.

National Thoroughbred Racing Association
www.ntra.com
Links to race tracks in the United States, along with the latest news on the Breeders Cup and Triple Crown.

Parks Canada/Parcs Canada
www.parkscanada.gc.ca
Information about Canada's national parks, historic sites and heritage areas.

Scenic Highways
www.byways.org
Descriptions and maps of All-American Roads and National Scenic Byways.

Ski & Snowboard Canada
www.skicanada.org
Links to ski areas in Canada.

Theme Parks
www.themeparksonline.org
Information and links.

U.S. Department of State
www.state.gov
Information on passports, visas and travel abroad.

U.S. Department of Transportation
www.dot.gov
Information on road construction and conditions.

U.S. Fish & Wildlife Service
www.fws.gov
Links to National Wildlife Refuges.

U.S. Forest Service
www.fs.fed.us
Information and links to the national forests and grasslands nationwide.

U.S. National Park Service
www.nps.gov
Links to individual parks as well as campground and tour reservations

U.S. National Weather Service
www.nws.noaa.gov
National, regional and local weather information for the United States.

U.S. Postal Service
www.usps.com
Do you need to find a post office while on vacation or don't remember a zip code? This site will answer all of your U.S. Postal Service questions.

VIA Rail Canada
www.viarail.ca
Information on Canada's passenger rail system.

Virtual Museum Canada
www.virtualmuseum.ca
Information on museums and events in Canada.

BORDER CROSSING

Travel Advisory

As of December 31, 2006, all travelers to or from Canada, Mexico, Central and South America, and the Caribbean utilizing air or sea will be absolutely required to carry a passport. On December 31, 2007, this requirement will be extended to all land border crossings.

Canada

U.S. citizens entering Canada from the U.S. are required to present passports or proof of U.S. citizenship accompanied by photo identification. U.S. citizens entering from a third country must have a valid passport. Visas are not required for U.S. citizens entering from the U.S. for stays of up to 180 days. Naturalized citizens should travel with their naturalization certificates. Alien permanent residents of the U.S. must present their Alien Registration Cards. Individuals under the age of 18 and traveling alone should carry a letter from a parent or legal guardian authorizing their travel in Canada.

U.S. driver's licenses are valid in Canada, and U.S. citizens do not need to obtain an international driver's license. Proof of auto insurance, however, is required.

United States (from Canada)

Canadian citizens entering the U.S. are required to demonstrate proof of their citizenship, normally with a photo identification accompanied by a valid birth certificate or citizenship card. Passports or visas are not required for visits lasting less than six months; for visits exceeding six months, they are mandatory. Individuals under the age of 18 and traveling alone should carry notarized documentation, signed by both parents, authorizing their travel.

Canadian driver's licenses are valid in the U.S. for one year, and automobiles may enter free of payment or duty fees. Drivers need only provide customs officials with proof of vehicle registration, ownership, and insurance.

Mexico

U.S. citizens entering Mexico are required to present passports or proof of U.S. citizenship accompanied by photo identification. Passports are strongly recommended. Visas are not required for stays of up to 180 days. Naturalized citizens should travel with their naturalization certificates, and alien permanent residents must present their Alien Registration Cards. Individuals under the age of 18 traveling alone, with one parent, or with other adults must carry notarized parental authorization or valid custodial documents. All U.S. citizens visiting for up to 180 days must also procure a tourist card, obtainable from Mexican consulates, tourism offices, border crossing points, and airlines serving Mexico. However, tourist cards are not needed for visits shorter than 72 hours to areas within the Border Zone (extending approximately 25 km into Mexico)

U.S. driver's licenses are valid in Mexico.

Visitors who wish to drive beyond the Baja California Peninsula or the Border Zone must obtain a temporary import permit for their vehicles. To acquire a permit, one must submit evidence of citizenship and of the vehicle's title and registration, as well as a valid driver's license. A processing fee must be paid. Permits are available at any Mexican Army Bank (Banjercito) located at border crossings or selected Mexican consulates. Mexican law also requires the posting of a refundable bond, via credit card or cash, at the Banjercito to guarantee the departure of the vehicle. Do not deal with any individual operating outside of official channels.

All visitors driving in Mexico should be aware that U.S. auto insurance policies are not valid and that buying short-term tourist insurance is mandatory. Many U.S. insurance companies sell Mexican auto insurance. American Automobile Association (for members only) and Sanborn's Mexico Insurance (800.638.9423) are popular companies with offices at most U.S. border crossings.

Published by GeoNova Publishing, Inc.

GeoNova Publishing, Inc. is the publisher of this Atlas. The information contained herein is derived from a variety of third party sources. While every effort has been made to verify the information contained in such sources, the publisher assumes no responsibility for inconsistencies or inaccuracies in the data nor liability for any damages of any type arising from errors or omissions.

2., aktualisierte Auflage 2010
ISBN 978-3-86871-900-0

Reiseland Nordamerika-Informationen

Siebenmeilenstiefel müsste man haben, um in alle Winkel der USA und Kanadas vorzudringen und deren Vielfalt kennen zu lernen – so enorm sind die Dimensionen des Kontinents.

Dabei sind auf dem Gebiet der Fortbewegungsmittel beträchtliche Fortschritte gemacht worden. Zunächst holperte der Pony Express durch die Prärie, dann ratterte die Eisenbahn durch die Schluchten der Rocky Mountains. Doch erst die Route 66 sorgte für den Reisehimmel auf Erden. Der durch sie beförderte Mythos der amerikanischen Landstraße brachte plötzlich Metropolen und verträumte Nester, Hochburgen der Musik und Gletscherspalten, Kunst und Kakteen in bequeme Reichweiten. Seit dem Zweiten Weltkrieg hat sich daraus eine immer perfektere Infrastruktur entwickelt, ein ausgeklügeltes Versorgungsnetz zum Reisen auf eigene Faust. Ohne die für europäische Verhältnisse gewaltigen Distanzen des Landes wäre diese beispiellose Bewegungsfreiheit nie entstanden, die heute die Mobilität der nordamerikanischen Gesellschaft auszeichnet.

In keiner anderen Nation scheint das *On-the-road*-Gefühl, das stetige Unterwegssein und Umziehen, so in Fleisch und Blut übergegangen zu sein wie in den USA. »Amerikaner sind Wesen auf vier Rädern«, heißt es oft. Das gilt für die Kids in ihren verrückten Kisten und auf ihren Kult-Harleys ebenso wie für Mom and Dad im Mittelklassewagen oder die grauen Panther in ihren Wohnmobilen auf der Suche nach der ewigen Sonne.

Vor allem die Nationalparks bekommen das zu spüren. Von den Sümpfen Floridas bis zu den Gletschern Alaskas zählen diese Refugien natürlicher Schönheit längst zum festen Fundus des amerikanischen Freizeitdrangs. Vor allem in den USA sind die Nationalparks Magneten für Millionen. Erst sehr viel später entdeckte man den Unterhaltungswert der Städte: anfangs nach zaghafter Denkmalpflege, zuletzt aber vehement durch aufwendige Neubauten in Gestalt glitzernder Konsumtempel, riesiger Vergnügungsparks und hypermoderner Aquarien. Nordamerika 2008: ein Füllhorn für den Tourismus? Schon. Nur, von Saison zu Saison wird auch klarer: Dort, wo alle hinwollen, steht man sich schnell auf den Füßen oder aber in langen Warteschlangen. »Die Amerikaner lieben ihre Naturparks zu Tode«, klagt ein Ranger im kalifornischen Yosemite National Park. An vielen Atlantik- und Pazifikstränden sieht es nicht anders aus, wenn dort an Wochenenden Millionen freizeithungriger *beach boys* ebenso einfallen wie kinderreiche Familien. Sogar die stillen Wüsten sind nicht mehr still: *dune buggies* und anderes schweres Motorengerät pflügen dröhnend durch karges Terrain. Kurz, in einer hochmobilen Gesellschaft, in der jeder sein eigenes Transitsystem ist, hat die Reiselust nach und nach eine Topographie der Fettnäpfchen geschaffen, mit der sich auch europäische Gäste möglichst früh vertraut machen sollten. Also, ein bisschen Planung kann nicht schaden. Ob Campingplatz oder Nobelrestaurant, Kanu-Tour oder Opernabend, Fähre oder Ferien auf der Ranch: ohne Reservierung läuft selten etwas. Das gehört ganz einfach zu den nordamerikanischen Spielregeln.

An- und Einreise

Zur Einreise in die USA benötigen Besucher aus Deutschland, Österreich und der Schweiz (auch Babys und Kinder) einen **maschinenlesbaren Pass**, der mindestens bis zum Ende der geplanten Reise gültig sein muss. Für deutsche Staatsangehörige ist nur der rote Europapass zulässig (Keine vorläufigen Reisepässe, Kinderausweise oder Einträge in den Pässen der Eltern). Reisepässe, die nach dem 25. Okt. 2006 ausgestellt werden, müssen zusätzlich über **biometrische Daten** in Chipform verfügen. Das gilt jedoch nicht für Reisende, die ein Visum besitzen.

Seit Januar 2009 müssen USA-Reisende zusätzlich und mindestens 72 Stunden vor Reiseantritt, besser eine Woche vorher, online eine sogenannte **ESTA-Genehmigung** *(Electronic System for Travel Authorization)* beantragen, dies gilt auch für Kinder. Gehen Sie über www.usembassy.de zu dieser Online-Reiseanmeldung, die dort derzeit kostenlos bearbeitet wird. Dazu ist ein Fragebogen mit persönlichen und anderen Daten auszufüllen, der bisher während des Flugs ausgeteilt wurde. Die ESTA-Genehmigungsnummer wird dem Reisenden per E-Mail zugeschickt. Sie ist bis zu zwei Jahren oder bis zum Ablauf des Passes für mehrere Reisen gültig.

Am besten erkundigt man sich vor seiner Abreise nach den aktuellsten Bestimmungen unter www.usembassy.de.

Zu den strengeren Sicherheitsbestimmungen seit dem 11. Sept. 2001 gehört auch, dass **verschlossene Gepäckstücke** mit großer Wahrscheinlichkeit von den Behörden mit Gewalt aufgebrochen werden. Deshalb sollte man die Koffer besser mit einem Gurt sichern als ein Zahlenschloss zu benutzen.

Nonstopflüge verschiedener Fluggesellschaften erreichen aus Europa nach rund 7 Stunden Flugzeit (und 6 Stunden Zeitunterschied) meist am frühen Nachmittag die Ostküste: z. B. New York oder Washington. Die Westküste wird in ungefähr 11 Stunden (und 9 Stunden Zeitunterschied) angeflogen: z.B. Los Angeles oder San Francisco. Über preiswerte Sondertarife sowie Charterflüge informieren die Reisebüros.

Vor der Gepäckausgabe wartet der *immigration officer*, der Beamte der Einwanderungsbehörde, der einen **Fingerabdruck** ab- und ein **digitales Foto** aufnimmt. Er ist für die Festsetzung der Aufenthaltsdauer zuständig und erkundigt sich deshalb nach Zweck *(holiday)* und Dauer der Reise, häufig auch nach dem Rückflugticket und der finanziellen Ausstattung.

Die Autovermieter haben eigene, leicht erkennbare Pendelbusse, die Sie sofort und kostenlos zum jeweiligen Mietbüro bringen. An allen internationalen Flughäfen der USA und Kanadas gibt es Airport-Busse oder Schnellbahnen (San Francisco z.B.), die in die Stadt bzw. zu den wichtigsten Hotels fahren und erheblich preisgünstiger sind als Taxis. Oft haben die großen Hotelketten eigene *shuttle busses*, die Sie kostenlos vom Flughafen abholen. In den Schalterhallen finden Sie meist entsprechende (und gebührenfreie) Telefone für die Wagenbestellung.

Ärztliche Vorsorge

In den USA und in Kanada ist man automatisch Privatpatient, und die Arzt- bzw. Krankenhauskosten sind extrem hoch. Man sollte also tunlichst vorsorgen und sich zunächst bei seiner Krankenkasse nach einer Kostenerstattung erkundigen. Falls nicht alle in den USA erbrachten Leistungen übernommen werden, ist unbedingt eine **Auslandskrankenversicherung** anzuraten, die für Urlaubsreisen preiswert zu haben ist. Allerdings: auch wenn Sie versichert sind, in beiden Ländern Nordamerikas muss beim Arzt oder im Krankenhaus sofort bezahlt werden, meist sogar im Voraus.

Für solche Notfälle erweist sich eine Kreditkarte als unersetzlich. Erkundigen Sie sich gegebenenfalls auch bei Ihrem Kreditkartenunternehmen, welche Leistungen Ihre (oder eine andere) Karte im Krankheitsfall im Ausland einschließt.

Apotheken *(pharmacy)* sind meist in *drugstores*, Supermärkten und Kaufhäusern zu finden. Ständig benötigte Medikamente sollte man schon von zu Hause mitbringen (Arzt-Attest ausstellen lassen für den Fall, dass der Zoll Fragen stellt). Viele Medikamente, die in Europa rezeptfrei zu haben sind, müssen in den USA vom Arzt verschrieben werden.

Auskunft

Die meisten Orte in den USA und Kanada besitzen gut ausgeschilderte **Visitors Bureaus, Tourist Information** und/oder eine **Chamber of Commerce**, die Tipps für Unternehmungen und Veranstaltungshinweise geben, auch telefonisch. **Landkarten** und **Stadtpläne** bekommt man oft an den Tankstellen, in vielen *drugstores* und Buchhandlungen.

Automiete/Autofahren

Bei der Landung in den USA oder Kanada sollten Sie die Frage Auto- oder Campmobilmiete schon beantwortet haben. **In jedem Fall nämlich sollten Sie den Wagen bereits durch Ihr Reisebüro mieten lassen und vor Antritt der Reise bezahlen.** Das ist preisgünstiger.

Wenn man seinen Wagen nicht dort zurückgibt, wo man ihn angemietet hat, wird in den meisten Fällen eine zusätzliche **Einweggebühr** *(drop off charge oder Inter City Fee)* fällig. Die Höhe richtet sich im Allgemeinen nach der Entfernung. Einwegmiete NYC–SFO zwischen $ 500 und $ 1000.

Mit dem PKW ist man besonders in den Städten flexibler, an Bord eines Campmobils häufiger an der frischen Luft, beweglicher, was die Zeiteinteilung angeht und insgesamt – vor allem in Hinsicht auf die Verpflegung – ein bisschen billiger dran. Anfragen z.B. wegen Wochenpauschalen, Freikilometern und Überführungsgebühren richtet man an das Reisebüro oder die internationalen Autovermieter. Bedenken Sie bei der Reservierung, dass es außer Nichtraucherautos auch solche für Behinderte gibt.

In Kanada sind die führenden internationalen Autovermieter an allen großen Flughäfen und in vielen Städten vertreten.

Bei der Anmietung des Fahrzeugs vor Ort muss man den nationalen **Führerschein** und eine anerkannte **Kreditkarte** präsentieren (ohne sie muss man im Voraus bezahlen und eine Kaution hinterlegen). Außerdem ist eine konkrete Adresse in den USA/Kanada oder zu Hause gefragt. Die angebotene Vollkaskoversicherung – *Collision Damage Waiver* (CDW) bzw. *Loss Damage Waiver* (LDW) – ist in den Mietpreisen der Reiseveranstalter bereits eingeschlossen. Alle Personen, die auf der Reise das von Ihnen gemietete Auto fahren wollen (Familienmitglieder, mitreisende Freunde oder Bekannte), sollten sich aus Haftungsgründen im Mietvertrag vor Ort namentlich unter Vorlage ihres Führerscheins und einer Kreditkarte eintragen lassen.

Achtung bei verdeckten Kosten! Die Autovermieter jubeln dem Besucher (über den CDW hinaus) gern weitere Versicherungen unter. Prüfen Sie vorher, ob diese nicht durch Ihre sonstigen Versicherungsleistungen (Haftpflicht, Kreditkarten) oder bereits mit dem Gutschein für die Automiete *(voucher)* abgedeckt sind. Um die Steuern werden Sie allerdings auf keinen Fall herumkommen. Sie schwanken je nach Region zwischen 5 und 19 Prozent.

Den übernommenen Wagen sollte man zunächst überprüfen (Reserverad etc.) und sich insbesondere beim Campmobil alles genau erklären lassen. Zur Standardausstattung gehören: Automatikschaltung, Klimaanlage, Servolenkung, Bremsverstärker, Tempomat

und (mehr und mehr) Airbags. Getankt wird grundsätzlich bleifreies Benzin *(unleaded gas)*. Bitte bedenken Sie, dass Sie sich nach einem langen Flug erst umstellen und beim Autofahren mit Konzentrationsschwierigkeiten rechnen müssen (Thema: Jetlag). Vorbeugend sollten Sie auf schwarzen Tee, Kaffee oder Alkohol während des Fluges verzichten und sich auf Wasser beschränken.

Als europäischer Autofahrer hat man auf den nordamerikanischen Highways leichtes Spiel. Man fährt dort vergleichsweise rücksichtsvoll und vor allem gemächlich. Meistens jedenfalls.

Einige Verkehrsregeln unterscheiden sich von denen in Europa:

– Die **Höchstgeschwindigkeit** ist ausgeschildert: auf Interstate Highways je nach Bundesstaat 55–75 m.p.h. (Meilen pro Stunde oder 89–121 km/h) bzw. außerhalb von Städten auf freien Strecken 65 m.p.h. (105 km/h); auf US- und State Highways 55 m.p.h., in Ortschaften 25–30 m.p.h. (40–48 km/h).

– In Kanada liegt das Tempolimit generell bei 80 bis 100 km/h. Es herrscht Gurtpflicht.

– **Schulbusse** mit blinkender Warnanlage, die Kinder ein- und aussteigen lassen, dürfen nicht passiert werden. Das gilt auch für Fahrzeuge aus der Gegenrichtung!

– **Rechtsabbiegen an roten Ampeln** ist in allen US-Staaten außer in New York City erlaubt, aber erst nach vollständigem Stopp und der Vergewisserung, dass kein Fußgänger oder andere Verkehrsteilnehmer behindert werden. (Ausnahme: bei Verkehrszeichen mit einem durchgestrichenen Rechtsabbiegerpfeil oder der Aufschrift NO TURN ON RED.)

– Außerhalb von Ortschaften muss man zum **Parken** oder **Anhalten** mit dem Fahrzeug vollständig von der Straße herunter.

– CAR POOL LANES heißen Fahrspuren auf Interstate Highways, die nur von Bussen, Taxis und Autos mit mindestens zwei oder drei Insassen benutzt werden dürfen. Solche Fahrspuren sind ausgeschildert und mit Rauten markiert.

– Fußgänger, besonders Kinder, haben immer Vorrang!

– Polizeikontrollen in den USA laufen im Gegensatz zu Mitteleuropa etwas anders ab. Wenn sich ein Polizeiauto mit Blaulicht oder Sirene nähert, halten Sie an, stellen den Motor ab und öffnen das Wagenfenster. Die »Cops« legen Wert darauf, Ihre Hände deutlich sehen zu können. Es besteht offiziell absolutes Alkoholverbot.

Die Hierarchie der Straßen sieht in allen Bundesstaaten gleich aus. Die **Interstate Highways** (z.B. I-10) mit ungeraden Nummern durchqueren den Kontinent in Nord-Süd-Richtung, die mit geraden in Ost-West-Richtung. Sie sind den europäischen Autobahnen vergleichbar, d.h. gut ausgebaute, kreuzungsfreie Strecken.

Die **US-Federals** (z.B. US 17) sind interstaatlich, aber nicht ganz so aufwendig und (vor allem im Osten) mit Kreuzungen und Ampeln versehen. Schließlich gibt es die **State Routes** (z.B. S 1 oder SR 1), Landstraßen innerhalb eines Bundesstaates. Außerdem existieren Provinzrouten (**County** plus Nummer) und natürlich jede Menge *dirt roads*, unbefestigte Schotterstraßen, die man mit einem Standardmietwagen ohne Not nicht befahren sollte. Geländewagen und/oder Vierradantrieb wären da schon zu empfehlen.

In den USA markieren die **Farben an den Bordsteinkanten** verschiedene Park- und Haltezonen:

Rot: Halteverbot
Gelb: LOADING ZONE – Ladezone für Lieferwagen
Gelb und Schwarz: LKW-Ladezone
Blau: Parkplatz für Behinderte
Grün: 10 Minuten Parken
Weiß: PASSENGER LOADING ZONE – nur Ein- und Aussteigen

Nachfolgende Schilder sollte man deuten können:

Parkverbot (USA)

Parkverbot (Kanada)

Halteverbot (USA)

Halteverbot (Kanada)

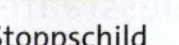

Stoppschild

Wenden verboten

Umleitung

Geschwindigkeitsbeschränkung (USA)

Geschwindigkeitsbeschränkung (Kanada)

Vorfahrt achten (Kanada)

HANDICAPPED PARKING – nur für Behindertenfahrzeuge
RESTRICTED PARKING ZONE – zeitlich begrenztes Parken; bei Hydranten herrscht ein ebenso striktes Park-Tabu wie in den *tow away zones*, wo man einen Strafzettel *(ticket)* bekommt und abgeschleppt wird. *Tickets* gibt's auch, sobald die Parkuhr *(parking meter)* abgelaufen ist *(expired)* und bei zu schnellem Fahren *(speeding)*.
DEAD END oder NO THROUGH STREET – Sackgasse
YIELD – Vorfahrt achten
RIGHT OF WAY – Vorfahrt
WATCH FOR PEDESTRIANS – auf Fußgänger achten
SLIPPERY WHEN WET – Rutschgefahr bei Nässe
DIP – Bodensenke
MPH – Meilen pro Stunde
SPEED LIMIT – Geschwindigkeitsbeschränkung
MAXIMUM SPEED – Höchstgeschwindigkeit
MERGE – einfädeln
U-TURN –Wendemöglichkeit
NO PASSING – Überholverbot
ROAD CONSTRUCTION AHEAD – Baustelle
FLAGMAN AHEAD – Baustelle (Straßenarbei-

ter mit roter Warnflagge)
MEN WORKING – Straßenarbeiten
DETOUR – Umleitung
RV – *Recreational vehicle* (Campmobil)
X-ing – etwas kreuzt (Fußgänger, Enten, Schildkröten, Wild)

An **Tankstellen** muss man oft **im Voraus bezahlen** (PAY FIRST) bzw. eine Kreditkarte hinterlegen. Die Preise variieren: gegen Barzahlung und/oder bei Selbstbedienung (SELF SERVE) gibt es mehr Sprit als auf Kreditkarte und/oder beim Tankwart (FULL SERVE). Getankt werden in den USA Gallonen (1 Gallone entspricht 3,79 Liter), auf die sich auch die angezeigten Preise beziehen, wohingegen man in Kanada die gewohnten Literangaben anzeigt.

Besonders im Osten der USA gibt es zahlreiche gebührenpflichtige Straßen *(toll roads)*, Tunnel, Brücken etc. So genannte turnpikes und parkways belasten meistens die Reisekasse. Hierfür sollte man immer Kleingeld *(change)* parat halten.

Bei **Pannen** sollte man als erstes seine **Mietfirma** anrufen, um die weiteren Schritte abzusprechen. An den Interstates stehen Notrufsäulen in kurzen Abständen zur Verfügung, von denen aus man sich mit der *Highway Patrol* in Verbindung setzen kann. Diese informiert dann Abschleppdienst, Notarzt etc. Auch der AAA unterhält einen eigenen Pannendienst, den man als Mitglied des ADAC, ÖAMTC und anderer Clubs beanspruchen kann. In nahezu allen Bundesstaaten besteht Gurtpflicht für alle Insassen.

Beachten Sie, dass auch in Nordamerika der Zusammenhang von Alkoholgenuss und Autofahren inzwischen sehr ernst genommen wird. DON'T DRINK AND DRIVE heißt es immer wieder. Mit einschlägigen Polizeikontrollen muss gerechnet werden.

Unterhaltsam wirken mitunter Sprachspiele, die viele Amerikaner mit ihren Nummernschildern betreiben, mit den *personal licence plates*: wenn z.B. ein Rolls-Royce mit dem Kennzeichen PROFIT durch Beverly Hills rauscht oder ein Wagen mit GMICUTE. Mit etwas phonetischer Fantasie wird daraus: *Gee, am I cute!* (»Mensch, bin ich süß!«).

Essen und Trinken

Die kulinarische Vielfalt Nordamerikas quillt vor allem aus den Töpfen der ethnischen Küchen und hat sich inzwischen auch bei solchen Europäern herumgesprochen, die bisher glaubten, Amerikaner verschlängen grundsätzlich nur Hamburger und *hot dogs*. Kreolisch, chinesisch oder thailändisch, *southern*, *Tex-Mex* oder *Californian cuisine* – die Palette der Leckerbissen ist unerschöpflich. Nicht überall, aber zumindest in einigen Gourmet-Hochburgen, z.B. New York, Philadelphia, Montreal, Toronto, New Orleans, Los Angeles, San Francisco, Dallas, Houston und Vancouver. Übrigens: viele *fast food outlets*, die schnellen Restaurantketten und Imbissstationen am Highway, sind besser als ihr Ruf. Im Osten des Landes wird **Wendy's** wegen seines handfesten *chili con carne* gelobt. Im Westen haben sich die Futter-Filialen von **Denny's** (mit dem 24-Stunden-Wahlspruch »*never closes*« oder »*always open*«) etabliert und bieten eine zuverlässige und preiswerte Frühstück- und Lunch-Karte sowie Salate und leichte Gerichte.

Der Trend zu fleischloser Kost hat in Ansätzen inzwischen auch Nordamerika erreicht. Dass die feinen Adressen *(white table cloth restaurants)* mehr und mehr auf Obst und Gemüse setzen, wundert dabei weniger als die Tatsache, dass selbst *fast food outlets* und *truckstops* mitziehen: mit Salatbars, *veggie (vegetable) burgers, veggie sandwiches, veggie fajitas*. Wer allerdings lieber der Fleischeslust frönt, dem sei besonders das *grain-fed beef*, das Fleisch der mit Korn gefütterten Rinder Albertas, ans Herz gelegt. Diese Spezialität ist allerdings Kanada-Reisenden vorbehalten.

Da der Ausschank von alkoholischen Getränken in einigen südlichen Bundesstaaten an Sonntagen gesetzlich eingeschränkt, überhaupt verboten oder nur aufgrund von Sonderlizenzen erlaubt ist, haben **viele Restaurants sonntags geschlossen**.

Bevor es im Restaurant etwas zu essen gibt, muss sich der Gast in der Regel einer kleinen kulturellen Aufnahmeprüfung unterziehen. Meist steht am Eingang schon ein Schild WAIT TO BE SEATED, was nichts anderes heißt, als dass man nicht geradewegs auf den nächsten leeren Tisch zustürzen, sondern auf die/den Empfangsdame/-herren warten soll, die/der einen Tisch zuweist. Warten bereits andere Gäste, tritt eines der auffälligsten angelsächsischen Rituale in Kraft: das geduldige Anstehen, das *standing in line*. Wer's nicht tut, wird schon mal sanft angemahnt: *You have to stand in line*. So etwas kann besonders Europäern (Briten ausgenommen) leicht passieren, denn nicht immer wird sofort klar, dass es sich bei der kleinsten Ansammlung von Leuten im Grunde schon um eine *line* handelt. Also fragt man im Zweifelsfall lieber: *Excuse me, is this a line?* Amerikaner lieben *lines* – im Gasthaus, bei der Post, an Bankschaltern, Kinokassen, an der Rezeption im Hotel. Sie hassen Drängelei und Klumpenbildung. Mit gutem Grund, denn *lines* schonen Nerven und ersparen unnötige Reibereien.

Neben dem üppigen Frühstück sind besonders die Lunch-Gerichte vielfältig, schmackhaft und preisgünstig. Alle Portionen, die abends erst recht, sind reichlich bemessen. Man wird keineswegs schräg angesehen, wenn man sich große Portionen teilt oder sich den unbewältigten Rest einpacken lässt *(Could you wrap this, please?)*.

Im Vergleich zu Europa **isst man in Nordamerika früh zu Abend**. Vor allem in kleineren Orten heißt das: bis 21 Uhr. Aber selbst in Städten fällt es mitunter schwer, nach 22 Uhr noch ein offenes Restaurant zu finden bzw. noch etwas zu bestellen.

Fürs Picknick oder auch für die Abend-Vesper im Hotelzimmer empfiehlt es sich, gleich zu Beginn der Reise einen ausreichend geräumigen ***cooler*** für den Kofferraum zu kaufen (ab 20 Liter). Eis gibt's reichlich in Supermärkten und Tankstellen.

Angesichts der vielen unvorhergesehenen Ausgaben (Parken, Maut, Eintritt, Steuern, Trinkgeld etc.), sollte man wissen, dass einige Bars und Lounges meist zwischen 17–19 Uhr zur ***happy hour*** kostenlos Snacks *(freebies* oder *munchies)* zu den Drinks servieren.

Bei Jugendlichen wird das Mindestalter von 21 Jahren beim Besuch in Bars, Discos und Spielkasinos in der Regel sehr ernst genommen! Normalerweise gilt der US-Führerschein *(driver's licence)* als Ausweis *(ID, identification)*. Da man in den USA keine Personalausweise kennt, kann es mitunter schwierig werden zu beweisen, dass man 21 Jahre oder älter ist.

Für Kleinigkeiten und Zwischenmahlzeiten sind die meisten **Supermärkte** wahre Fundgruben, weil sie Gemüse, Obst, Sandwiches, Gebäck usw. frisch, lecker und preiswert anbieten – oft zu jeder Tages- und Nachtzeit. Auch die Shops der Tankstellen sind als Versorgungsstationen nicht zu verachten.

Nichtraucher-Zonen sind in den allermeisten Restaurants und *coffee shops* gang und gäbe. Und die Missachtung des Nichtrauchergebots gilt keineswegs als Kavaliersdelikt. Auch wenn es vielen nicht passt: besonders die USA haben sich zu einem Nichtraucherland entwickelt. Auf allen inner-amerikanischen Flügen gilt völliges Rauchverbot. In Kalifornien und in New York darf in keinem Restaurant, Bar, Büro und öffentlichen Raum mehr geraucht werden!

Im Gegensatz zu Europa, wo um jedes kühlende zusätzliche **Eisstückchen** gekämpft werden muss, quellen US-Getränke vor Eis nahezu über: ob *ice tea, ice water, coke* oder sonst ein *soft drink* – kleine Eisbomben sind sie alle und für manche Zähne gewöhnungsbedürftig.

Die Amerikaner befinden sich seit geraumer Zeit in einem wahren **Kaffeerausch**. Die Zeit der »Plörre« scheint abgelaufen, ebenso wie die der *endless cup*, die unendliche *refills* von Labberkaffee ermöglichte. Vor allem im Westen (eingeleitet durch die in Seattle, Oregon, ansässige Kaffeerösterei »Starbucks«) sind in den letzten Jahren zahlreiche duftende Kaffee-Boutiquen entstanden, in denen Espresso, Cappuccino, Café Latte etc. neben frischen Backwaren und Sandwiches angeboten werden. Die neue amerikanische Kaffeehauskultur mit ihren süßen Theken erstreckt sich inzwischen von Küste zu Küste, oft in Kombination mit Buchhandlungen oder Zeitungsläden. Die Einrichtung ist meist anheimelnd und zu wichtigen sozialen Treffpunkten geworden.

Feiertage/Feste

Einen Grund zu feiern gibt es in einem Vielvölkerstaat wie den USA fast immer. Da viele US-Feiertage auf einen Montag fallen, entstehen lange Wochenenden und dadurch oft touristische Staus. Das *Super Bowl Weekend* im Januar z.B. ist stets besonders fest in amerikanischer Hand; dasselbe gilt für Festivals aller Art. Banken, öffentliche Gebäude, Sehenswürdigkeiten und viele Museen sind feiertags geschlossen.

Offizielle Feiertage:
Neujahrstag (1. Januar)
Martin Luther King Jr. Day (3. Mo im Januar)
Presidents' Day (3. Mo im Februar)
Memorial Day (letzter Mo im Mai, Beginn der Hauptsaison)
Unabhängigkeitstag (4. Juli)
Labor Day (1. Mo im September, Ende der Reisesaison)
Columbus Day (2. Mo im Oktober)
Veterans' Day (11. November)
Thanksgiving (4. Do im November)
Weihnachten (25. Dezember)

Richtig und öffentlich gefeiert wird davon eigentlich nur der 4. Juli. Termingerecht macht sich an diesem Tag der enorme Patriotismus der Amerikaner Luft.

Anders verhält es sich bei den lokalen Partys und ethnischen Festivals, zu denen die Amerikaner stets in Scharen mit Kind und Kegel anrücken – zu den vielen Rodeos, Musikfesten, Mummenschanz-Paraden, mexikanischen *Cinco-de-Mayo*-Feiern, zu Halloween, dem japanischen Kirschblütenfest und der allgegenwärtigen *Country Fair*. Solche Gelegenheiten sollte man sich auf keinen Fall entgehen lassen, denn nirgendwo präsentiert sich der Mikrokosmos der amerikanischen Gesellschaft besser.

Auch nördlich der Grenze zu den USA gibt es zahlreiche Feiertage, die zum Teil mit attraktiven Festen und folkloristischen Ereignissen verbunden sind. Hier die wichtigsten **kanadischen** Feiertage:

Neujahr
Karfreitag
Ostermontag
Victoria Day (letzter Mo vor dem 25. Mai)
Canada Day (1. Juli)
Labour Day (1. Mo im September)
Thanksgiving (2. Mo im Oktober)
Remembrance Day (11. November)
Weihnachten

Geld/Devisen/Reisekosten

Die Reisekasse verteilt man am besten auf drei Zahlungsmittel: **US- bzw. kanadische Dollar** als **Bargeld**, **Reiseschecks** *(traveler's checks)*, die auf diese Währung ausgestellt sind, und (eine oder mehrere) **Kreditkarten** (Mastercard/Eurocard, Visa oder American Express). Es besteht keine Beschränkung hinsichtlich des Geldbetrags (bar, Reiseschecks), der in die USA ein- bzw. ausgeführt werden darf. Jedoch ist beim Zoll (s.u.) eine Erklärung abzugeben, wenn man mit einem Betrag von mehr als $ 10 000 ein- oder ausreist. In Kanada werden oft sogar Euroscheckkarten akzeptiert.

Reiseschecks einzulösen ist unproblematisch. Man zahlt damit im Restaurant, an der Tankstelle oder im Hotel und bekommt den Restbetrag bar zurück. Euro-Reiseschecks und Bargeld in Euro werden selbst in den Großstädten nur am internationalen Flughafen und – zu normalen Banköffnungszeiten – in einigen wenigen Wechselstuben umgetauscht. Allerdings: Viele Banken geben Bargeld gegen Vorlage einer geläufigen Kreditkarte und des Reisepasses ab.

Der US-Dollar sowie sein kanadisches Pendant ist in 100 Cent unterteilt. Es gibt **Münzen** zu 1 *cent (penny)*, 5 *cent (nickel)*, 10 *cent (dime)*, 25 *cent (quarter)*, 50 *cent (half dollar)* und 1 Dollar.

Vorsicht: die **US-Dollar-Scheine** *(bills, notes)*, die es im Wert von 1, 2, 5, 10, 20, 50 und 100 Dollar (in Kanada auch 500 und 1 000 Dollar) gibt, sind alle gleich groß und grün, außer der pfirsichfarbenen 20-$-Note (in Kanada sind die Scheine farbig). Größere Geldscheine und Reiseschecks (z.B. schon Hunderter) werden ungern gesehen und in manchen Läden und Tankstellen (vor allem nachts) nicht akzeptiert. Lieber im Hotel wechseln lassen oder von zu Hause bereits Reiseschecks in $-20- und $-50-Stückelung mitnehmen.

In den USA muss man nicht nur bei der Automiete mit verdeckten Kosten rechnen. So ist es z.B. üblich, dass Preise grundsätzlich ohne Umsatzsteuer angegeben werden, man also immer mehr bezahlt, als ausgewiesen ist. D.h., **auf alle ausgezeichneten Beträge kommen, je nach Region und Kommune, mindestens 6 Prozent *(sales tax)* hinzu!** Viele Hotels (besonders in den Großstädten) erheben zusätzlich eine Parkgebühr, die bis zu $ 20 pro Übernachtung betragen kann.

Wer eine Reise durch mehrere Nationalparks plant, sollte beim ersten Park die Gelegenheit nutzen, einen **America the Beautyful - the National Parks and Federal Recreation Lands Pass** ($ 80) zu kaufen; in vielen Fällen kommt das billiger als jeweils gesondert Eintritt zu bezahlen. Der Pass berechtigt ein Jahr lang zum Besuch aller National Parks, National Monuments und National Historical Parks, ganz gleich in welchem Bundesstaat.

Gepäck/Klima/Kleidung

Im Allgemeinen ist eine lockere **Freizeitkleidung** überall in Nordamerika passend. Wer allerdings in den großen Städten schick ausgehen will, braucht eine noblere Garderobe. Insgesamt aber entspricht man mit Jeans, T-Shirts, Freizeithemden und Turnschuhen dem Alltag am besten.

Für Frühjahr und Herbst (erst recht für den Winter) sowie für die nördlichen Regionen der USA und Kanadas, in den Höhenlagen der Appalachen, des Colorado Plateau und der Rocky Mountains sind wärmere Pullover und Jacken gefragt. Gleiches gilt auch in trockenen Wüstenzonen, die nachts stark abkühlen.

Je heißer es draußen ist, um so eisiger empfinden besonders die meisten Europäer die Klimaanlagen, die für sie ungewohnt und nicht ohne gesundheitliches Risiko sind. Deshalb sollte man mit entsprechender Kleidung vorbereitet sein. Für Kanada gilt der Sommer als die beste Reisezeit, zumindest, was den Nordteil des Landes angeht. Die Südhälfte lässt sich klimatisch am besten im Frühjahr, Sommer und Herbst bereisen.

Wenn man mit eigenem Rasierapparat oder Fön anreist (die auf 110 Volt umgestellt werden können), sollte man auch einen **Adapter** für amerikanische Steckdosen im Gepäck haben. In den USA und Kanada muss man oft lange danach suchen.

Auch **Filme** kauft man besser zu Hause, da die Preise in Nordamerika höher liegen und die Entwicklung nicht eingeschlossen ist.

Hinweise für Behinderte

In den USA und Kanada sind die Einrichtungen für Rollstuhlfahrer insgesamt erheblich besser als in Deutschland und Europa. Allgemein kann man sich darauf verlassen, dass alle öffentlichen Gebäude (z.B. Rathäuser, Postämter) mit Rampen versehen sind. Das gilt auch für die meisten Supermärkte, Museen, Sehenswürdigkeiten und Vergnügungsparks. Durchweg sind die Bordsteine an den Fußgängerüberwegen abgeflacht. In vielen Hotels und Hotelketten (z.B. **Motel 6**) gibt es Rollstuhlzimmer. Fast überall sind behindertengerechte Toiletten vorhanden.

Einige Autovermieter bieten spezielle Fahrzeuge mit Handbedienung für Körperbehinderte an – ohne Aufpreis.

Kinder

Die Amerikaner und auch Kanadier sind durchweg kinderfreundlich. Kindermenüs, eigene Sitzkissen, Stühle und Kindertische in den Restaurants sowie billige, wenn nicht gar kostenlose Unterbringung in Hotels und Motels sind selbstverständlich.

Besonders mit dem Campmobil macht den Kindern die Rundfahrt Spaß: Grillen oder auch kleine Wanderungen lassen Langeweile nicht aufkommen. Auch die Nordamerikaner reisen viel mit Kindern, so dass Kontaktmöglichkeiten sich leichter ergeben. Wenn man mit Kind(ern) reist, empfiehlt es sich, die Tagesplanung etwas lockerer zu gestalten.

Das zuständige *Visitors Bureau* und die Hotels in den Städten vermitteln Babysitter.

Maße und Gewichte

Hier bleibt vorerst alles beim Alten: *inch* und *mile*, *gallon* und *pound*. Man muss sich also wohl oder übel umstellen. Die Tabellen (siehe nächste Seite) können dabei – auch was Bekleidungsgrößen angeht – helfen.

In Kanada gelten die gleichen Maß- und Gewichtsangaben wie in Mitteleuropa.

Längenmaße:	1 inch (in.)	=	2,54 cm
	1 foot (ft.)	=	30,48 cm
	1 yard (yd.)	=	0,9 m
	1 mile	=	1,6 km
Flächenmaße:	1 square foot	=	930 cm²
	1 acre	=	0,4 Hektar (= 4 047 m²)
	1 square mile	=	259 Hektar (= 2,59 km²)
Hohlmaße:	1 pint	=	0,47 l
	1 quart	=	0,95 l
	1 gallon	=	3,79 l
Gewichte:	1 ounce (oz.)	=	28,35 g
	1 pound (lb.)	=	453,6 g
	1 ton	=	907 kg

Temperaturen:												
°F (Fahrenheit)	104	100	90	86	80	70	68	50	40	32		
°C (Celsius)	40	37,8	32,2	30	26,7	21,1	20	10	4,4	0		
Bekleidungsmaße:												
Herrenkonfektion												
Deutsch	46	48	50	52	54	56	58					
Amerikanisch	36	38	40	42	44	46	48					
Damenkonfektion												
Deutsch	38	40	42	44	46	48						
Amerikanisch	10	12	14	16	18	20						
Kinderbekleidung												
Deutsch	98	104	110	116	122							
Amerikanisch	3	4	5	6	6x							
Kragen/collars												
Deutsch	35–36	37	38	39	40/41	42	43					
Amerikanisch	14	14½	15	15½	16	16½	17					
Strümpfe/stockings												
Deutsch	35	36	37	38	39	40	41					
Amerikanisch	8	8½	9	9½	10	10½	11					
Schuhe/shoes												
Deutsch	36	37	38	39	40	41	42	43	44	45	46	47
Amerikanisch	5	5¾	6½	7¼	8	8¾	9½	10¼	11	11¾	12½	13¼

Verkehrsmittel

Effiziente **U- und Straßenbahnen** verkehren in New York, Chicago, Washington, Philadelphia, Baltimore, Atlanta und San Francisco; ansonsten nur mehr oder weniger umständliche Busse (besonders unerfreulich: Los Angeles und Houston) oder nostalgische Straßenbahnen (New Orleans, San Francisco, San Diego).

Taxi-Unternehmen in den Städten entnehmen Sie bitte den gelben Telefonbuchseiten bzw. dem Wissensstand der Hotelportiers. Nur in einigen Städten (z.B. New York, Chicago, Philadelphia, Washington, New Orleans und San Francisco) kann man Taxis leicht durch Heranwinken an der Straße bekommen. In der Regel aber ergattert man ein Taxi nur per Telefon oder an Hoteleingängen. Achten Sie stets darauf, dass bei Beginn der Fahrt das Taxameter angestellt wird.

Gute **Flugverbindungen** sind für ein schier grenzenloses Land wie Kanada unabdingbar. Air Canada verfügen in Ergänzung mit regionalen Linien über ein enges Netz. Für **Bahnreisen** ist die »VIA Rail Canada« und für **Busreisen** »Greyhound Canada« der beste Ansprechpartner.

Post

Das Postnetz in Nordamerika ist sehr dicht. Für die USA und Kanada gilt: Postämter gibt es sogar in den winzigsten Orten. Und je kleiner das Nest ist, desto weniger muss man warten, will man Briefmarken kaufen oder ein Päckchen aufgeben. Eine Postkarte in die Heimat ist inzwischen oft länger als eine Woche unterwegs.

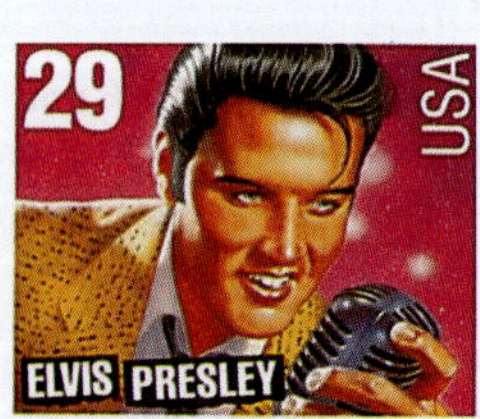

Man kann sich postlagernde Sendungen zuschicken lassen, die wie folgt adressiert sind:

Name (Familienname unterstrichen)
c/o General Delivery
Main Post Office
(Ort, z.B. New Orleans, LA, Toronto...)
USA bzw. Kanada

Das Telefonsystem hat mit dem Postwesen in den USA nichts zu tun, weshalb man in den Postämtern auch keine Telefonzellen findet. Telegramme können bei der **Western Union Telegraph Company** aufgegeben werden (auch telefonisch).

Presse/Radio/TV

Die führenden **Zeitungen** der Nation lassen sich an einer Hand abzählen: *New York Times*, *Washington Post* und *Los Angeles Times* sind sicher darunter. Stadt- und staatsübergreifend ist die *USA Today*, die sich für den europäischen Besucher nicht nur als gut verständlich und am übersichtlichsten erweist, sondern auch an den meisten Straßenecken und Hoteleingängen zu haben ist.

Gleichwohl: Internationale politische Nachrichten darf man auch hier nicht erwarten, schon gar keine aus Old Germany, es sei denn, ein Studienrat aus Betzdorf hat sich von seiner Frau scheiden lassen, weil sie schon zum dritten Mal aus dem Fenster springen wollte.

Nichts spricht dagegen, beim Autofahren so oft wie möglich vom **Radio** Gebrauch zu machen: Man hört sich in die Sprache (und jeweils lokale Aussprache) ein, erfährt das eine oder andere und genießt nebenbei exzellente Musik.

Das **TV** ist selbst in den einfachsten Hotels ein Schaufenster der Landeskunde, abgesehen davon, dass die großen Sender wie NBC oder ABC (aber auch CNN und andere) aktuelle Nachrichten und natürlich (und ausgiebig) Wetterberichte senden. Viele Hotels bieten den werbefreien Kanal HBO *(home box office)* oder andere Pay-TV-Sender an.

Shopping

Shop til you drop: Kaufen bis zum Umfallen! Kein Land der Welt macht sich diese Devise so zu eigen wie die USA. Sie sind, aufs Ganze gesehen, ein gigantischer Supermarkt, der fast überall rund um die Uhr geöffnet ist, Sonn- und Feiertage eingeschlossen.

Besonders faszinierend sind die riesigen **Shopping Centers** und Shopping Malls, innerhalb der Städte oder an deren Rand auf der grünen Wiese, sowie die neueren eleganten Konsumtempel, die neben Top-Boutiquen und großen Warenhausketten jede Menge Cafés, Restaurants, Kinos, Fitnesszentren und sogar Joggingpfade auf den Dächern bieten. In der Regel sind sie Mo–Sa 9–18 Uhr geöffnet.

Spezifisch amerikanisch und außerordentlich unterhaltsam sind die lokalen **Märkte** – ob mit Kunstwerken *(arts and crafts show)*, Obst und Gemüse *(farmers market)* oder mit Krempel auf Flohmärkten *(flea market)* sowie samstags auf *swap meets* (Tauschmärkte) und *garage sales* (private Entrümpelungsaktionen überfüllter Garagen), bei denen so manches Schnäppchen zu machen ist.

Kanada ist kommerziell nicht annähernd so weit erschlossen wie die USA. Die Geschäfte schließen in der Regel um 18 Uhr, Freitag und Samstag oft erst um 21 Uhr. Neben den üblichen Einkaufszentren gibt es Spezialgalerien, in denen sich die beliebten Kunstwerke der Inuit und Indianer erstehen lassen.

Sicherheitshinweise

Zu beurteilen, wie sicher ein Ort ist fällt um so schwerer, je weiter dieser vom eigenen Lebenskreis entfernt liegt. Die internationale Presse, die z.B. über Gewaltverbrechen in Miami berichtet, verdrängt damit die nicht weniger ängstigende Tatsache, dass viele Straßen in der eigenen Stadt ebenso tödlich sein können. So lässt sich sagen, dass trotz der deprimierenden Kriminalstatistik mancher US-Metropolen die USA insgesamt ein sicheres Reiseland sind. Tagsüber auf jeden Fall, aber auch abends. Ethnische Wohnviertel bergen die meisten Gefahren, besonders für den Fußgänger; aber auch mit dem Auto kann es böse Überraschungen geben. Und man muss ja nicht nach dem Abendessen oder Barbesuch noch einmal »um den Block« spazieren oder zum Hotel zu Fuß zurücklaufen. Nehmen Sie ein Taxi!

Bei **Erdbeben** in der Stadt sollte man sich von allen Fenstern und Glastüren fernhalten und unter einen Türrahmen oder in eine Ecke stellen. Auf keinen Fall auf den Balkon gehen, den Aufzug benutzen oder das Haus verlassen! Denn die größte Gefahr während und nach einem Erdbeben sind herumfliegendes Glas, abfallendes Mauerwerk und abstürzende Hochspannungsleitungen. Auch sollten – wegen Gasexplosionsgefahr – keine Streichhölzer oder Feuerzeuge benutzt werden. Wenn die Erschütterungen aufhören, ist daran zu denken, dass weitere folgen können.

Auch Gottes freie Natur birgt Risiken, die an Parks und Stadtwälder gewöhnte Mitteleuropäer meist unterschätzen. Die **Wildnisregionen** in den USA und vor allem Kanadas eignen sich nur bedingt zur Kaffeefahrt oder zum unbekümmerten Spaziergang! Skorpione, Klapperschlangen, bösartige Moskitos, Bären und Wölfe können den Urlaub ebenso verhageln wie plötzliche Regengüsse und die in den Wüsten des Westens so gefürchteten *washes*, durch überraschende Regenfälle entstandene Sturzbäche, die alles mit sich reißen. Wussten Sie z.B., dass in der Wüste mehr Menschen ertrinken als verdursten? Informieren Sie sich also bei den Rangern der Nationalparks über die potentiellen Gefahren und wie man sie vermeidet! Achten Sie auch darauf, dass Sie im heißen Südwesten der USA stets genügend Trinkwasser mit sich führen. Festes Schuhwerk ist unumgänglich.

Telefonieren

An öffentlichen Telefonen mangelt es in keiner nordamerikanischen Stadt. Benutzen Sie sie! Auskünfte, Reservierungen und Voranmeldungen per Telefon ersparen Enttäuschungen und Zeitverlust. Hilfreich ist stets der *Operator* (»0«), der/die Rufnummern vermittelt, Vorwahlnummern *(area codes)* durchgibt und auch die Preiseinheiten für Ferngespräche nennt.

Das Telefonieren aus der Telefonzelle, dem *payphone*, erfordert etwas Übung. Ortsgespräche *(local calls)* sind einfach. Man wirft 25 ¢ ein und wählt die siebenstellige Nummer. Ferngespräche *(long distance calls)* werden meist in der Aufschrift am Telefon erläutert. Für Gespräche außerhalb des eigenen Vorwahlbezirks benötigt man den gewünschten *area code* und wählt davor eine 1: also 1, *area code* und Nummer. Bevor das Gespräch zustande kommt, meldet sich der Operator oder eine Computerstimme und gibt die Gebühr für die ersten 3 Minuten an. Spricht man länger, kommt die Stimme wieder und möchte mehr Geld. Es empfiehlt sich also, 25 ¢-Stücke zu horten, um allzeit telefonbereit zu sein.

Rufnummern, die vor ihrer siebenstelligen Zahl eine 800 (oder 866, 877, 888) haben, sind gebührenfrei. Auch bei ihnen wählt man zuvor eine 1. (Also: 1-800-...)

Um eine Telefonnummer herauszufinden, ruft man die *directory assistance*, die man im eigenen Vorwahlbezirk unter der Nummer 411 erreicht, an; für andere Bezirke wählt man die jeweilige Vorwahl (...) und dann die 555-1212. Auskünfte über die gebührenfreien 1-800-Nummern gibt es unter 1-800-555-1212.

Gespräche nach Europa kosten für 3 Minuten ca. $ 6–8. Man lässt sich vom Operator verbinden oder wählt 011, die Landesvorwahl (Deutschland: 49), Stadtvorwahl (ohne die erste Null) und Nummer. Man kann sich in US-Telefonzellen auch zurückrufen lassen.

Vom Hotel/Motel aus kann man entweder über den Hotel-Operator oder direkt innerhalb der USA bzw. Kanada und auch nach Europa telefonieren. Falls man über einen Code (auf dem Apparat angegeben, oft 7 oder 8) eine Amtsleitung bekommt, fragt meist eine freundliche Stimme nach der Zimmernummer, damit das Gespräch abgerechnet werden kann.

Die »Direkt«-Gespräche ins Ausland sind von Telefonzellen aus so bequem, weil man Deutsch sprechen kann und noch nicht einmal für die Vermittlung Münzen braucht, da der Empfänger automatisch die Gebühr – die allerdings recht hoch ist – zahlt:

Deutschland Direkt
1-800-292-0049 und Nummer
Austria Direkt
1-800-624-0043 und Nummer
Schweiz Direkt
1-800-305- 0041 und Nummer

Die ***calling cards*** diverser Telefongesellschaften bringen eine Reihe von Vorteilen: Man kann mit der Karte praktisch von jeder Straßenecke aus den Rest der Welt erreichen, ohne pfundweise Kleingeld bei sich tragen zu müssen. Außerdem spart man die erheblichen Zuschläge der Hotels auf die Gebühreneinheiten. Die Handhabung ist denkbar simpel, und man bekommt über alle geführten Gespräche eine detaillierte Rechnungsaufstellung mit angerufener Nummer, Datum, Ort, Zeit und Gebühr.

Angesichts der verwirrenden Telefontarife in den USA empfiehlt sich gleich zu Beginn der Reise der Kauf einer **Prepaid-Telefonkarte**. Solche Karten gibt es speziell für *international calls* teilweise mit extrem günstigen

Tarifen (z.B. 3 ¢ pro Minute nach Deutschland). Erhältlich sind diese Karten vor allem in Supermärkten (die *World Card* z.B. bei Filialen von 7 Eleven), Tankstellen oder Telefonshops zu $ 5-, 10-, 50- etc. Beträgen. Minutenpreise und sonstige Konditionen (z.B. *minimum fee*) sowie Reichweite unbedingt vergleichen.

Europäische Handys funktionieren in den USA wie zu Hause, wenn es sich um sogenannte **Mehrband-Mobiltelefone** handelt (siehe Bedienungsanleitung oder beim Provider direkt zu erfragen). Allerdings zahlt man je nach Anbieter sowohl für Telefonate nach Hause wie auch für den Empfang eines Gesprächs 1–2 € je Minute. Grundsätzlich kann man mit einem Mobiltelefon auch Prepaid-Telefonkarten wie oben beschrieben benutzen, wenn bei dem eigenen Provider das kostenlose Anwählen von 1-800er Nummern in den USA möglich ist. Sollte die Einwahl kostenlos sein, dann haben Sie über die Kombination der Telefonkarte mit dem eigenem Handy eine kostengünstige Möglichkeit, in den USA zu telefonieren.

Wer eine längere Tour unternimmt, kann auch bei einem der amerikanischen Mobilfunkbetreiber eine Sim-Karte für das dortige GSM-Netz kaufen und in das aus Europa mitgebrachte (entsperrte!) Handy einlegen. Oder man kauft sich für 20–60 $ ein einfaches Prepaid-Handy vor Ort. Man erhält in beiden Fällen eine örtliche Nummer in den USA. Es empfiehlt sich die Telefonnummer in der Stadt/Region zu nehmen, in der man überwiegend sein wird, denn dann kann man von günstigen Ortstarifen profitieren. Sim-Karten gibt es bei Anbietern wie T-Mobile oder Cingular.

Handys heißen in den USA *cell phone* oder *mobile phone*.

Trinkgeld

Dies ist ein Thema für sich, weil Nordamerikaner es anders handhaben als Europäer. Zwar sind Trinkgelder dort wie hier freiwillige Zahlungen, aber dennoch sollte man wissen: Grundsätzlich sind in den Rechnungsbeträgen (Restaurants, Taxis etc.) keine Trinkgelder enthalten; Bedienungen in den USA und Kanada aber leben im Wesentlichen von ihnen und nicht von ihren Gehältern.

Daraus folgt, die landesüblichen Sätze möglichst nicht zu unterschreiten, es sei denn, man ist wirklich schlecht behandelt worden, was erfahrungsgemäß äußerst selten vorkommt. In Restaurants lässt man rund 15 Prozent des Rechnungsbetrages als *tip* auf dem Tisch liegen. Das ist die Untergrenze!

Man gibt auch im Hotel: den *bellboys* und den Kofferträgern je nach Hotelklasse etwa 50 ¢ bis $ 1 pro großem Gepäckstück, Taxifahrern und Frisören etwa 15–20 Prozent vom Rechnungsbetrag, in den Bars etwa 50 ¢ je Drink und dem Zimmermädchen bei mehrtägigem Aufenthalt $ 3–4.

Zum Trost: eine der wenigen Gelegenheiten, wo kein Trinkgeld erwartet wird, sind die Serviceleistungen an Tankstellen.

Unterkunft

Hotels und **Motels** in Nordamerika sind in der Regel einwandfrei, zuverlässig und, von wenigen Engpässen abgesehen, in ausreichender Anzahl und in allen Preisklassen vertreten.

Die meisten Hotels oder Motels können von Europa aus reserviert werden. In den USA benutzt man dazu die gebührenfreie 800er-Nummer, nicht zuletzt auch deshalb, weil man dadurch günstigere Zimmerpreise gewährt bekommt. Zimmerreservierung ist in jedem Fall in der Hauptreisezeit Juni, Juli, August oder an Wochenenden und Feiertagen, zu Zeiten des so genannten *tourist frenzy*, anzuraten, besonders für dann gewöhnlich überlaufene Gebiete wie alle National Parks, State Parks oder Disneyland etc.

Auch bei der Hotelreservierung ist sowohl in den USA als auch in Kanada eine Kreditkartennummer praktisch unumgänglich (an Wochenenden und Feiertagen auf jeden Fall). Die Karte garantiert das Zimmer. Wird eine Reservierung ohne Karte akzeptiert, muss man bis **spätestens 18 Uhr** einchecken. Bei der kurzfristigen Zimmersuche sind die örtlichen *Visitor Bureaus* behilflich.

Bei allen Motels oder Hotels auf dem Lande ist Parken frei, bei Hotels in den Innenstädten sind Parkgebühren von täglich $ 10–20 zusätzlich zum Zimmerpreis keine Seltenheit.

In fast allen Zentren der großen Städte bieten die Hotels günstige Wochenendpauschalen *(weekend specials)*, um ihre geringe Auslastung zu kompensieren.

Preise gelten stets für einen *double room*. Einzelzimmer sind nur unwesentlich billiger, während man für ein zusätzliches Bett etwa $ 5–10 zuzahlen muss. Für Kinder, die im Zimmer der Eltern schlafen, wird meist kein Aufpreis berechnet.

Für Nichtraucher: fragen Sie nach einem *non smoking room* – die meisten Hotels bieten solche Zimmer ohne Aufpreis an.

Als besonders preisgünstig, sauber und dazu noch meist verkehrsgünstig gelegen gelten die Motels der Kette **Motel 6**. Der Übernachtungspreis liegt z.Zt. um die $ 30–50 für eine Person, die zweite zahlt rund $ 6 extra. Außerdem: für $ 1.50 kann man sich ein Zimmer im nächsten Zielort reservieren lassen, so dass man sich mit der Anreise nicht so sehr beeilen muss.

Bed & Breakfast ist das angelsächsische Pendant zum Hotel garni: Zimmer mit Frühstück also, und zwar meist in historischem Rahmen. Bei den Amerikanern stehen sie hoch im Kurs. Offenbar wissen viele das gemütliche Frühstück mit hausgemachter Marmelade zu schätzen und ziehen das Flair nostalgischer Räumlichkeiten den stereotypen Motelräumen vor. Außerdem wirkt das im Preis eingeschlossene Frühstück (so mager es sein mag), als spare man Kosten. Deshalb schmücken sich neuerdings sogar einige Motelketten mit dem Zusatz »Inn« und servieren ein kostenloses Mini-Frühstück *(complimentary breakfast)*. Europäischen Besuchern bieten B&Bs unter Umständen den Vorteil, dass sie Gespräche und Kontakte finden.

Nicht minder unterhaltsam sind auch die Aufenthalte auf einer **Ranch**. In Texas, Arizona und anderen, meist westlichen Bundesstaaten erfreut sich diese Version von Ferien auf dem Bauernhof wachsender Beliebtheit: mit zünftigem Cowboy-Frühstück und *cookouts*, Ausritten und anderen Freizeitaktivitäten für die ganze Familie.

Camping ist überall außerhalb der großen Städte beliebt. Die im Allgemeinen großzügig angelegten Plätze bieten oft eine herrliche Lage und den direkten Anschluss an Wanderwege und Strände. Der Wohnwagen befreit von den täglichen Hotel- und Restaurantritualen und bringt Abwechslung auf die Speisekarte, weil man die preiswerten und oft hervorragenden Obst- und Gemüseangebote der Supermärkte nutzen kann. Außerdem fördert Camping die Bekanntschaft mit Gleichgesinnten.

Die staatlichen Campingplätze liegen meist in State Parks, haben Feuerstellen, Holzbänke und -tische sowie Waschanlagen. Vorbestellung ist oft nicht möglich, daher sollte man so früh wie möglich einchecken. Die privaten Campingplätze sind meist vorzüglich ausgestattet, mit sauberen Duschen, Grillplätzen und oft mit kleinem Laden. Die Übernachtungspreise schwanken zwischen $ 15–30 für zwei Personen pro Nacht.

Wildcampen für mehrere Tage wird nicht so gern gesehen, doch kann man durchaus über Nacht sein Motorhome auf einem Parkplatz oder – nach Rücksprache am *front desk* – im Einzelfall auch auf Hotel- und Motelparkplätzen, hinter Tankstellen und auf Supermarktparkplätzen abstellen (möglichst auf solchen, die 24 Stunden geöffnet sind).

Beim **US National Park Service** gibt es eine zentrale und kostenlose Reservierungsnummer, unter der man für jeweils einen Tag im Voraus einen Campingplatz in einem der Nationalparks reservieren kann: ✆ 1-800-444-6777 und http://reservations.nps.gov.

Noch von Europa aus kann man einen bzw. mehrere der **KOA** (www.koa.com) Campingplätze reservieren. Auf Anfrage bekommt man Unterlagen zurück, in die man die gewünschten Daten gegen eine geringe Gebühr eintragen kann.

Zeitzonen

Das Territorium der USA erstreckt sich über vier verschiedene Zeitzonen: *Eastern Time, Central Time, Mountain Time, Pacific Time*. Zwischen Ende April und November wird, von einigen speziellen Regionen abgesehen, die Uhr ähnlich wie in Europa um eine Stunde auf Sommerzeit *(daylight saving time, DST)* vorgestellt. Hawai'i hat seine eigene Zeitzone: *Hawai'i Standard Time* (MEZ minus 11 Std.). In Alaska gilt *Alaska Time* = MEZ minus 10 Stunden.

Neben den oben genannten Zeitzonen gibt es für Kanada noch eine Zone für Newfoundland, eine für die anderen Maritimes (Atlantik-Provinzen) und die *Yukon Time* = MEZ minus 9 Std.

Zoll

Zollfrei in die USA mitbringen darf man außer der persönlichen Reiseausrüstung (Kleidung, Kamera etc.) pro Person (bei Abweichungen gelten für Kanada die in Klammern angegebenen Mengen):

- 200 Zigaretten oder 50 Zigarren (aber bitte nicht aus Kuba!) oder 3 Pfund Tabak (200 Gramm)
- 1 Liter Alkohol (1,14 Liter)
- Geschenke im Wert bis zu $ 100 (€ 60)

Tierische und pflanzliche Frischprodukte (Obst, Wurst, Gemüse) dürfen nicht eingeführt werden. Die Zollbeamten sind da unerbittlich – Wurststulle und Orange werden konfisziert. Dagegen sind Gebäck, Käse und Süßigkeiten (keine Schnapspralinen!) erlaubt.

Den eigenen Wagen darf man bis zu einem Jahr mitbringen, was sich aber nur ab einer Aufenthaltsdauer von mindestens 2 Monaten lohnt. Bleibt man länger als 12 Monate, muss das Fahrzeug nach den amerikanischen Sicherheitsbestimmungen umgerüstet werden. Wer seinen Wagen nach einer Reise in den USA verkaufen möchte, muss ebenfalls umrüsten und zusätzlich Zoll bezahlen.

Bei speziellen Fragen zu den amerikanischen Zollbestimmungen setzt man sich am besten mit dem nächsten US- oder dem kanadischen Konsulat in Verbindung.

Bei der **Rückreise** dürfen für den persönlichen Bedarf abgabefrei eingeführt werden:
– 200 Zigaretten oder 100 Zigarillos oder 50 Zigarren oder 250 g Tabak
– 1 Liter Spirituosen mit einem Alkoholgehalt von mehr als 22 Vol.-% oder 2 Liter mit einem Alkoholgehalt von maximal 22 Vol.-%
– andere Mitbringsel bis zu einem Warenwert von g 430.

Überschreiten die Reisemitbringsel die Reisefreimengen, so fallen Einfuhrabgaben an. Am besten die Kaufbelege aufbewahren, ansonsten wird der Wert geschätzt. Bis zu einem Wert von € 700 werden pauschal 17,5 % Zoll erhoben, bei allem, was darüber liegt, wird genauer gerechnet. Auskünfte erhält man beim Informationsmanagement Zoll unter ✆ (03 51) 448 34-510, www.zoll.de.

Wichtige Adressen

In Deutschland:

Botschaft der Vereinigten Staaten von Amerika
Pariser Platz 2
D-4191 Berlin
Tel. 030/830 50
www.usembassy.de

Amerikanisches Generalkonsulat
Gießener Str. 30
D-60435 Frankfurt/Main
Tel. 069/75 35-0

Amerikanisches Generalkonsulat
Willi-Becker-Allee 10
D-40227 Düsseldorf
Tel. 02 11/788 89 27, Fax 02 11/788 89 38

Amerikanisches Generalkonsulat
Alsterufer 27/28
D-20354 Hamburg
Tel. 040/411 71-100
Fax 040/411 71-222

Amerikanisches Generalkonsulat
Wilhelm-Seyfferth-Str. 4
D-04107 Leipzig
Tel. 03 41/21 38 40
leipzig@usconsulate.de

Amerikanisches Generalkonsulat
Königinstr. 5
D-80539 München
Tel. 089/28 88-0, Fax 089/280-99 98
consmunich@state.gov

USA-Infoline
Tel. 0190/78 00 78
(gebührenpflichtig)

Visit USA Committee Germany e. V.
Uferstr. 47
D-55116 Mainz
Tel. 07 00/84 74 88 72
Fax 07 00/10 12 714
www.vusa.travel

Kanadische Botschaft
Leipziger Platz 17, D-10117 Berlin
Tel. 030/203 12-0, Fax 030/20 31 25 90
www.kanada.de

Canadian Tourism Commission
Eichenheege 1-5
D-63477 Maintal
Tel. 018 05/52 62 32
www.travelcanada.ca

Konsulate von Kanada befinden sich in Düsseldorf, Hamburg, München und Stuttgart.

In Österreich:

Botschaft der Vereinigten Staaten von Amerika
Boltzmanngasse 16
A-1090 Wien
Tel. 01/313 39-0
Fax 01/310 06 82
www.usembassy.at

Kanadische Botschaft
Laurenzerberg 2
A-1010 Wien
Tel. 01/531 38 30 00, Fax 01/531 38 33 21
www.kanada.at

In der Schweiz:

Botschaft der Vereinigten Staaten von Amerika
Jubiläumsstr. 93
CH-3005 Bern
Tel. 031/357 70 11
Fax 031/357 73 44
http://bern.usembassy.gov

Kanadische Botschaft
Kirchenfeldstr. 88
Case postale
CH-3005 Bern
Tel. 031/357 32 00, Fax 031/357 32 10

In den USA:

Deutsche Botschaft
4645 Reservoir Road N.W.
Washington, DC 20007
Tel. +1/202/298-4000
Fax +1/202/298-4249
www.washington.diplo.de

Botschaft von Österreich
3524 International Court N.W.
Washington, DC 20008
Tel. +1/202/895-6700
Fax +1/202/895-6750
www.austria.org

Botschaft der Schweiz
2900 Cathedral Avenue N.W.
Washington, DC 20008
Tel. +1/202/745-7900
Fax +1/202/387-2564
www.eda.admin.ch/washington

In Kanada:

Deutsche Botschaft
1 Waverly Street
Ottawa, ON K2P 0T8
Tel. +1/613/232-1101
Fax +1/616/594-9330
www.ottawa.diplo.de

Botschaft von Österreich
445 Wilbrod Street
Ottawa, ON K1N 6M7
Tel. +1/613/789-1444
Fax +1/613/789-3431
www.austro.org

Botschaft der Schweiz
5 Marlborough Avenue
Ottawa, ON K1N 8E6
Tel. +1/613/235-1837
Fax +1/613/563-1394
www.eda.admin.ch/canada

Entfernungstabelle

Distances in chart are in miles. To convert miles to kilometers, multiply the distance in miles by 1.609

Example: New York, NY to Boston, MA = 215 miles or 346 kilometers (215 x 1.609)

	ALBUQUERQUE, NM	ATLANTA, GA	BALTIMORE, MD	BILLINGS, MT	BIRMINGHAM, AL	BISMARCK, ND	BOISE, ID	BOSTON, MA	BUFFALO, NY	BURLINGTON, VT	CHARLESTON, SC	CHARLESTON, WV	CHARLOTTE, NC	CHEYENNE, WY	CHICAGO, IL	CINCINNATI, OH	CLEVELAND, OH	DALLAS, TX	DENVER, CO	DES MOINES, IA	DETROIT, MI	EL PASO, TX	HOUSTON, TX	INDIANAPOLIS, IN	JACKSON, MS	KANSAS CITY, MO	LAS VEGAS, NV	LITTLE ROCK, AR	LOS ANGELES, CA	LOUISVILLE, KY	MEMPHIS, TN	MIAMI, FL	MILWAUKEE, WI	MINNEAPOLIS, MN	MONTRÉAL, QC	NASHVILLE, TN	NEW ORLEANS, LA	NEW YORK, NY	OKLAHOMA CITY, OK	OMAHA, NE	ORLANDO, FL	PHILADELPHIA, PA	PHOENIX, AZ	PITTSBURGH, PA	PORTLAND, ME	PORTLAND, OR	RAPID CITY, SD	RENO, NV	RICHMOND, VA	ST. LOUIS, MO	SALT LAKE CITY, UT	SAN ANTONIO, TX	SAN DIEGO, CA	SAN FRANCISCO, CA	SEATTLE, WA	TAMPA, FL	TORONTO, ON	VANCOUVER, BC	WASHINGTON,DC	WICHITA, KS
ALBUQUERQUE, NM		1490	1902	991	1274	1333	966	2240	1808	2178	1793	1568	1649	538	1352	1409	1619	754	438	1091	1608	263	994	1298	1157	894	578	900	806	1320	1033	2155	1426	1339	2172	1248	1276	2015	546	973	1934	1954	466	1670	2338	1395	841	1020	1876	1051	624	818	825	1111	1463	1949	1841	1597	1896	707
ATLANTA, GA	1490		679	1889	150	1559	2218	1100	910	1158	317	503	238	1482	717	476	726	792	1403	967	735	1437	800	531	386	801	2067	528	2237	419	389	661	813	1129	1241	242	473	869	944	989	440	782	1868	676	1197	2647	1511	2440	527	549	1916	1000	2166	2618	2705	455	958	2838	636	989
BALTIMORE, MD	1902	679		1959	795	1551	2401	422	370	481	583	352	441	1665	708	521	377	1399	1690	1031	532	2045	1470	600	1032	1087	2445	1072	2705	602	933	1109	805	1121	564	716	1142	192	1354	1168	904	104	2366	246	520	2830	1626	2623	152	841	2100	1671	2724	2840	2775	960	565	2908	38	1276
BILLINGS, MT	991	1889	1959		1839	413	626	2254	1796	2181	2157	1755	2012	455	1246	1552	1597	1433	554	1007	1534	1255	1673	1432	1836	1088	965	1530	1239	1547	1625	2554	1175	839	2093	1648	1955	2049	1227	904	2333	2019	1199	1719	2352	889	379	960	2053	1341	548	1500	1302	1176	816	2348	1762	949	1953	1067
BIRMINGHAM, AL	1274	150	795	1839		1509	2170	1215	909	1241	466	578	389	1434	667	475	725	647	1356	919	734	1292	678	481	241	753	1852	381	2092	369	241	812	763	1079	1289	194	351	985	729	941	591	897	1723	763	1313	2599	1463	2392	678	501	1868	878	2021	2472	2657	606	958	2791	758	838
BISMARCK, ND	1333	1559	1551	413	1509		1039	1846	1388	1773	1749	1347	1604	594	838	1144	1189	1342	693	675	1126	1597	1582	1024	1548	801	1378	1183	1702	1139	1337	2224	767	431	1685	1315	1734	1641	1136	616	2003	1611	1662	1311	1944	1301	320	1372	1645	1053	960	1599	1765	1749	1229	2018	1354	1362	1545	934
BOISE, ID	966	2218	2401	626	2170	1039		2697	2239	2624	2520	2182	2375	737	1708	1969	2040	1711	833	1369	1977	1206	1952	1852	2115	1376	760	1808	1033	1933	1954	2883	1748	1465	2535	1976	2234	2491	1506	1234	2662	2462	993	2161	2795	432	930	430	2496	1628	342	1761	1096	646	500	2677	2204	633	2395	1346
BOSTON, MA	2240	1100	422	2254	1215	1846	2697		462	214	1003	741	861	1961	1003	862	654	1819	2004	1326	741	2465	1890	940	1453	1427	2757	1493	3046	964	1353	1529	1100	1417	313	1136	1563	215	1694	1463	1324	321	2706	592	107	3126	1921	2919	572	1181	2395	2092	3065	3135	3070	1380	570	3204	458	1616
BUFFALO, NY	1808	910	370	1796	909	1388	2239	462		375	899	431	695	1502	545	442	197	1393	1546	868	277	2039	1513	508	1134	995	2299	1066	2572	545	927	1425	642	958	397	716	1254	400	1262	1005	1221	414	2274	217	560	2667	1463	2460	485	749	1936	1665	2632	2677	2612	1276	106	2745	384	1184
BURLINGTON, VT	2178	1158	481	2181	1241	1773	2624	214	375		1061	782	919	1887	930	817	567	1763	1931	1253	652	2409	1916	878	1479	1366	2684	1437	2957	915	1297	1587	1027	1343	92	1086	1588	299	1632	1390	1383	371	2644	587	233	3052	1848	2845	630	1119	2322	2036	3020	3062	2997	1438	419	3130	517	1554
CHARLESTON, SC	1793	317	583	2157	466	1749	2520	1003	899	1061		468	204	1783	907	622	724	1109	1705	1204	879	1754	1110	721	703	1102	2371	900	2554	610	760	583	1003	1319	1145	543	783	773	1248	1290	379	685	2184	642	1101	2948	1824	2741	428	850	2218	1310	2483	2934	2973	434	1006	3106	539	1291
CHARLESTON, WV	1568	503	352	1755	578	1347	2182	741	431	782	468		265	1445	506	209	255	1072	1367	802	410	1718	1192	320	816	764	2122	745	2374	251	606	994	601	918	822	395	926	515	1022	952	790	454	2035	217	839	2610	1422	2403	322	512	1880	1344	2393	2620	2571	845	537	2705	346	953
CHARLOTTE, NC	1649	238	441	2012	389	1604	2375	861	695	919	204	265		1637	761	476	520	1031	1559	1057	675	1677	1041	575	625	956	2225	754	2453	464	614	730	857	1173	1003	397	713	631	1102	1144	525	543	2107	438	959	2802	1678	2595	289	704	2072	1241	2405	2759	2827	581	802	2960	397	1145
CHEYENNE, WY	538	1482	1665	455	1434	594	737	1961	1502	1887	1783	1445	1637		972	1233	1304	979	100	633	1241	801	1220	1115	1382	640	843	1076	1116	1197	1217	2147	1012	881	1799	1240	1502	1755	773	497	1926	1725	1004	1425	2059	1166	305	959	1760	892	436	1046	1179	1176	1234	1941	1468	1368	1659	613
CHICAGO, IL	1352	717	708	1246	667	838	1708	1003	545	930	907	506	761	972		302	346	936	1015	337	283	1543	1108	184	750	532	1768	662	2042	299	539	1382	89	409	841	474	935	797	807	474	1161	768	1819	467	1101	2137	913	1930	802	294	1406	1270	2105	2146	2062	1176	510	2196	701	728
CINCINNATI, OH	1409	476	521	1552	475	1144	1969	862	442	817	622	209	476	1233	302		253	958	1200	599	261	1605	1079	116	700	597	1955	632	2215	106	493	1141	398	714	815	281	820	636	863	736	920	576	1876	292	960	2398	1219	2191	530	350	1667	1231	2234	2407	2368	935	484	2501	517	785
CLEVELAND, OH	1619	726	377	1597	725	1189	2040	654	197	567	724	255	520	1304	346	253		1208	1347	669	171	1854	1328	319	950	806	2100	882	2374	356	742	1250	443	760	588	531	1070	466	1073	806	1045	437	2085	136	751	2469	1264	2262	471	560	1738	1481	2437	2478	2413	1101	303	2547	370	995
DALLAS, TX	754	792	1399	1433	647	1342	1711	1819	1393	1763	1109	1072	1031	979	936	958	1208		887	752	1218	647	241	913	406	554	1331	327	1446	852	466	1367	1010	999	1772	681	525	1589	209	669	1146	1501	1077	1246	1917	2140	1077	1933	1309	635	1410	271	1375	1827	2208	1161	1441	2342	1362	367
DENVER, CO	438	1403	1690	554	1356	693	833	2004	1546	1931	1705	1367	1559	100	1015	1200	1347	887		676	1284	701	1127	1088	1290	603	756	984	1029	1118	1116	2069	1055	924	1843	1162	1409	1799	681	541	1847	1744	904	1460	2102	1261	404	1054	1688	855	531	946	1092	1271	1329	1862	1512	1463	1686	521
DES MOINES, IA	1091	967	1031	1007	919	675	1369	1326	868	1253	1204	802	1057	633	337	599	669	752	676		606	1283	992	481	931	194	1429	567	1703	595	720	1632	378	246	1165	725	1117	1121	546	136	1411	1091	1558	791	1424	1798	629	1591	1126	436	1067	1009	1766	1807	1822	1426	834	1956	1025	390
DETROIT, MI	1608	735	532	1534	734	1126	1977	741	277	652	879	410	675	1241	283	261	171	1218	1284	606		1799	1338	318	960	795	2037	891	2310	366	752	1401	380	697	564	541	1079	622	1062	743	1180	592	2074	292	838	2405	1201	2198	627	549	1675	1490	2373	2415	2350	1194	233	2483	526	984
EL PASO, TX	263	1437	2045	1255	1292	1597	1206	2465	2039	2409	1754	1718	1677	801	1543	1605	1854	647	701	1283	1799		758	1489	1051	1085	717	974	801	1499	1112	1959	1617	1530	2363	1328	1118	2235	737	1236	1738	2147	432	1893	2563	1767	1105	1315	1955	1242	864	556	730	1181	1944	1753	2032	2087	2008	898
HOUSTON, TX	994	800	1470	1673	678	1582	1952	1890	1513	1916	1110	1192	1041	1220	1108	1079	1328	241	1127	992	1338	758		1033	445	795	1474	447	1558	972	586	1201	1193	1240	1892	801	360	1660	449	910	980	1572	1188	1366	1988	2381	1318	2072	1330	863	1650	200	1487	1938	2449	995	1561	2583	1433	608
INDIANAPOLIS, IN	1298	531	600	1432	481	1024	1852	940	508	878	721	320	575	1115	184	116	319	913	1088	481	318	1489	1033		675	485	1843	587	2104	112	464	1196	279	596	872	287	826	715	752	618	975	655	1764	370	1038	2280	1101	2073	641	239	1549	1186	2122	2290	2249	990	541	2383	596	674
JACKSON, MS	1157	386	1032	1836	241	1548	2115	1453	1134	1479	703	816	625	1382	750	700	950	406	1290	931	960	1051	445	675		747	1735	269	1851	594	211	915	835	1151	1514	423	185	1223	612	935	694	1135	1482	988	1550	2544	1458	2337	914	505	1813	644	1780	2232	2612	709	1183	2746	996	771
KANSAS CITY, MO	894	801	1087	1088	753	801	1376	1427	995	1366	1102	764	956	640	532	597	806	554	603	194	795	1085	795	485	747		1358	382	1632	516	536	1466	573	441	1359	559	932	1202	348	188	1245	1141	1360	857	1525	1805	710	1598	1085	252	1074	812	1695	1814	1872	1259	1028	2007	1083	192
LAS VEGAS, NV	578	2067	2445	965	1852	1378	760	2757	2299	2684	2371	2122	2225	843	1768	1955	2100	1331	756	1429	2037	717	1474	1843	1735	1358		1478	274	1874	1611	2733	1808	1677	2596	1826	1854	2552	1124	1294	2512	2500	285	2215	2855	1188	1035	442	2444	1610	417	1272	337	575	1256	2526	2265	1390	2441	1276
LITTLE ROCK, AR	900	528	1072	1530	381	1183	1808	1493	1066	1437	900	745	754	1076	662	632	882	327	984	567	891	974	447	587	269	382	1478		1706	526	140	1190	747	814	1446	355	455	1262	355	570	969	1175	1367	920	1590	2237	1093	2030	983	416	1507	600	1703	2012	2305	984	1115	2439	1036	464
LOS ANGELES, CA	806	2237	2705	1239	2092	1702	1033	3046	2572	2957	2554	2374	2453	1116	2042	2215	2374	1446	1029	1703	2310	801	1558	2104	1851	1632	274	1706		2126	1839	2759	2082	1951	2869	2054	1917	2820	1352	1567	2538	2760	369	2476	3144	971	1309	519	2682	1856	691	1356	124	385	1148	2553	2538	1291	2702	1513
LOUISVILLE, KY	1320	419	602	1547	369	1139	1933	964	545	915	610	251	464	1197	299	106	356	852	1118	595	366	1499	972	112	594	516	1874	526	2126		386	1084	394	711	920	175	714	739	774	704	863	678	1786	394	1062	2362	1215	2155	572	264	1631	1125	2144	2372	2364	878	589	2497	596	705
MEMPHIS, TN	1033	389	933	1625	241	1337	1954	1353	927	1297	760	606	614	1217	539	493	742	466	1116	720	752	1112	586	464	211	536	1611	140	1839	386		1051	624	940	1306	215	396	1123	487	724	830	1035	1500	780	1451	2382	1247	2175	843	294	1652	739	1841	2144	2440	845	975	2574	896	597
MIAMI, FL	2155	661	1109	2554	812	2224	2883	1529	1425	1587	583	994	730	2147	1382	1141	1250	1367	2069	1632	1401	1959	1201	1196	915	1466	2733	1190	2759	1084	1051		1478	1794	1671	907	874	1299	1609	1654	232	1211	2390	1167	1627	3312	2176	3105	954	1214	2581	1401	2688	3140	3370	274	1532	3504	1065	1655
MILWAUKEE, WI	1426	813	805	1175	763	767	1748	1100	642	1027	1003	601	857	1012	89	398	443	1010	1055	378	380	1617	1193	279	835	573	1808	747	2082	394	624	1478		337	939	569	1020	894	880	514	1257	865	1892	564	1198	2063	842	1970	899	367	1446	1343	2145	2186	1991	1272	607	2124	799	769
MINNEAPOLIS, MN	1339	1129	1121	839	1079	431	1465	1417	958	1343	1319	918	1173	881	409	714	760	999	924	246	697	1530	1240	596	1151	441	1677	814	1951	711	940	1794	337		1255	886	1337	1211	793	383	1573	1181	1805	881	1515	1727	606	1839	1216	621	1315	1257	2014	2055	1654	1588	924	1788	1115	637
MONTRÉAL, QC	2172	1241	564	2093	1289	1685	2535	313	397	92	1145	822	1003	1799	841	815	588	1772	1843	1165	564	2363	1892	872	1514	1359	2596	1446	2869	920	1306	1671	939	1255		1094	1632	383	1625	1300	1466	454	2637	607	282	2963	1758	2756	714	1112	2232	2043	2931	2972	2907	1522	330	3041	600	1547
NASHVILLE, TN	1248	242	716	1648	194	1315	1976	1136	716	1086	543	395	397	1240	474	281	531	681	1162	725	541	1328	801	287	423	559	1826	355	2054	175	215	907	569	886	1094		539	906	703	747	686	818	1715	569	1234	2405	1269	2198	626	307	1675	954	2056	2360	2463	701	764	2597	679	748
NEW ORLEANS, LA	1276	473	1142	1955	351	1734	2234	1563	1254	1588	783	926	713	1502	935	820	1070	525	1409	1117	1079	1118	360	826	185	932	1854	455	1917	714	396	874	1020	1337	1632	539		1332	731	1121	653	1245	1548	1108	1660	2663	1643	2431	1002	690	1932	560	1846	2298	2731	668	1302	2865	1106	890
NEW YORK, NY	2015	869	192	2049	985	1641	2491	215	400	299	773	515	631	1755	797	636	466	1589	1799	1121	622	2235	1660	715	1223	1202	2552	1262	2820	739	1123	1299	894	1211	383	906	1332		1469	1258	1094	91	2481	367	313	2920	1716	2713	342	956	2189	1861	2839	2929	2864	1150	507	2998	228	1391
OKLAHOMA CITY, OK	546	944	1354	1227	729	1136	1506	1694	1262	1632	1248	1022	1102	773	807	863	1073	209	681	546	1062	737	449	752	612	348	1124	355	1352	774	487	1609	880	793	1625	703	731	1469		463	1388	1408	1012	1124	1792	1934	871	1727	1331	505	1204	466	1370	1657	2002	1403	1295	2136	1350	161
OMAHA, NE	973	989	1168	904	941	616	1234	1463	1005	1390	1290	952	1144	497	474	736	806	669	541	136	743	1236	910	618	935	188	1294	570	1567	704	724	1654	514	383	1300	747	1121	1258	463		1433	1228	1440	928	1561	1662	525	1455	1263	440	932	927	1630	1672	1719	1448	971	1853	1162	307
ORLANDO, FL	1934	440	904	2333	591	2003	2662	1324	1221	1383	379	790	525	1926	1161	920	1045	1146	1847	1411	1180	1738	980	975	694	1245	2512	969	2538	863	830	232	1257	1573	1466	686	653	1094	1388	1433		1006	2169	963	1422	3091	1955	2884	750	993	2360	1180	2467	2918	3149	82	1327	3283	860	1434
PHILADELPHIA, PA	1954	782	104	2019	897	1611	2462	321	414	371	685	454	543	1725	768	576	437	1501	1744	1091	592	2147	1572	655	1135	1141	2500	1175	2760	678	1035	1211	865	1181	454	818	1245	91	1408	1228	1006		2420	306	419	2890	1686	2683	254	895	2160	1774	2779	2900	2835	1062	522	2968	140	1330
PHOENIX, AZ	466	1868	2366	1199	1723	1662	993	2706	2274	2644	2184	2035	2107	1004	1819	1876	2085	1077	904	1558	2074	432	1188	1764	1482	1360	285	1367	369	1786	1500	2390	1892	1805	2637	1715	1548	2481	1012	1440	2169	2420		2136	2804	1335	1308	883	2343	1517	651	987	358	750	1513	2184	2307	1655	2362	1173
PITTSBURGH, PA	1670	676	246	1719	763	1311	2161	592	217	587	642	217	438	1425	467	292	136	1246	1460	791	292	1893	1366	370	988	857	2215	920	2476	394	780	1167	564	881	607	569	1108	367	1124	928	963	306	2136		690	2590	1386	2383	341	611	1859	1519	2494	2599	2534	1019	321	2668	240	1046
PORTLAND, ME	2338	1197	520	2352	1313	1944	2795	107	560	233	1101	839	959	2059	1101	960	751	1917	2102	1424	838	2563	1988	1038	1550	1525	2855	1590	3144	1062	1451	1627	1198	1515	282	1234	1660	313	1792	1561	1422	419	2804	690		3223	2019	3016	670	1279	2493	2189	3162	3233	3168	1478	668	3301	556	1714
PORTLAND, OR	1395	2647	2830	889	2599	1301	432	3126	2667	3052	2948	2610	2802	1166	2137	2398	2469	2140	1261	1798	2405	1767	2381	2280	2544	1805	1188	2237	971	2362	2382	3312	2063	1727	2963	2405	2663	2920	1934	1662	3091	2890	1335	2590	3223		1268	578	2925	2057	771	2322	1093	638	170	3106	2633	313	2824	1775
RAPID CITY, SD	841	1511	1626	379	1463	320	930	1921	1463	1848	1824	1422	1678	305	913	1219	1264	1077	404	629	1201	1105	1318	1101	1458	710	1035	1093	1309	1215	1247	2176	842	606	1758	1269	1643	1716	871	525	1955	1686	1308	1386	2019	1268		1151	1720	963	628	1335	1372	1368	1195	1970	1429	1328	1620	712
RENO, NV	1020	2440	2623	960	2392	1372	430	2919	2460	2845	2741	2403	2595	959	1930	2191	2262	1933	1054	1591	2198	1315	2072	2073	2337	1598	442	2030	519	2155	2175	3105	1970	1839	2756	2198	2431	2713	1727	1455	2884	2683	883	2383	3016	578	1151		2718	1850	524	1870	642	217	755	2899	2426	898	2617	1568
RICHMOND, VA	1876	527	152	2053	678	1645	2496	572	485	630	428	322	289	1760	802	530	471	1309	1688	1126	627	1955	1330	641	914	1085	2444	983	2682	572	843	954	899	1216	714	626	1002	342	1331	1263	750	254	2343	341	670	2925	1720	2718		834	2194	1530	2684	2934	2869	805	660	3003	108	1274
ST. LOUIS, MO	1051	549	841	1341	501	1053	1628	1181	749	1119	850	512	704	892	294	350	560	635	855	436	549	1242	863	239	505	252	1610	416	1856	264	294	1214	367	621	1112	307	690	956	505	440	993	895	1517	611	1279	2057	963	1850	834		1326	968	1875	2066	2125	1008	782	2259	837	441
SALT LAKE CITY, UT	624	1916	2100	548	1868	960	342	2395	1936	2322	2218	1880	2072	436	1406	1667	1738	1410	531	1067	1675	864	1650	1549	1813	1074	417	1507	691	1631	1652	2581	1446	1315	2232	1675	1932	2189	1204	932	2360	2160	651	1859	2493	771	628	524	2194	1326		1419	754	740	839	2375	1902	973	2094	1044
SAN ANTONIO, TX	818	1000	1671	1500	878	1599	1761	2092	1665	2036	1310	1344	1241	1046	1270	1231	1481	271	946	1009	1490	556	200	1186	644	812	1272	600	1356	1125	739	1401	1343	1257	2043	954	560	1861	466	927	1180	1774	987	1519	2189	2322	1335	1870	1530	968	1419		1285	1737	2275	1195	1714	2410	1635	624
SAN DIEGO, CA	825	2166	2724	1302	2021	1765	1096	3065	2632	3020	2483	2393	2405	1179	2105	2234	2437	1375	1092	1766	2373	730	1487	2122	1780	1695	337	1703	124	2144	1841	2688	2145	2014	2931	2056	1846	2839	1370	1630	2467	2779	358	2494	3162	1093	1372	642	2684	1875	754	1285		508	1271	2481	2601	1414	2720	1531
SAN FRANCISCO, CA	1111	2618	2840	1176	2472	1749	646	3135	2677	3062	2934	2620	2759	1176	2146	2407	2478	1827	1271	1807	2415	1181	1938	2290	2232	1814	575	2012	385	2372	2144	3140	2186	2055	2972	2360	2298	2929	1657	1672	2918	2900	750	2599	3233	638	1368	217	2934	2066	740	1737	508		816	2933	2643	958	2834	1784
SEATTLE, WA	1463	2705	2775	816	2657	1229	500	3070	2612	2997	2973	2571	2827	1234	2062	2368	2413	2208	1329	1822	2350	1944	2449	2249	2612	1872	1256	2305	1148	2364	2440	3370	1991	1654	2907	2463	2731	2864	2002	1719	3149	2835	1513	2534	3168	170	1195	755	2869	2125	839	2275	1271	816		3164	2577	140	2769	1843
TAMPA, FL	1949	455	960	2348	606	2018	2677	1380	1276	1438	434	845	581	1941	1176	935	1101	1161	1862	1426	1194	1753	995	990	709	1259	2526	984	2553	878	845	274	1272	1588	1522	701	668	1150	1403	1448	82	1062	2184	1019	1478	3106	1970	2899	805	1008	2375	1195	2481	2933	3164		1383	3297	916	1448
TORONTO, ON	1841	958	565	1762	958	1354	2204	570	106	419	1006	537	802	1468	510	484	303	1441	1512	834	233	2032	1561	541	1183	1028	2265	1115	2538	589	975	1532	607	924	330	764	1302	507	1295	971	1327	522	2307	321	668	2633	1429	2426	660	782	1902	1714	2601	2643	2577	1383		2711	563	1217
VANCOUVER, BC	1597	2838	2908	949	2791	1362	633	3204	2745	3130	3106	2705	2960	1368	2196	2501	2547	2342	1463	1956	2483	2087	2583	2383	2746	2007	1390	2439	1291	2497	2574	3504	2124	1788	3041	2597	2865	2998	2136	1853	3283	2968	1655	2668	3301	313	1328	898	3003	2259	973	2410	1414	958	140	3297	2711		2902	1977
WASHINGTON, DC	1896	636	38	1953	758	1545	2395	458	384	517	539	346	397	1659	701	517	370	1362	1686	1025	526	2008	1433	596	996	1083	2441	1036	2702	596	896	1065	799	1115	600	679	1106	228	1350	1162	860	140	2362	240	556	2824	1620	2617	108	837	2094	1635	2720	2834	2769	916	563	2902		1272
WICHITA, KS	707	989	1276	1067	838	934	1346	1616	1184	1554	1291	953	1145	613	728	785	995	367	521	390	984	898	608	674	771	192	1276	464	1513	705	597	1655	769	637	1547	748	890	1391	161	307	1434	1330	1173	1046	1714	1775	712	1568	1274	441	1044	624	1531	1784	1843	1448	1217	1977	1272	